E.X.O.
SAGA ONE | PART ONE

# YOUNEEK
## STUDIOS

E.X.O.® - The Legend of Wale Williams
Part One

www.youneekstudios.com
ISBN 978-0-9966070-0-1

For All Inquiries Contact: info@youneekstudios.com

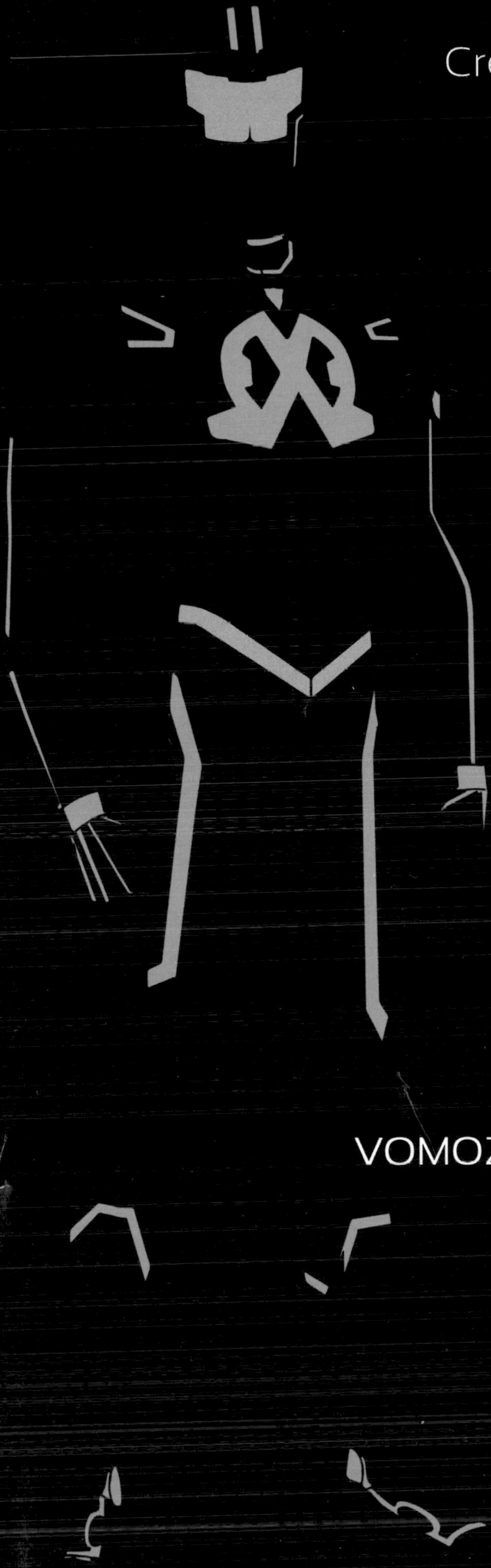

Creator, Writer & Art Director
# ROYE OKUPE

Editor
## AYODELE ELEGBA

Artist
## SUNKANMI AKINBOYE

Colorist
## RAPHAEL KAZEEM

Cover Art
## GODWIN AKPAN

Special Thanks
## MRS. SHERI WILLIAMS

Executive Producer
## VOMOZ COMMUNICATIONS INC.

Arise, O compatriots,

Nigeria's call obey

To serve our Fatherland

With **love and strength** and faith.

The **labour** of our **heroes** past

Shall **never** be in vain,

To **serve** with **heart and might**

One nation bound in freedom, **peace and unity**.


- National Anthem of Nigeria


CHAPTER

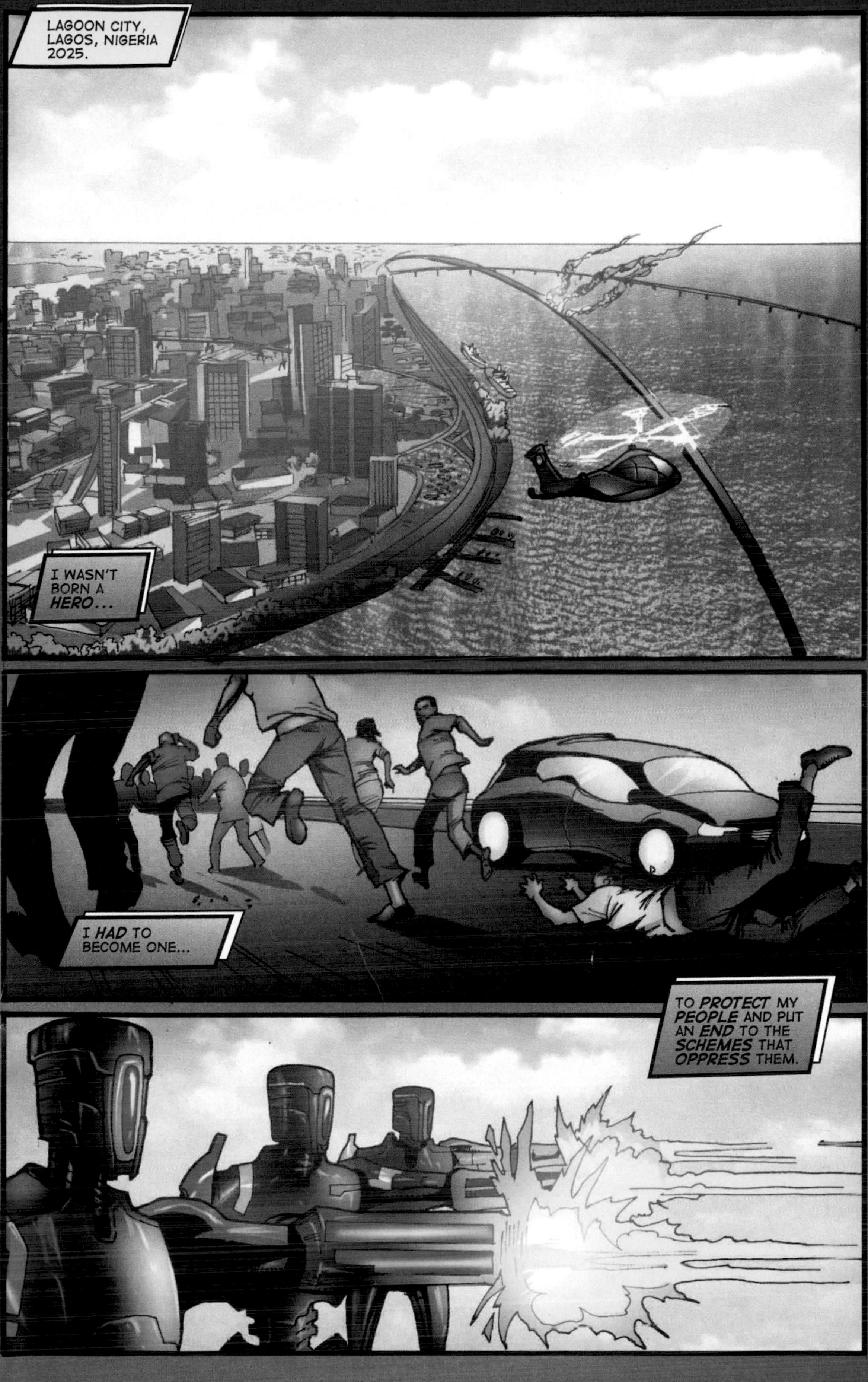
LAGOON CITY, LAGOS, NIGERIA 2025.
I WASN'T BORN A HERO...
I HAD TO BECOME ONE...
TO PROTECT MY PEOPLE AND PUT AN END TO THE SCHEMES THAT OPPRESS THEM.

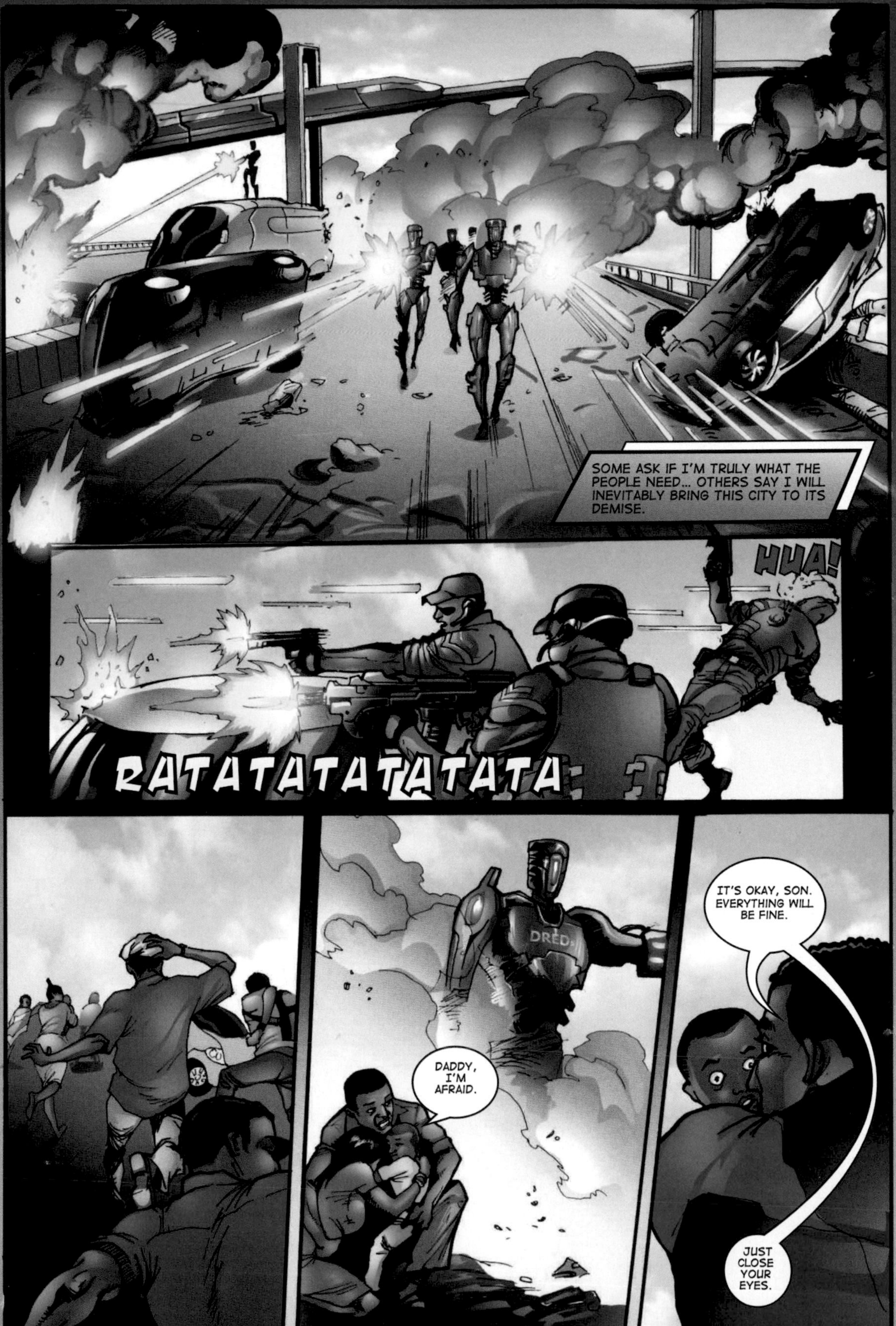
SOME ASK IF I'M TRULY WHAT THE PEOPLE NEED... OTHERS SAY I WILL INEVITABLY BRING THIS CITY TO ITS DEMISE.
HUA!
RATATATATATATATA
DREDs
DADDY, I'M AFRAID.
IT'S OKAY, SON. EVERYTHING WILL BE FINE.
JUST CLOSE YOUR EYES.

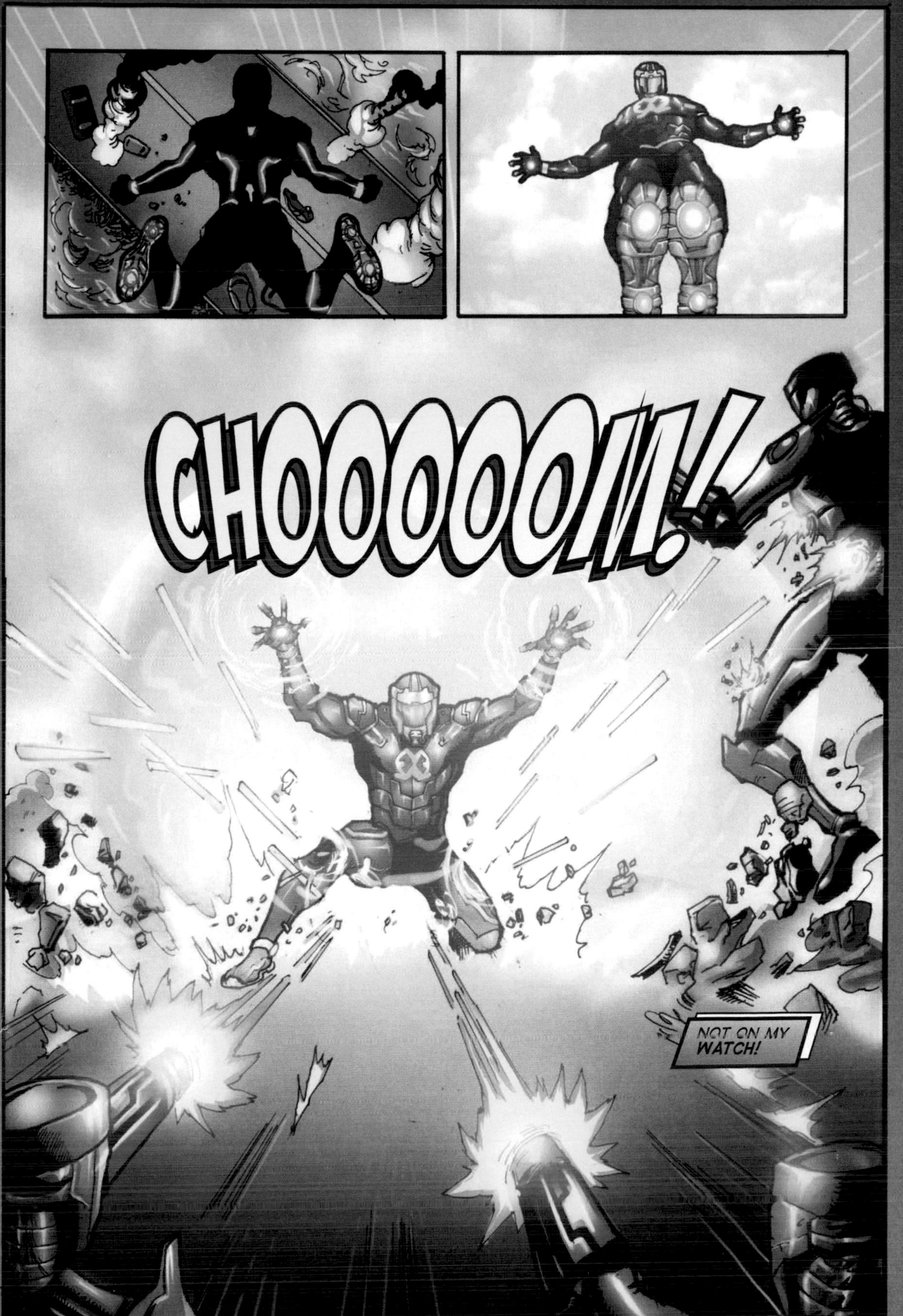
CHOOOOOM!
NOT ON MY WATCH!

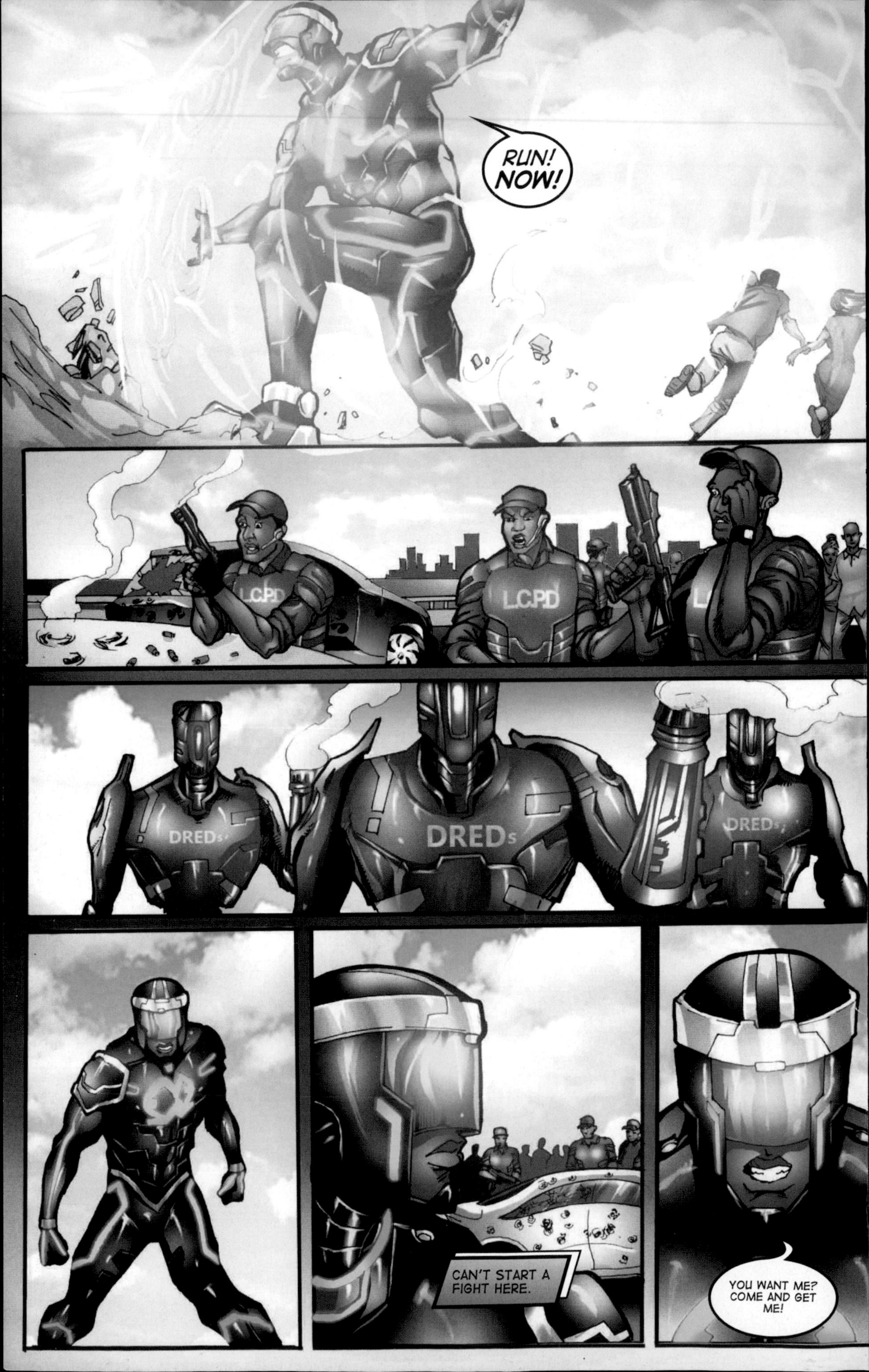
RUN! NOW!
L.C.P.D
L.C.P.D
DREDs
DREDs
DREDs
CAN'T START A FIGHT HERE.
YOU WANT ME? COME AND GET ME!

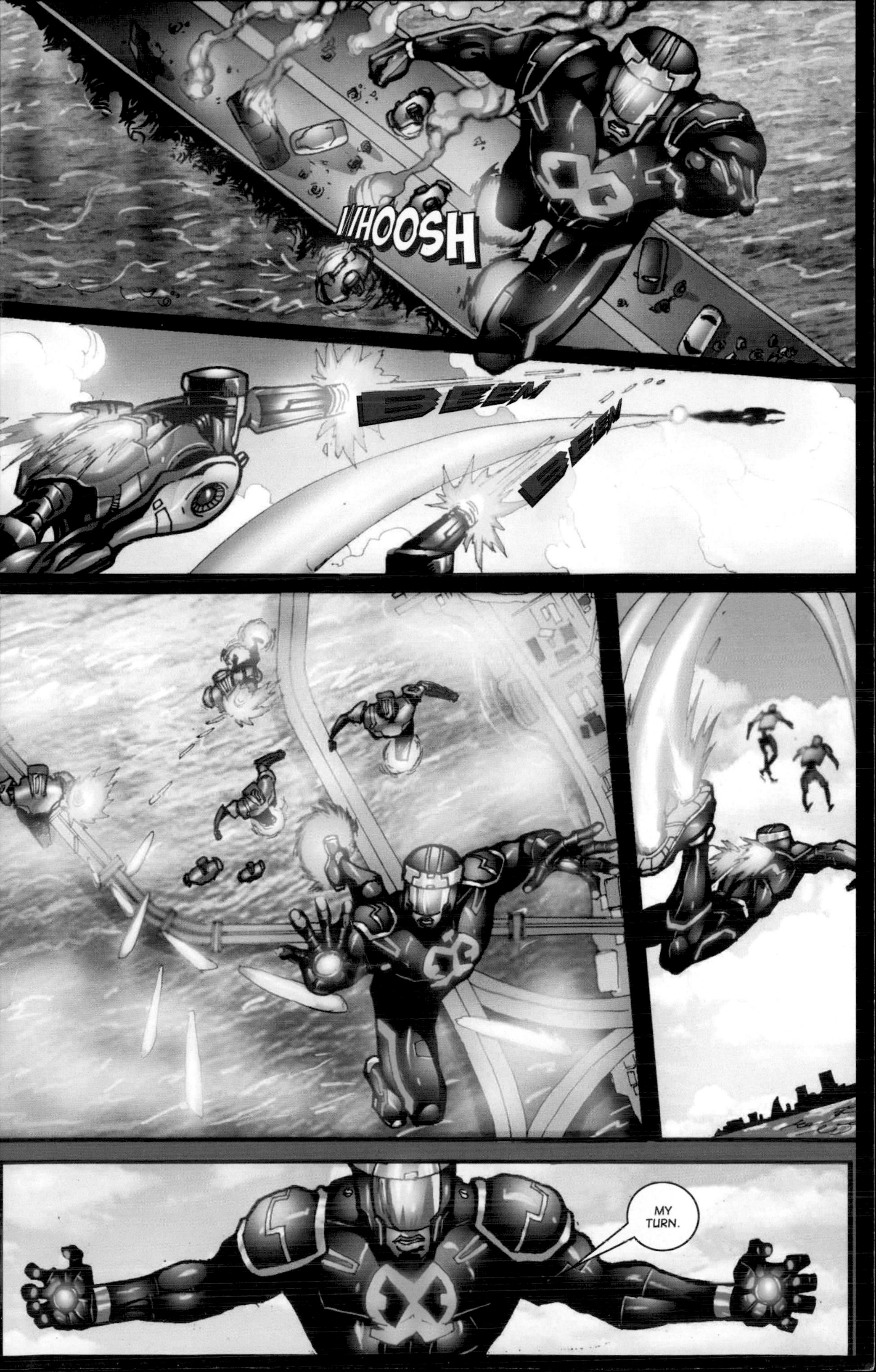
WHOOSH
BEEM
BEEM
MY TURN.

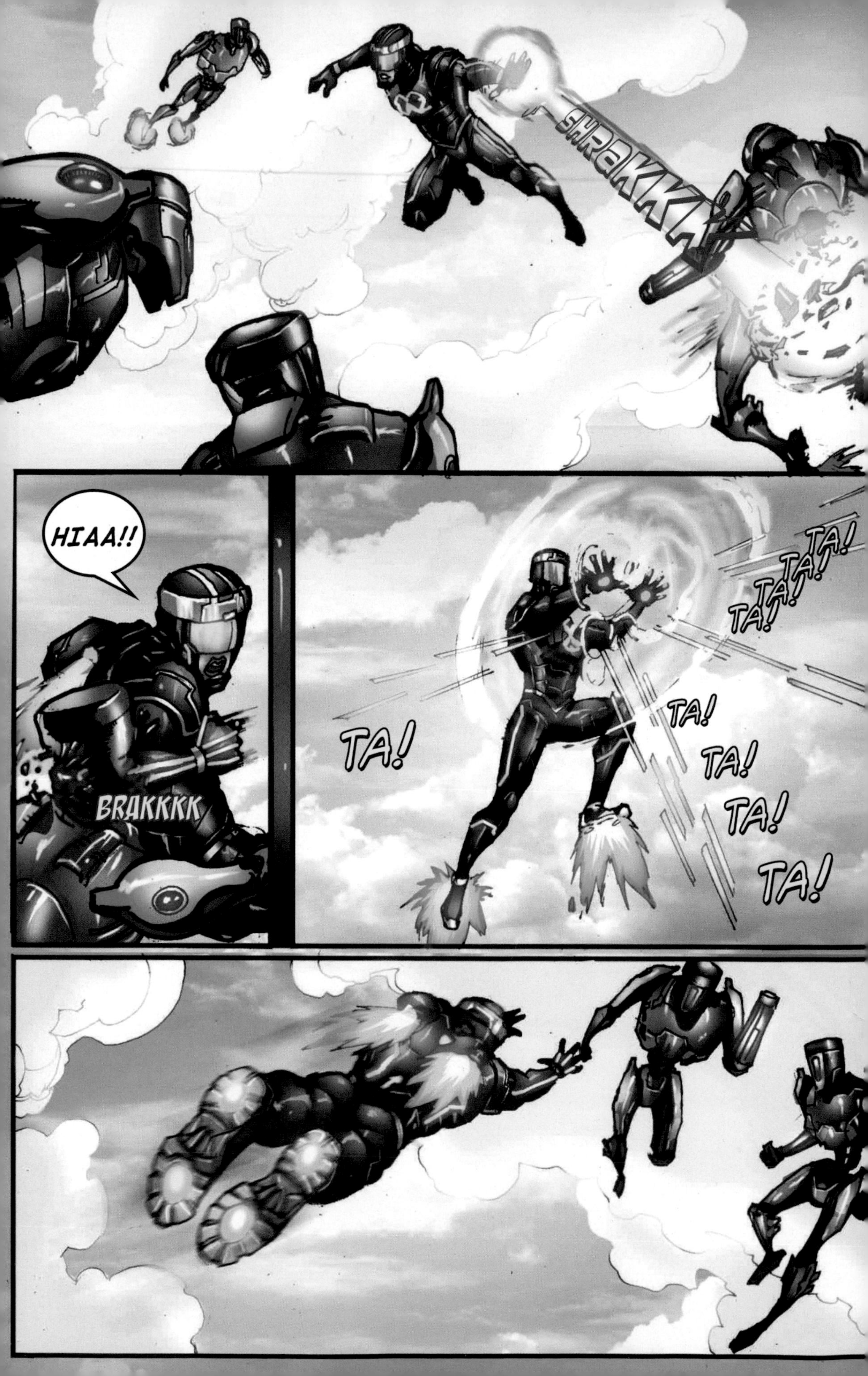
SHRAKKK
HIAA!!
BRAKKKK
TA! TA! TA! TA!
TA!
TA!
TA!
TA!
TA!

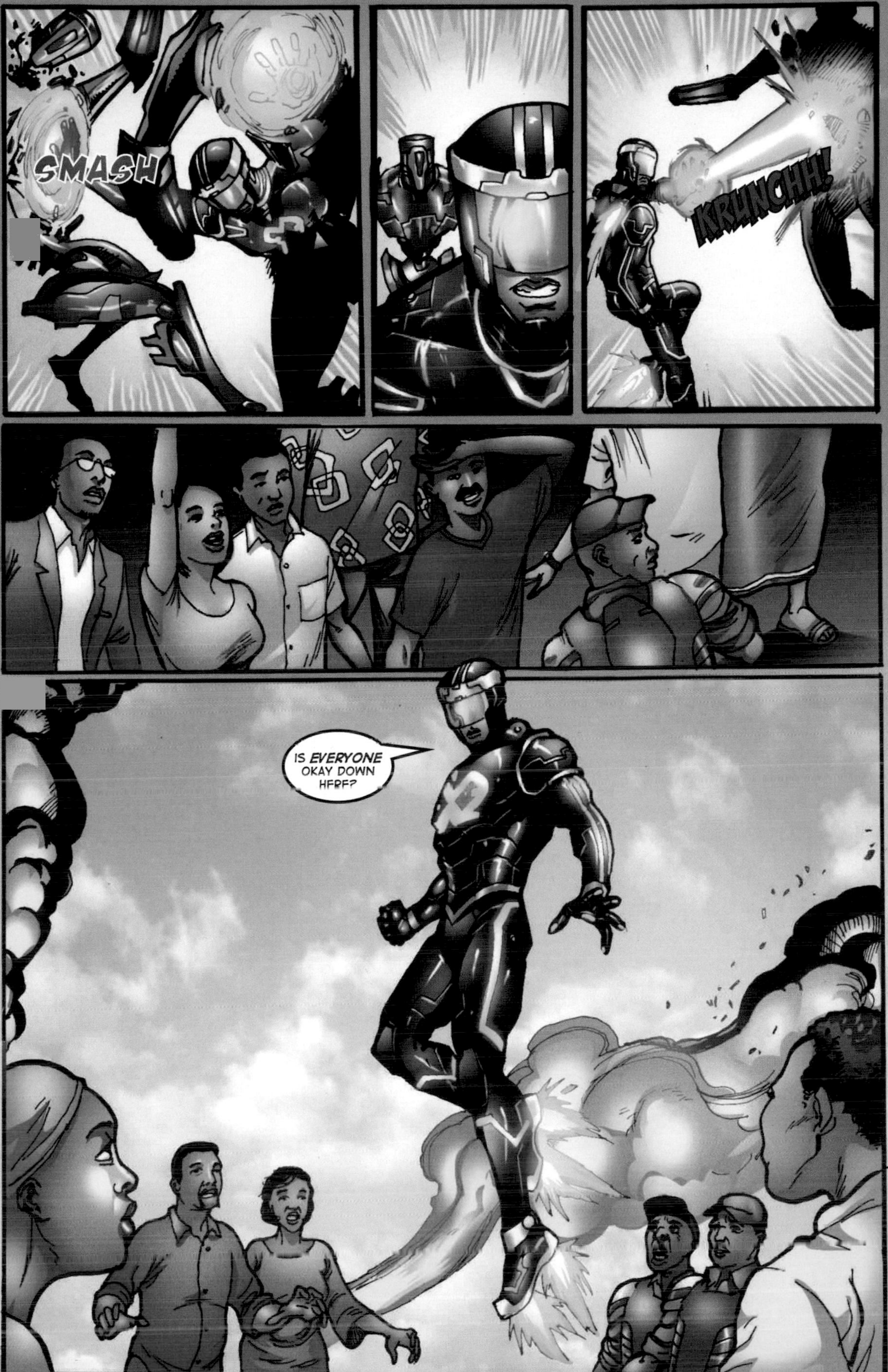
SMASH
KRUNCHH!
IS *EVERYONE* OKAY DOWN HERE?

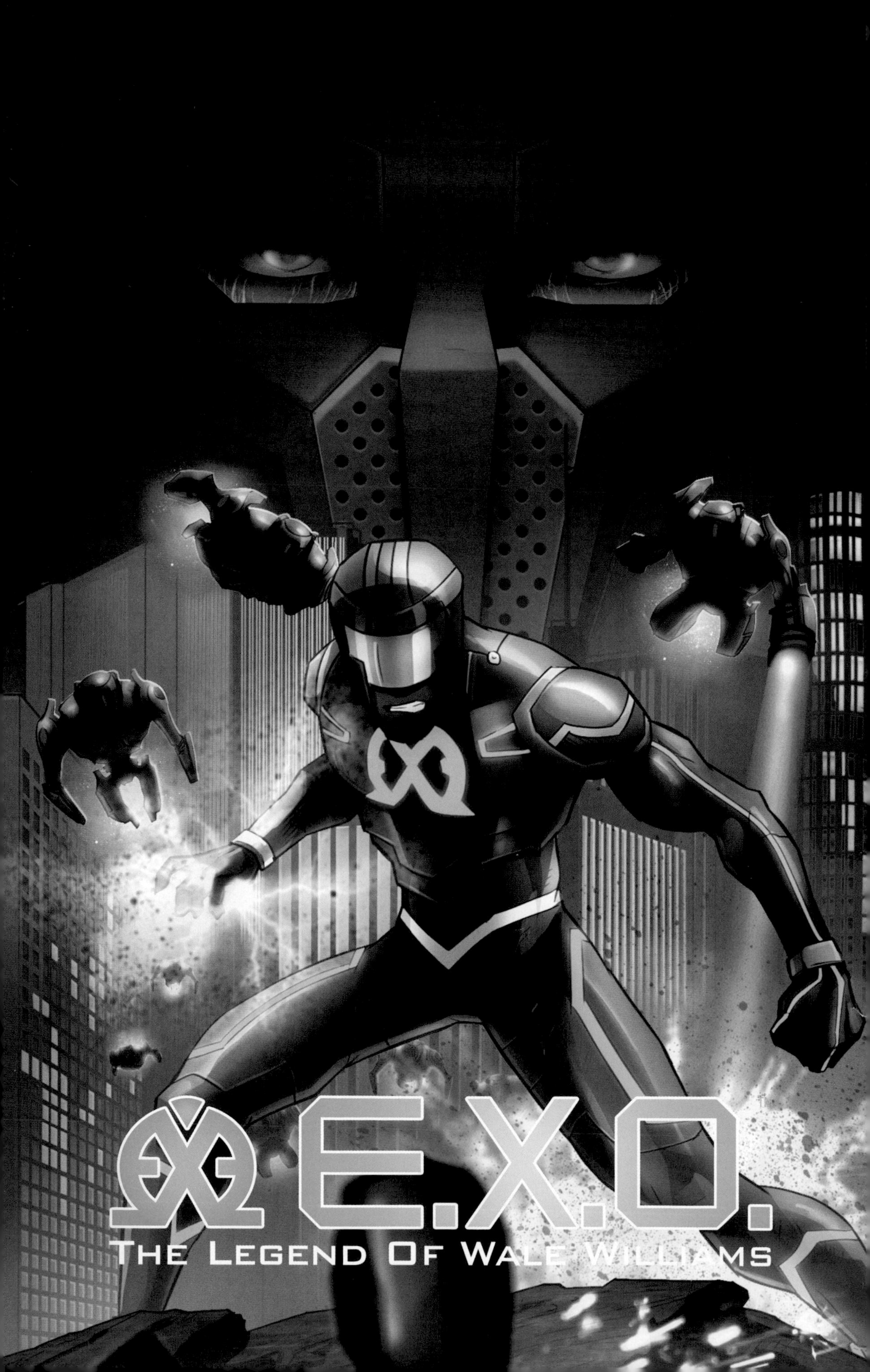
E.X.O.
THE LEGEND OF WALE WILLIAMS

# FIVE YEARS
## AGO

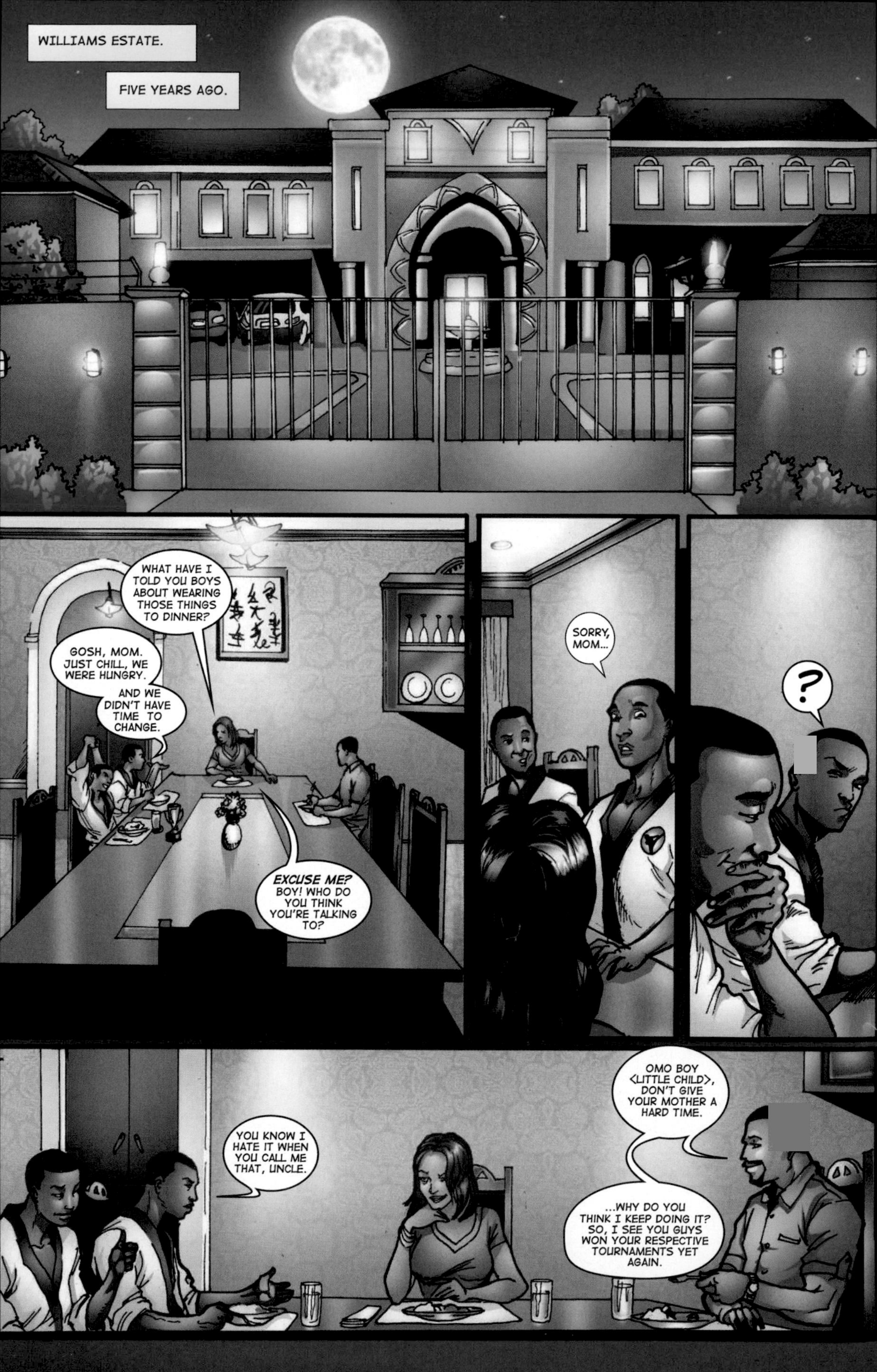
WILLIAMS ESTATE.
FIVE YEARS AGO.
WHAT HAVE I TOLD YOU BOYS ABOUT WEARING THOSE THINGS TO DINNER?
GOSH, MOM. JUST CHILL, WE WERE HUNGRY.
AND WE DIDN'T HAVE TIME TO CHANGE.
EXCUSE ME? BOY! WHO DO YOU THINK YOU'RE TALKING TO?
SORRY, MOM...
?
OMO BOY <LITTLE CHILD>, DON'T GIVE YOUR MOTHER A HARD TIME.
YOU KNOW I HATE IT WHEN YOU CALL ME THAT, UNCLE.
...WHY DO YOU THINK I KEEP DOING IT? SO, I SEE YOU GUYS WON YOUR RESPECTIVE TOURNAMENTS YET AGAIN.

YUP. *FIFTH* TIME IN A ROW FOR WALE. THEY'RE CALLING HIM A *PRODIGY.*

YOU KNOW WHAT, THAT REMINDS ME OF THE TIME WHEN I JOINED THE ARMY. I WAS---

UNCLE JIDE, YOU AND YOUR ARMY STORIES.

HEY, THAT'S MAJOR WILLIAMS TO YOU, BOY!

AT LEAST UNCLE JIDE IS *HERE* TO TELL US STORIES. UNLIKE OUR---

WALE!

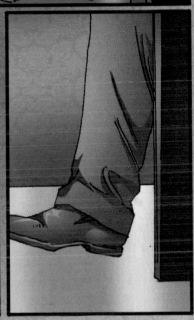

EVENING, *EVERYONE!* MY APOLOGIES FOR BEING *LATE.* WORK WAS SO BUSY TODAY.

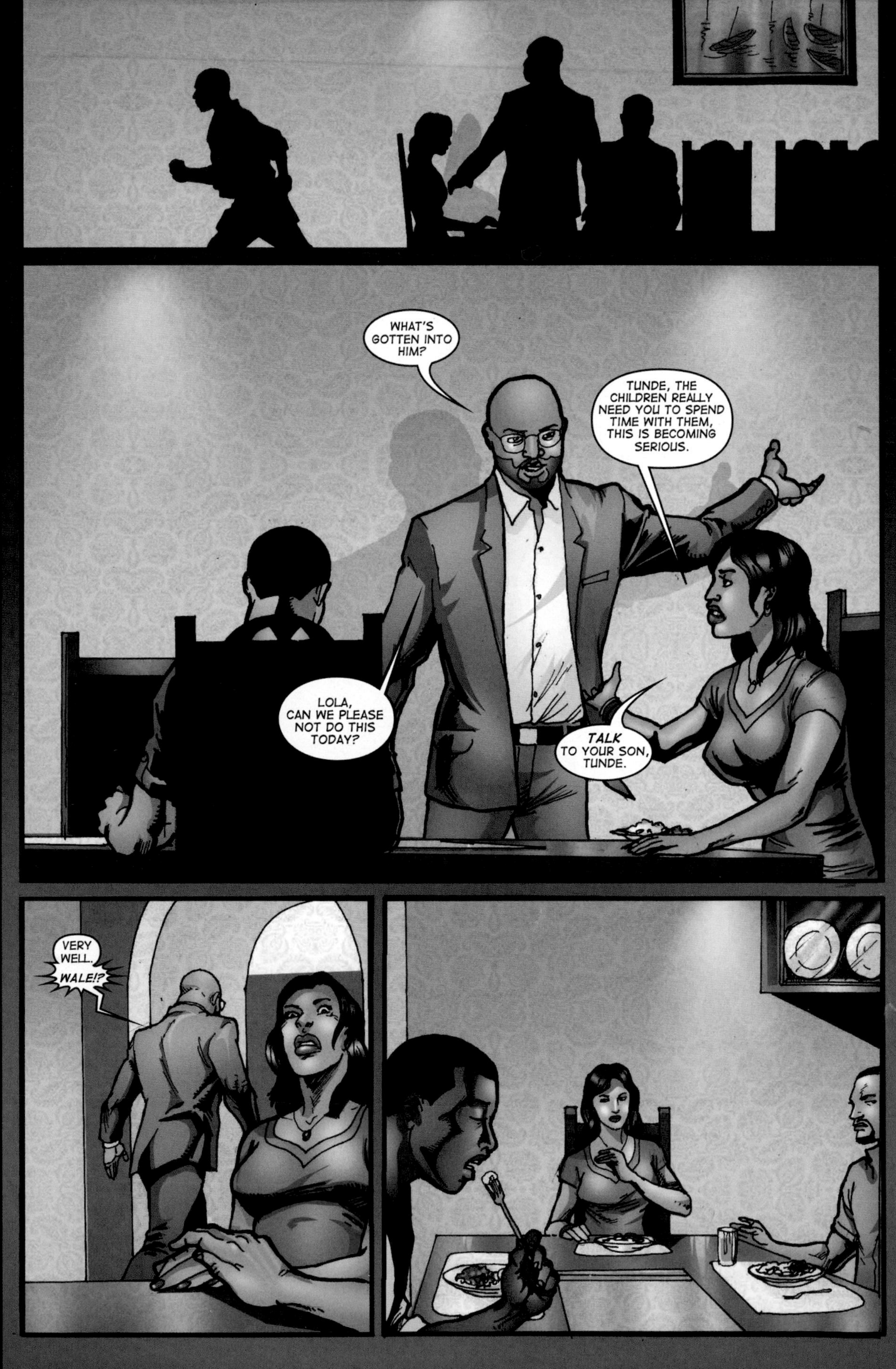
WHAT'S GOTTEN INTO HIM?
TUNDE, THE CHILDREN REALLY NEED YOU TO SPEND TIME WITH THEM, THIS IS BECOMING SERIOUS.
LOLA, CAN WE PLEASE NOT DO THIS TODAY?
TALK TO YOUR SON, TUNDE.
VERY WELL.
WALE!?

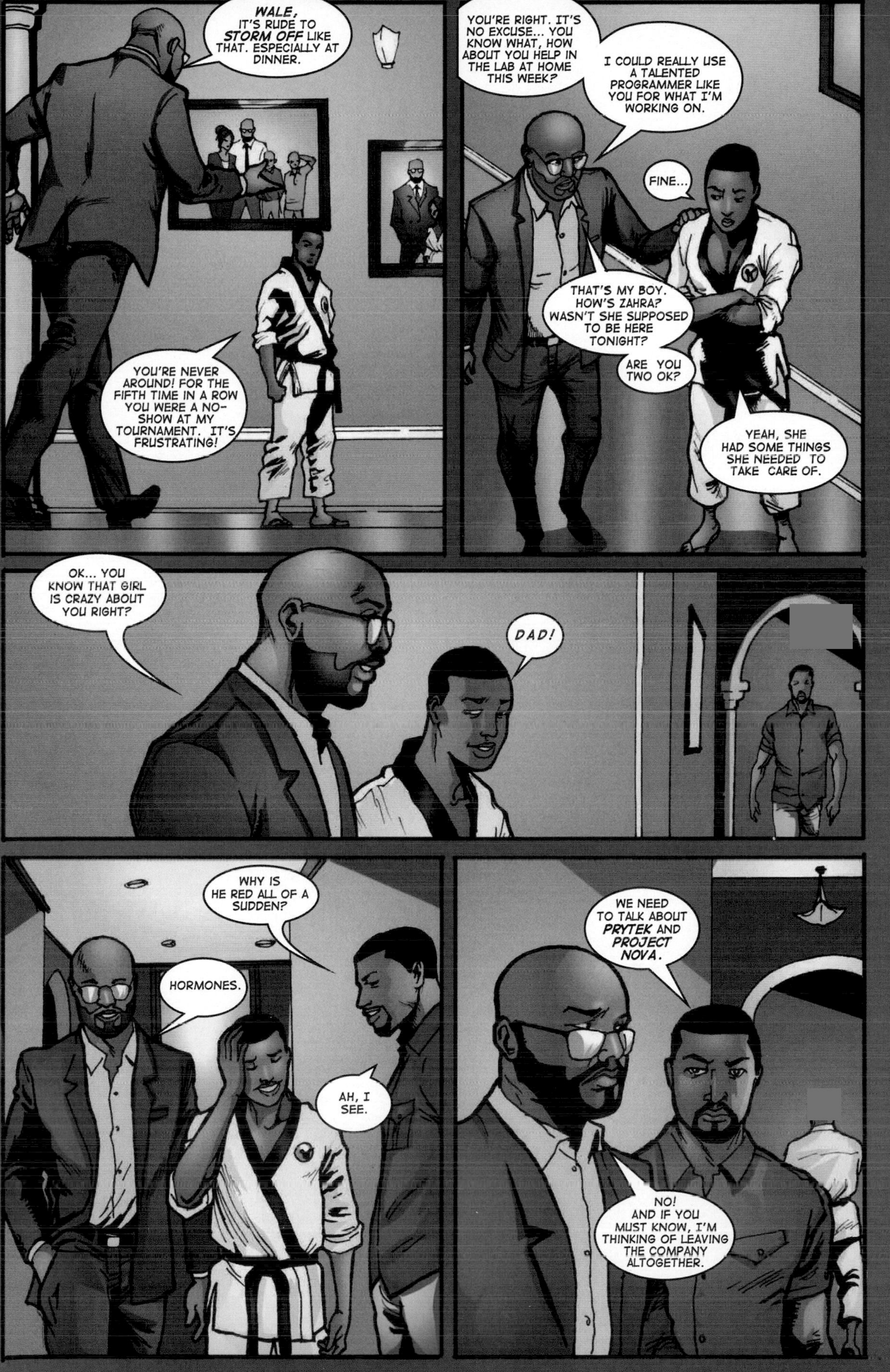
WALE, IT'S RUDE TO STORM OFF LIKE THAT. ESPECIALLY AT DINNER.
YOU'RE NEVER AROUND! FOR THE FIFTH TIME IN A ROW YOU WERE A NO-SHOW AT MY TOURNAMENT. IT'S FRUSTRATING!
YOU'RE RIGHT. IT'S NO EXCUSE... YOU KNOW WHAT, HOW ABOUT YOU HELP IN THE LAB AT HOME THIS WEEK?
I COULD REALLY USE A TALENTED PROGRAMMER LIKE YOU FOR WHAT I'M WORKING ON.
FINE...
THAT'S MY BOY. HOW'S ZAHRA? WASN'T SHE SUPPOSED TO BE HERE TONIGHT?
ARE YOU TWO OK?
YEAH, SHE HAD SOME THINGS SHE NEEDED TO TAKE CARE OF.
OK... YOU KNOW THAT GIRL IS CRAZY ABOUT YOU RIGHT?
DAD!
WHY IS HE RED ALL OF A SUDDEN?
HORMONES.
AH, I SEE.
WE NEED TO TALK ABOUT PRYTEK AND PROJECT NOVA.
NO! AND IF YOU MUST KNOW, I'M THINKING OF LEAVING THE COMPANY ALTOGETHER.

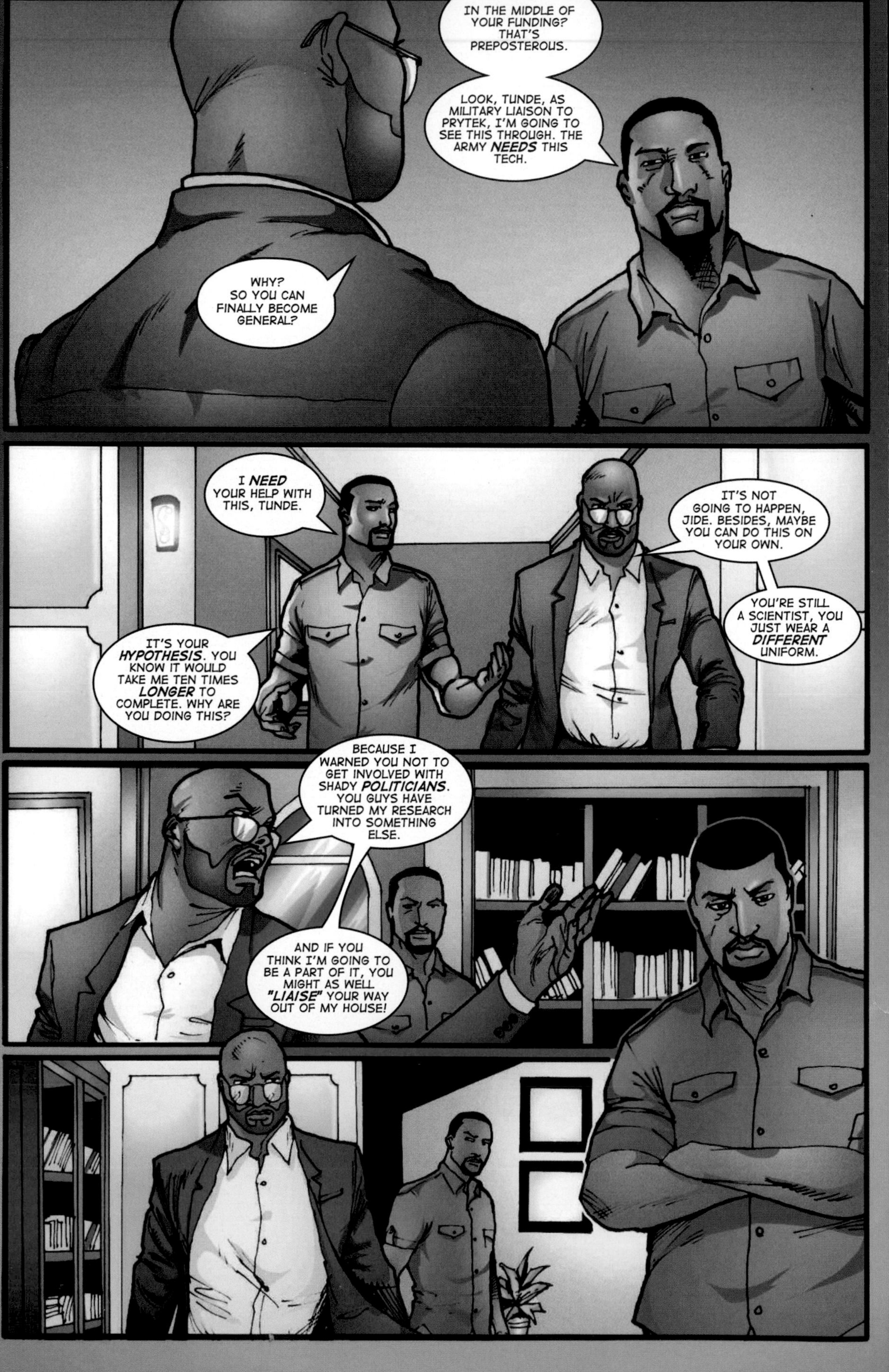
IN THE MIDDLE OF YOUR FUNDING? THAT'S PREPOSTEROUS.
LOOK, TUNDE, AS MILITARY LIAISON TO PRYTEK, I'M GOING TO SEE THIS THROUGH. THE ARMY NEEDS THIS TECH.
WHY? SO YOU CAN FINALLY BECOME GENERAL?
I NEED YOUR HELP WITH THIS, TUNDE.
IT'S NOT GOING TO HAPPEN, JIDE. BESIDES, MAYBE YOU CAN DO THIS ON YOUR OWN.
YOU'RE STILL A SCIENTIST, YOU JUST WEAR A DIFFERENT UNIFORM.
IT'S YOUR HYPOTHESIS. YOU KNOW IT WOULD TAKE ME TEN TIMES LONGER TO COMPLETE. WHY ARE YOU DOING THIS?
BECAUSE I WARNED YOU NOT TO GET INVOLVED WITH SHADY POLITICIANS. YOU GUYS HAVE TURNED MY RESEARCH INTO SOMETHING ELSE.
AND IF YOU THINK I'M GOING TO BE A PART OF IT, YOU MIGHT AS WELL "LIAISE" YOUR WAY OUT OF MY HOUSE!

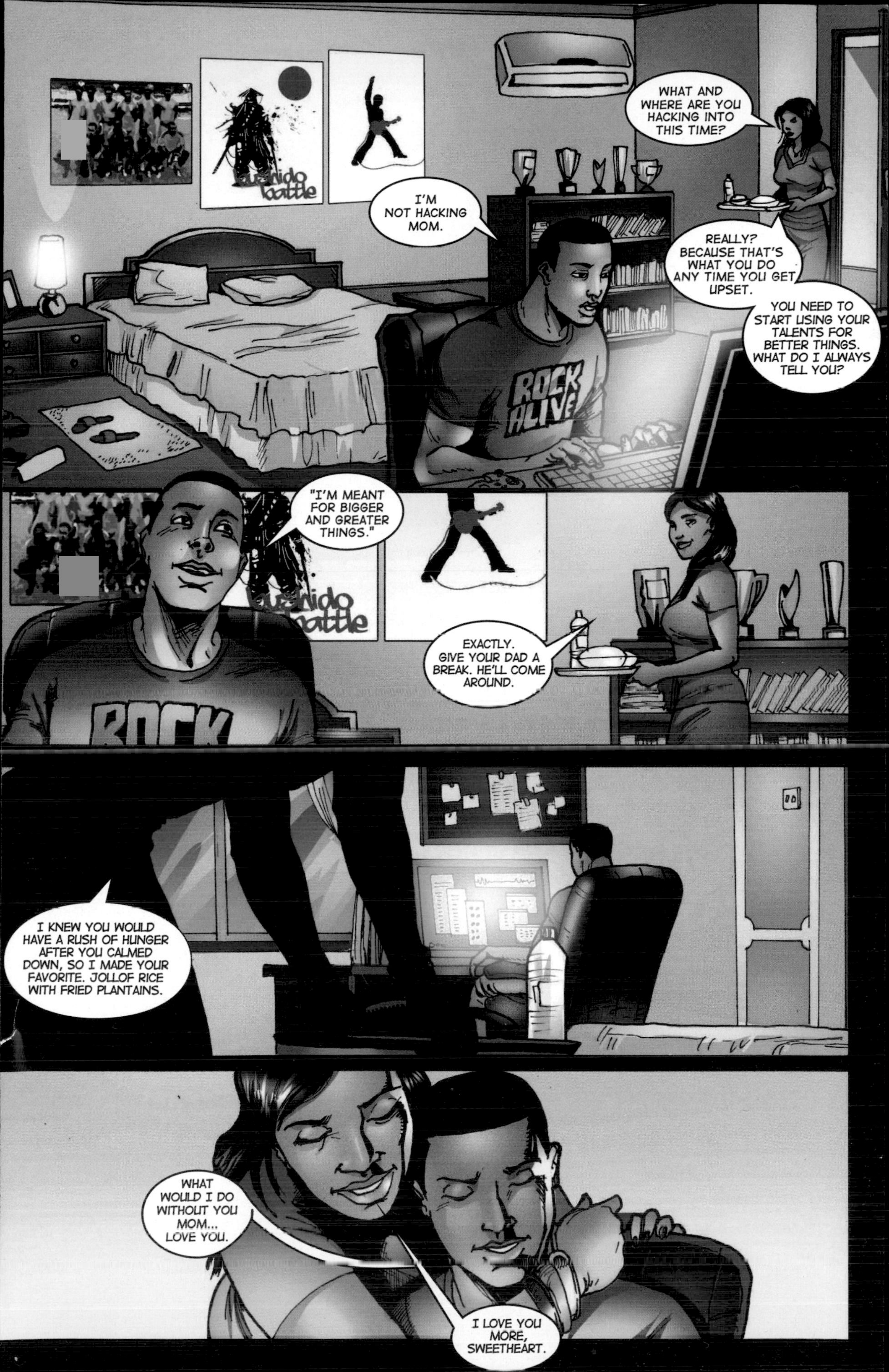
bushido battle
WHAT AND WHERE ARE YOU HACKING INTO THIS TIME?
I'M NOT HACKING MOM.
REALLY? BECAUSE THAT'S WHAT YOU DO ANY TIME YOU GET UPSET.
YOU NEED TO START USING YOUR TALENTS FOR BETTER THINGS. WHAT DO I ALWAYS TELL YOU?
ROCK ALIVE
"I'M MEANT FOR BIGGER AND GREATER THINGS."
EXACTLY. GIVE YOUR DAD A BREAK. HE'LL COME AROUND.
I KNEW YOU WOULD HAVE A RUSH OF HUNGER AFTER YOU CALMED DOWN, SO I MADE YOUR FAVORITE. JOLLOF RICE WITH FRIED PLANTAINS.
WHAT WOULD I DO WITHOUT YOU MOM... LOVE YOU.
I LOVE YOU MORE, SWEETHEART.

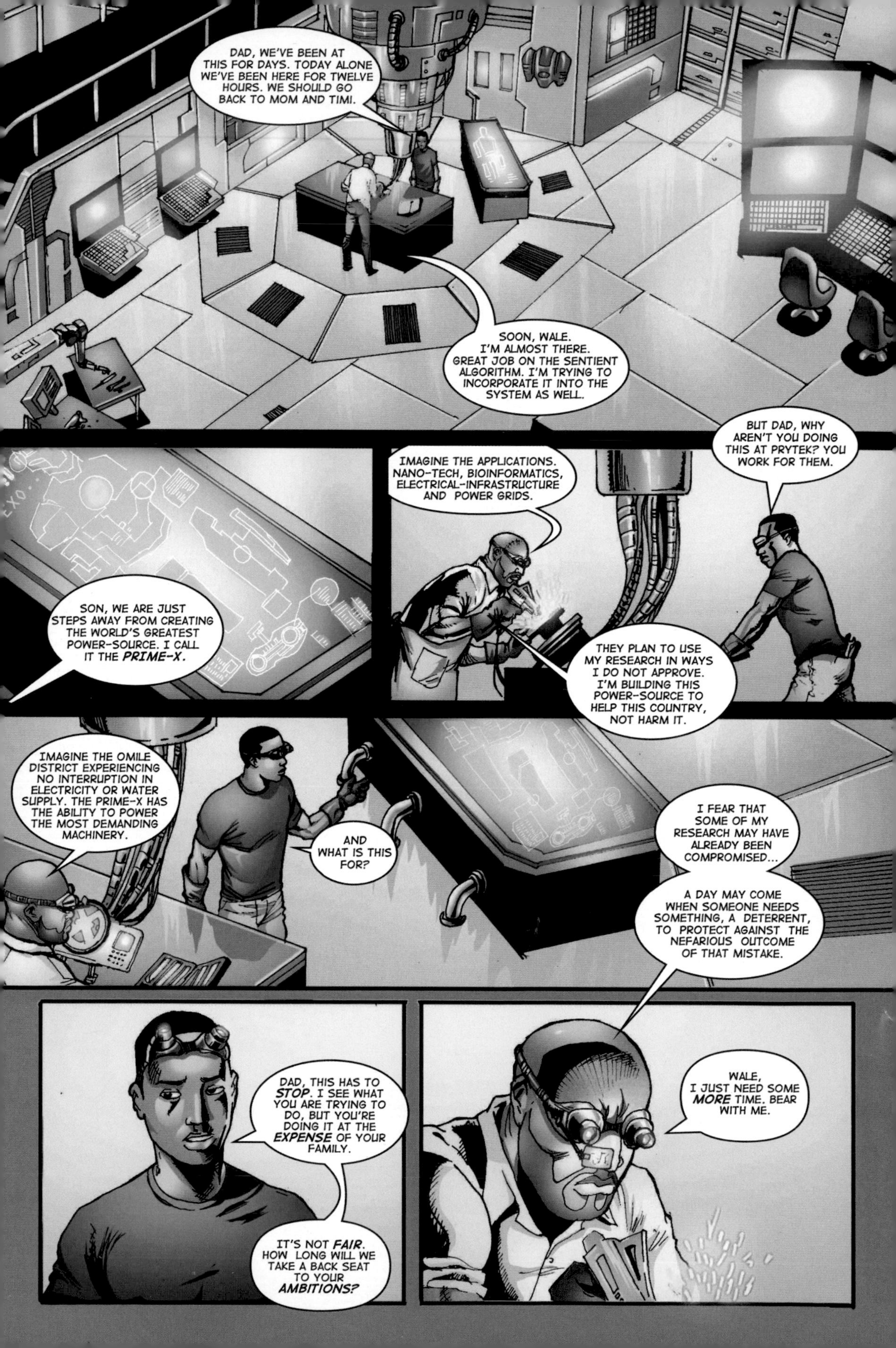
DAD, WE'VE BEEN AT THIS FOR DAYS. TODAY ALONE WE'VE BEEN HERE FOR TWELVE HOURS. WE SHOULD GO BACK TO MOM AND TIMI.
SOON, WALE. I'M ALMOST THERE. GREAT JOB ON THE SENTIENT ALGORITHM. I'M TRYING TO INCORPORATE IT INTO THE SYSTEM AS WELL.
SON, WE ARE JUST STEPS AWAY FROM CREATING THE WORLD'S GREATEST POWER-SOURCE. I CALL IT THE PRIME-X.
IMAGINE THE APPLICATIONS. NANO-TECH, BIOINFORMATICS, ELECTRICAL-INFRASTRUCTURE AND POWER GRIDS.
BUT DAD, WHY AREN'T YOU DOING THIS AT PRYTEK? YOU WORK FOR THEM.
THEY PLAN TO USE MY RESEARCH IN WAYS I DO NOT APPROVE. I'M BUILDING THIS POWER-SOURCE TO HELP THIS COUNTRY, NOT HARM IT.
IMAGINE THE OMILE DISTRICT EXPERIENCING NO INTERRUPTION IN ELECTRICITY OR WATER SUPPLY. THE PRIME-X HAS THE ABILITY TO POWER THE MOST DEMANDING MACHINERY.
AND WHAT IS THIS FOR?
I FEAR THAT SOME OF MY RESEARCH MAY HAVE ALREADY BEEN COMPROMISED...
A DAY MAY COME WHEN SOMEONE NEEDS SOMETHING, A DETERRENT, TO PROTECT AGAINST THE NEFARIOUS OUTCOME OF THAT MISTAKE.
DAD, THIS HAS TO STOP. I SEE WHAT YOU ARE TRYING TO DO, BUT YOU'RE DOING IT AT THE EXPENSE OF YOUR FAMILY.
IT'S NOT FAIR. HOW LONG WILL WE TAKE A BACK SEAT TO YOUR AMBITIONS?
WALE, I JUST NEED SOME MORE TIME. BEAR WITH ME.

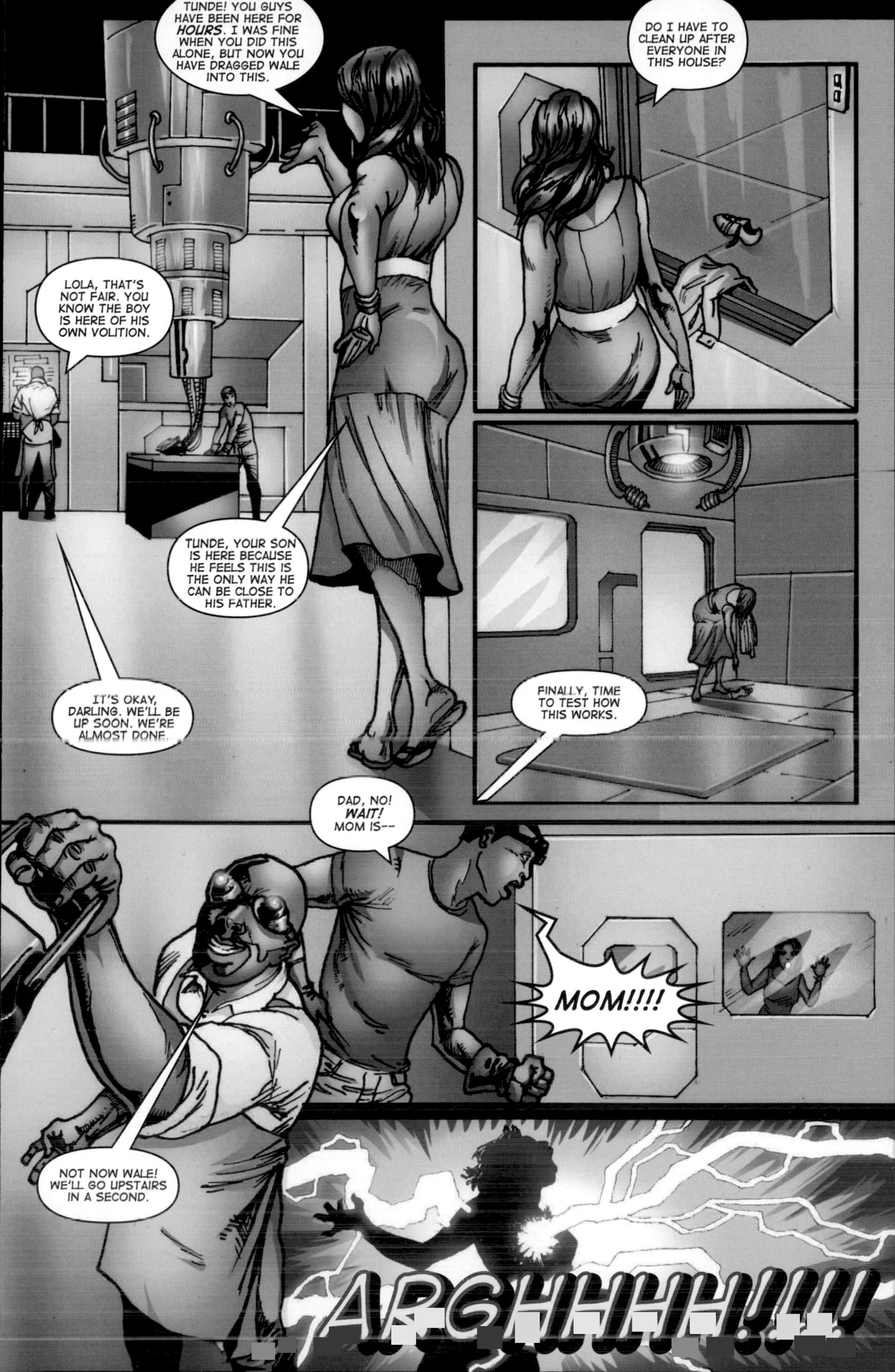
TUNDE! YOU GUYS HAVE BEEN HERE FOR HOURS. I WAS FINE WHEN YOU DID THIS ALONE, BUT NOW YOU HAVE DRAGGED WALE INTO THIS.
LOLA, THAT'S NOT FAIR. YOU KNOW THE BOY IS HERE OF HIS OWN VOLITION.
TUNDE, YOUR SON IS HERE BECAUSE HE FEELS THIS IS THE ONLY WAY HE CAN BE CLOSE TO HIS FATHER.
IT'S OKAY, DARLING. WE'LL BE UP SOON. WE'RE ALMOST DONE.
DO I HAVE TO CLEAN UP AFTER EVERYONE IN THIS HOUSE?
FINALLY, TIME TO TEST HOW THIS WORKS.
DAD, NO! WAIT! MOM IS--
MOM!!!!
NOT NOW WALE! WE'LL GO UPSTAIRS IN A SECOND.
ARGHHHH!!!!

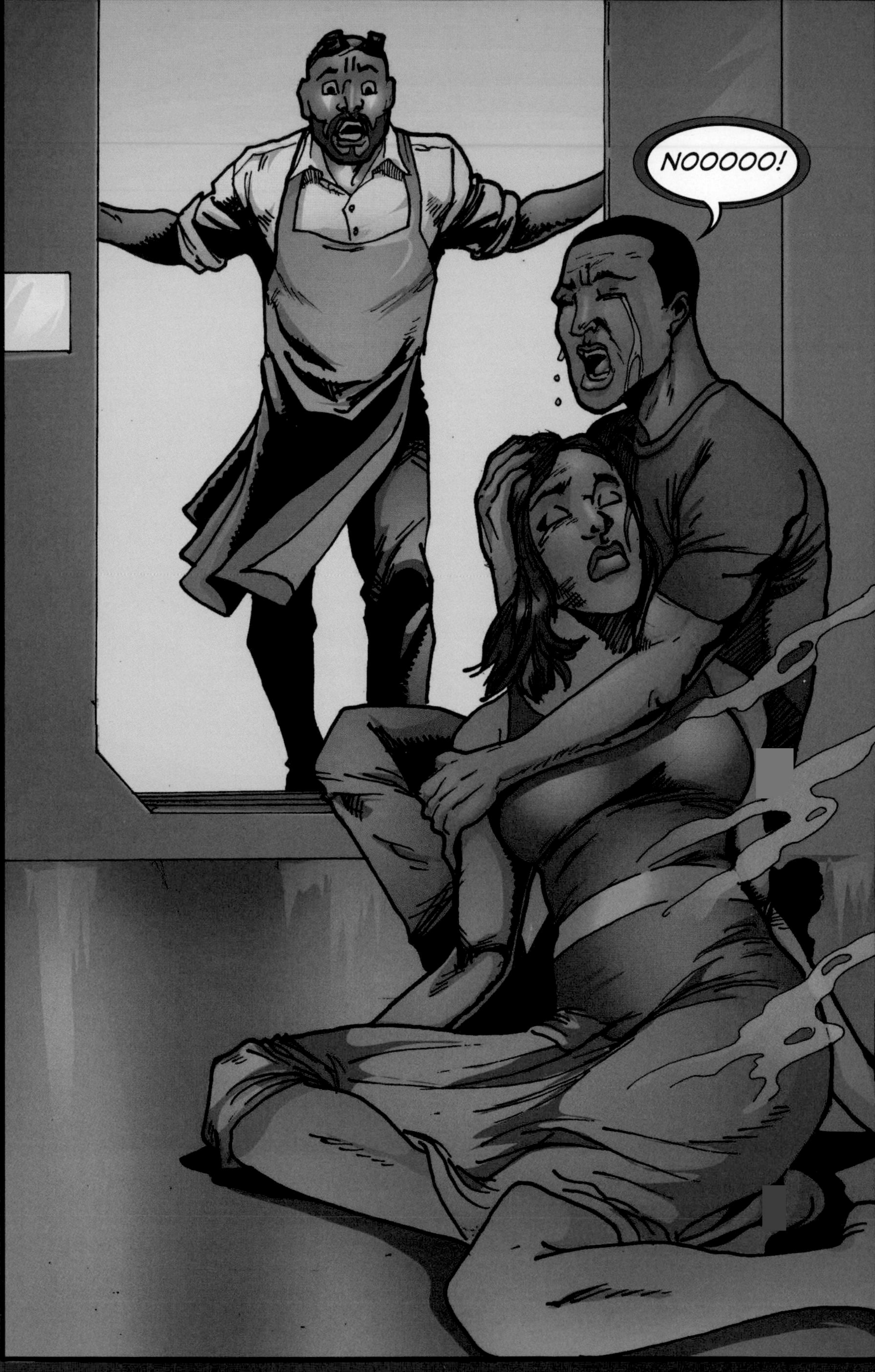
NOOOOO!

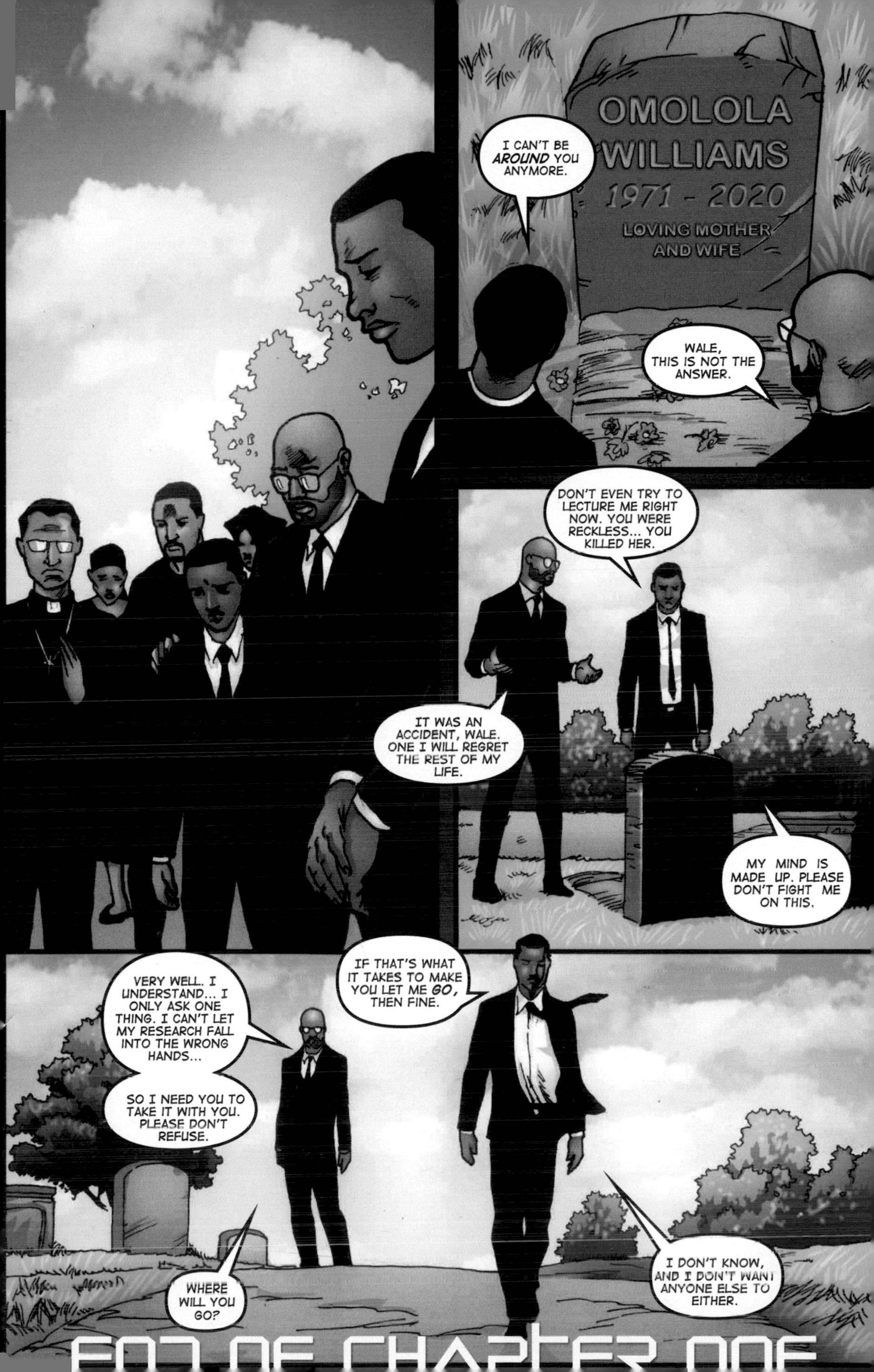
OMOLOLA WILLIAMS 1971 - 2020 LOVING MOTHER AND WIFE
I CAN'T BE *AROUND* YOU ANYMORE.
WALE, THIS IS NOT THE ANSWER.
DON'T EVEN TRY TO LECTURE ME RIGHT NOW. YOU WERE RECKLESS... YOU KILLED HER.
IT WAS AN ACCIDENT, WALE. ONE I WILL REGRET THE REST OF MY LIFE.
MY MIND IS MADE UP. PLEASE DON'T FIGHT ME ON THIS.
VERY WELL. I UNDERSTAND... I ONLY ASK ONE THING. I CAN'T LET MY RESEARCH FALL INTO THE WRONG HANDS...
SO I NEED YOU TO TAKE IT WITH YOU. PLEASE DON'T REFUSE.
IF THAT'S WHAT IT TAKES TO MAKE YOU LET ME *GO*, THEN FINE.
WHERE WILL YOU GO?
I DON'T KNOW, AND I DON'T WANT ANYONE ELSE TO EITHER.
END OF CHAPTER ONE

"I wasn't born a hero... I had to become one."

- *EXO*

# CHAPTER

# two

# back to the present [2025]

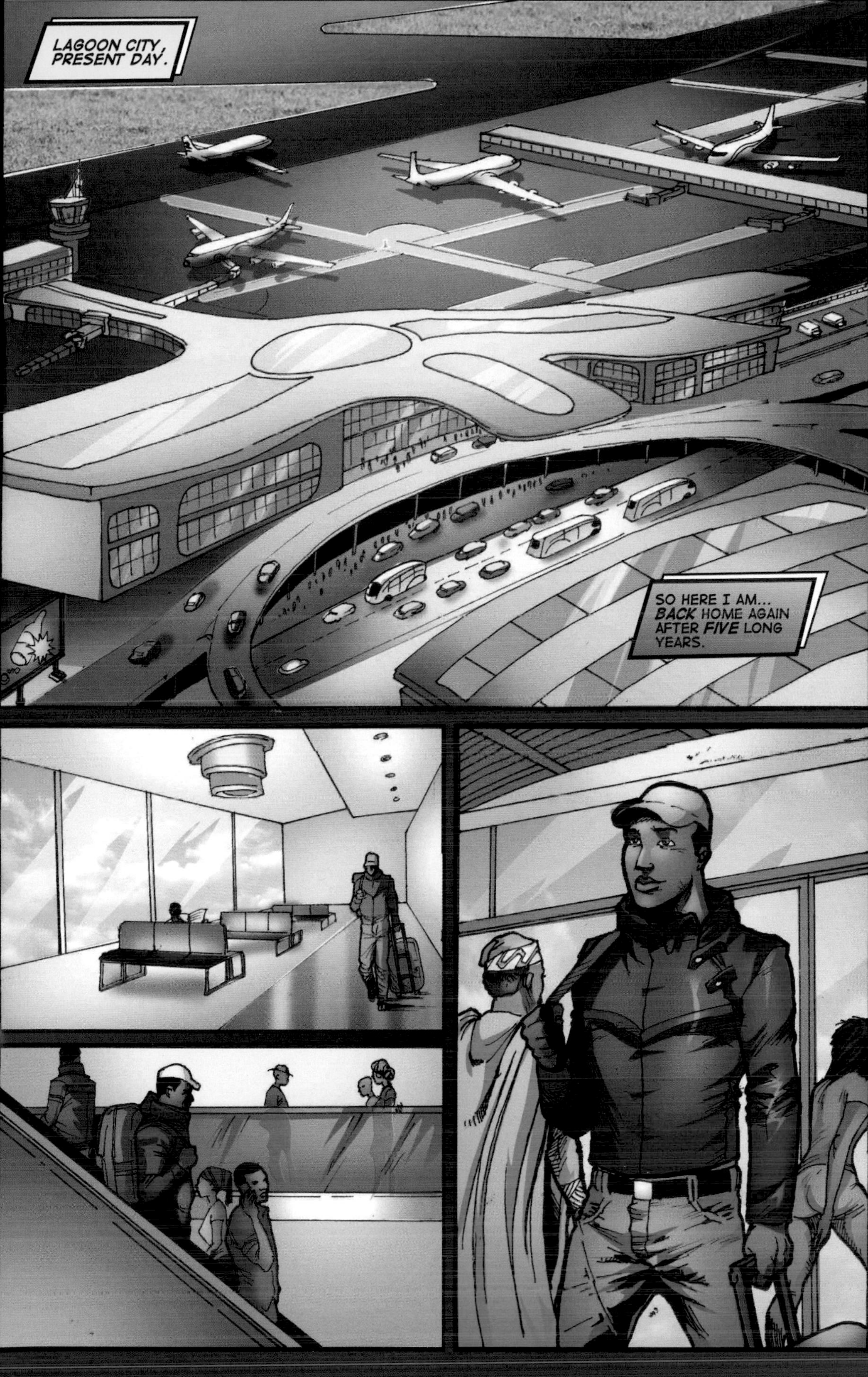
LAGOON CITY, PRESENT DAY.
SO HERE I AM... BACK HOME AGAIN AFTER FIVE LONG YEARS.

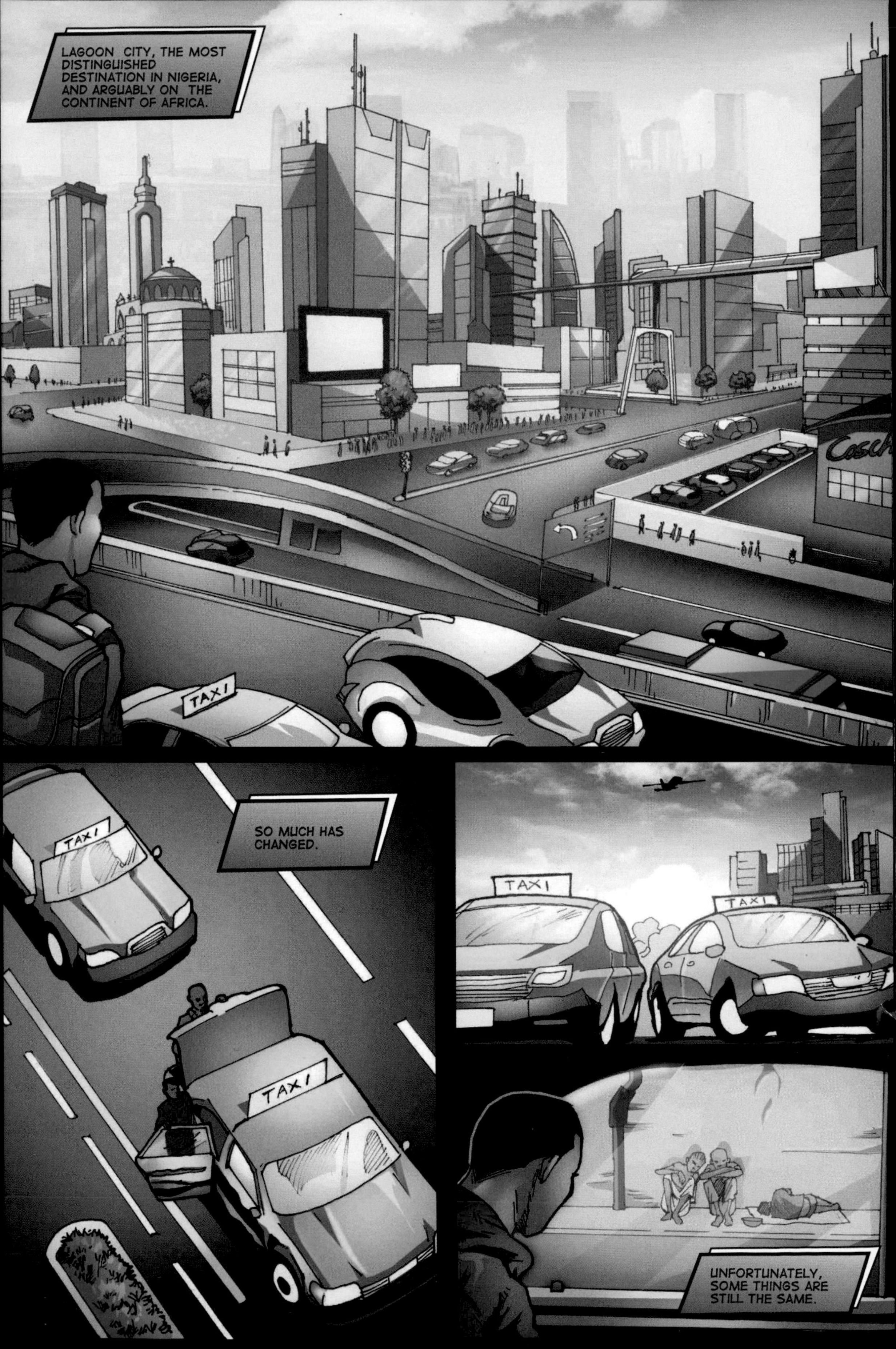

LAGOON CITY, THE MOST DISTINGUISHED DESTINATION IN NIGERIA, AND ARGUABLY ON THE CONTINENT OF AFRICA.
TAXI
SO MUCH HAS CHANGED.
TAXI
TAXI
TAXI
TAXI
UNFORTUNATELY, SOME THINGS ARE STILL THE SAME.

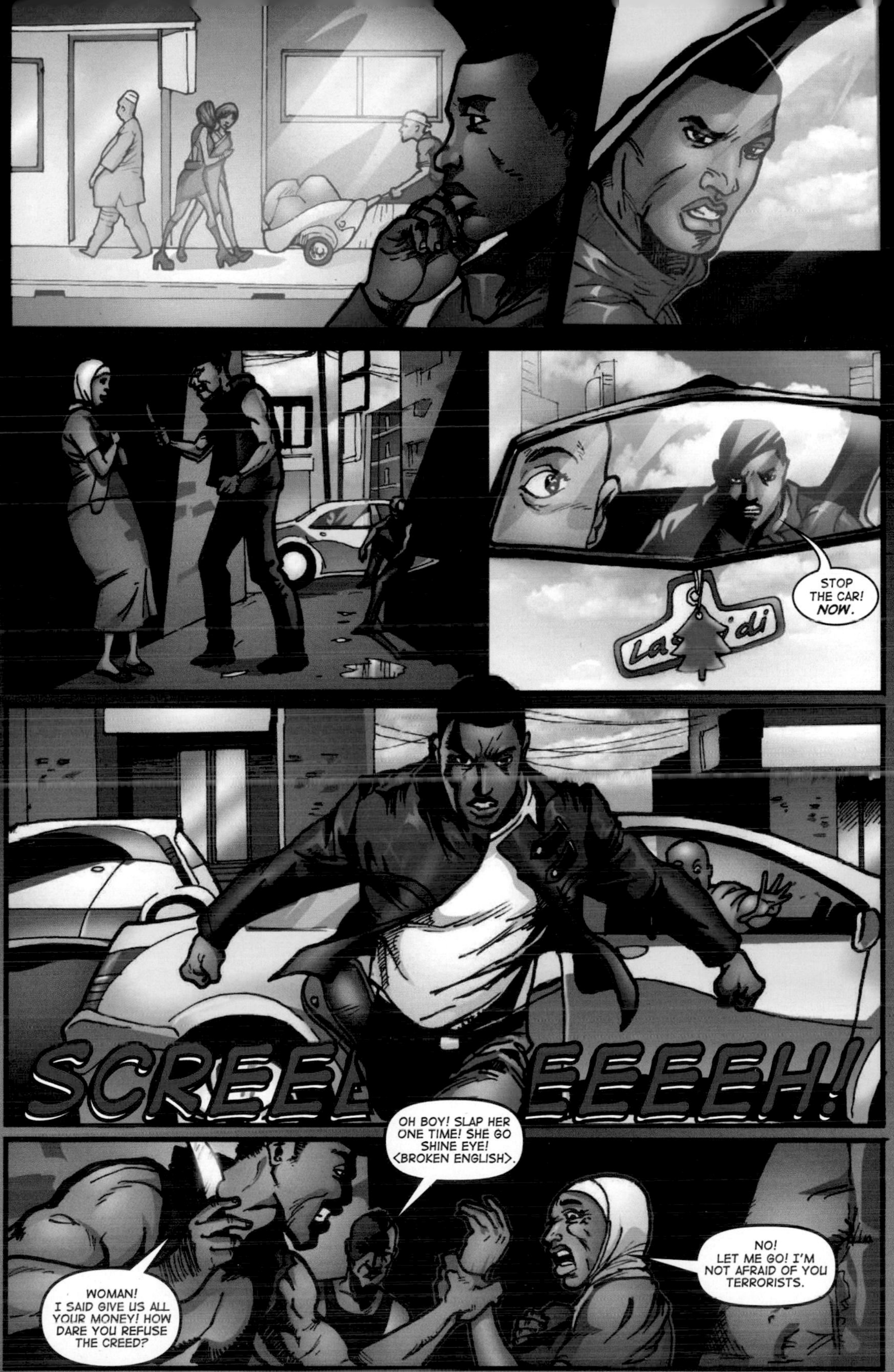
STOP THE CAR! *NOW*.
SCREEE EEEEEH!
OH BOY! SLAP HER ONE TIME! SHE GO SHINE EYE! <BROKEN ENGLISH>.
WOMAN! I SAID GIVE US ALL YOUR MONEY! HOW DARE YOU REFUSE THE CREED?
NO! LET ME GO! I'M NOT AFRAID OF YOU TERRORISTS.

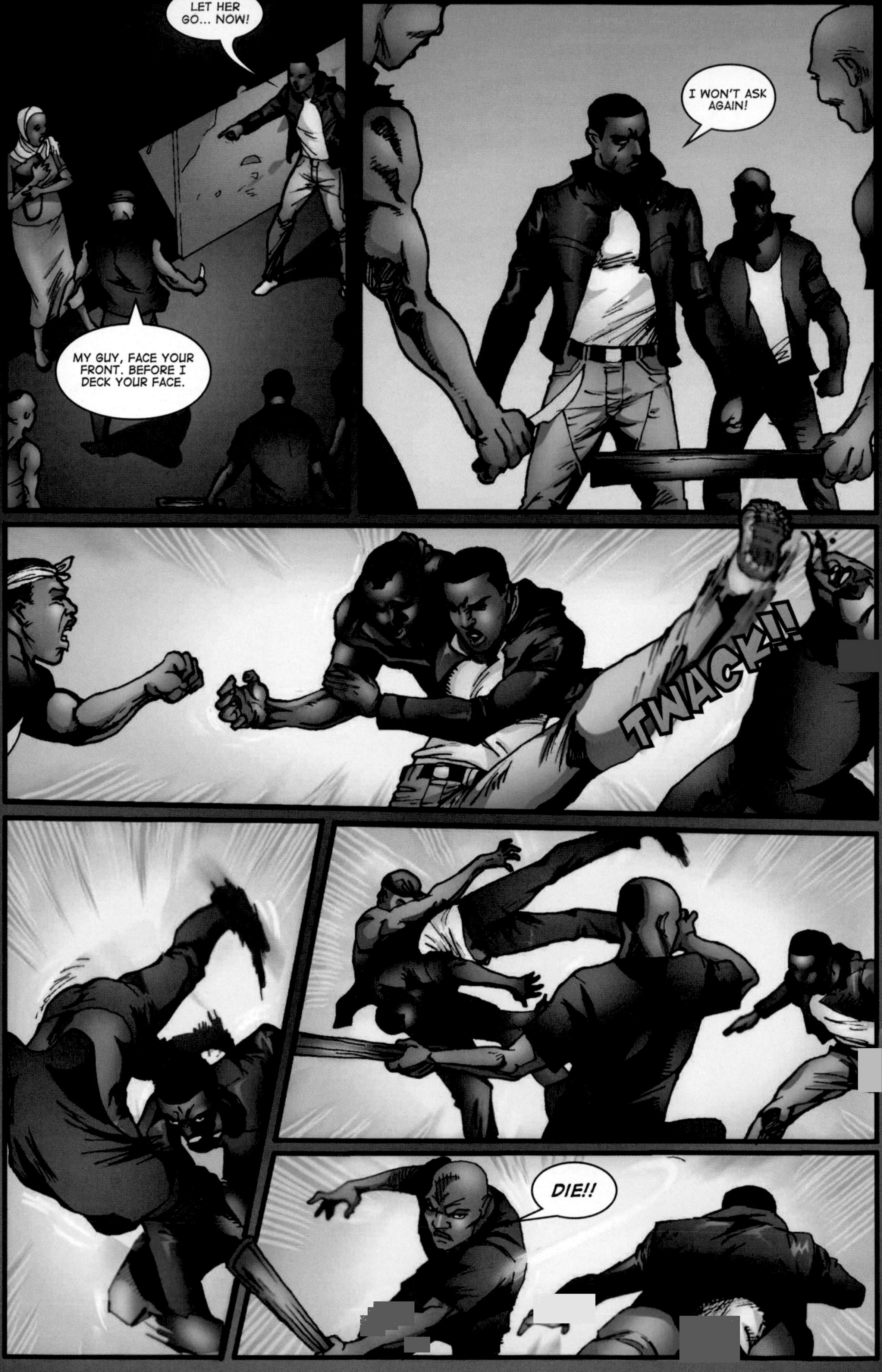
LET HER GO... NOW!
MY GUY, FACE YOUR FRONT. BEFORE I DECK YOUR FACE.
I WON'T ASK AGAIN!
TWACK!!
DIE!!

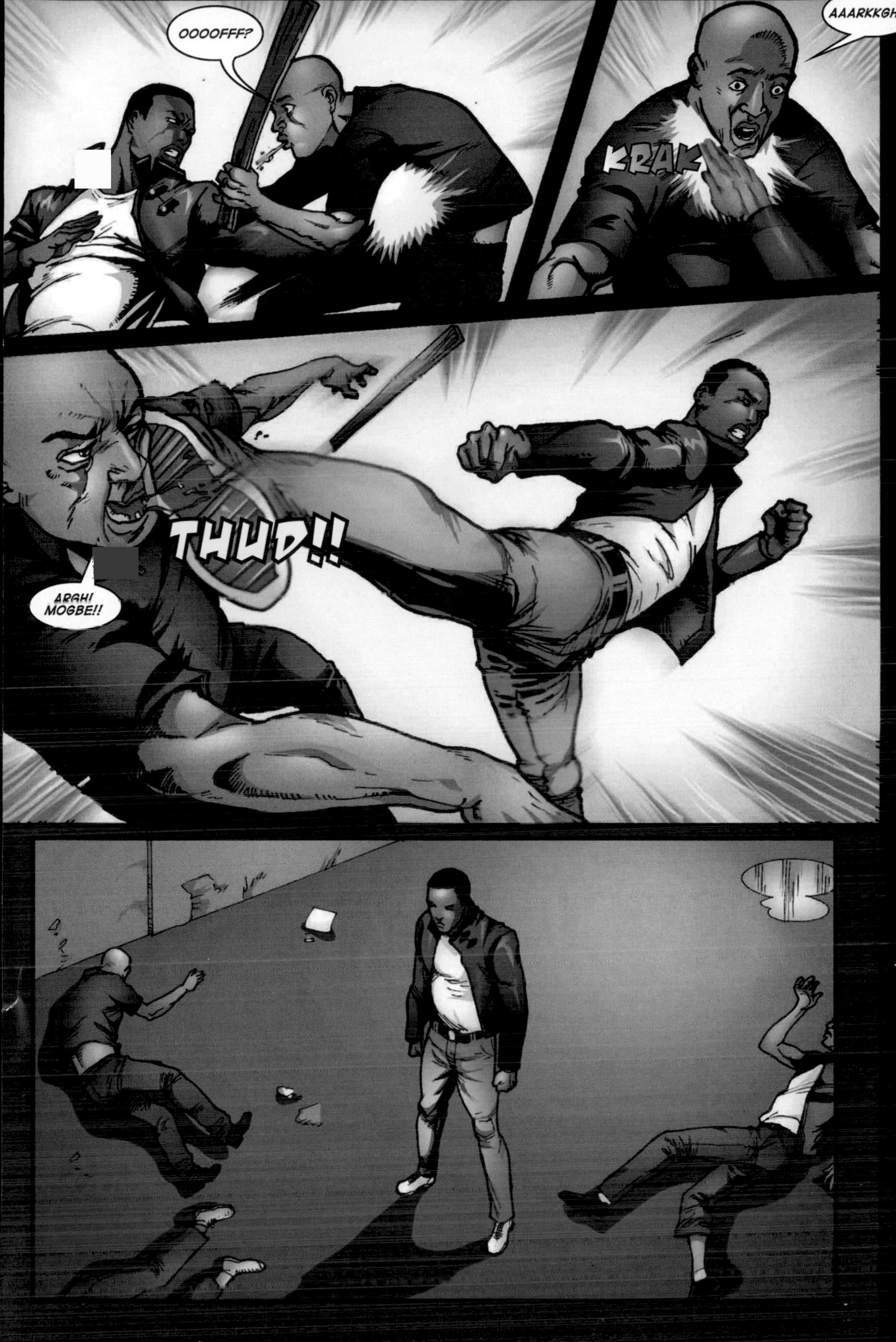
OOOOFFF?
AAARKKGH?
KRAK
THUD!!
ARGH! MOGBE!!

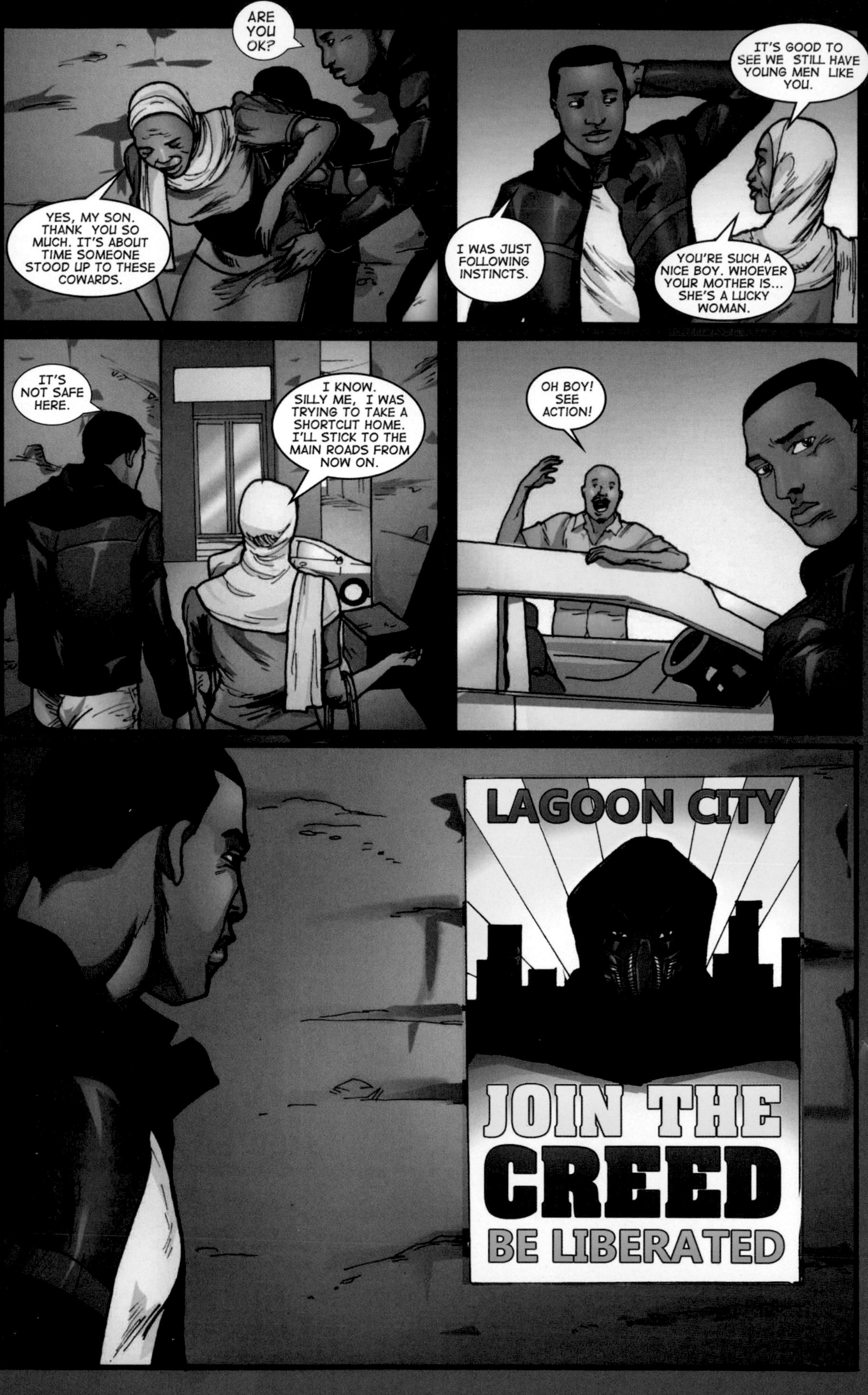
ARE YOU OK?
YES, MY SON. THANK YOU SO MUCH. IT'S ABOUT TIME SOMEONE STOOD UP TO THESE COWARDS.
IT'S GOOD TO SEE WE STILL HAVE YOUNG MEN LIKE YOU.
I WAS JUST FOLLOWING INSTINCTS.
YOU'RE SUCH A NICE BOY. WHOEVER YOUR MOTHER IS... SHE'S A LUCKY WOMAN.
IT'S NOT SAFE HERE.
I KNOW. SILLY ME, I WAS TRYING TO TAKE A SHORTCUT HOME. I'LL STICK TO THE MAIN ROADS FROM NOW ON.
OH BOY! SEE ACTION!
LAGOON CITY
JOIN THE
CREED
BE LIBERATED

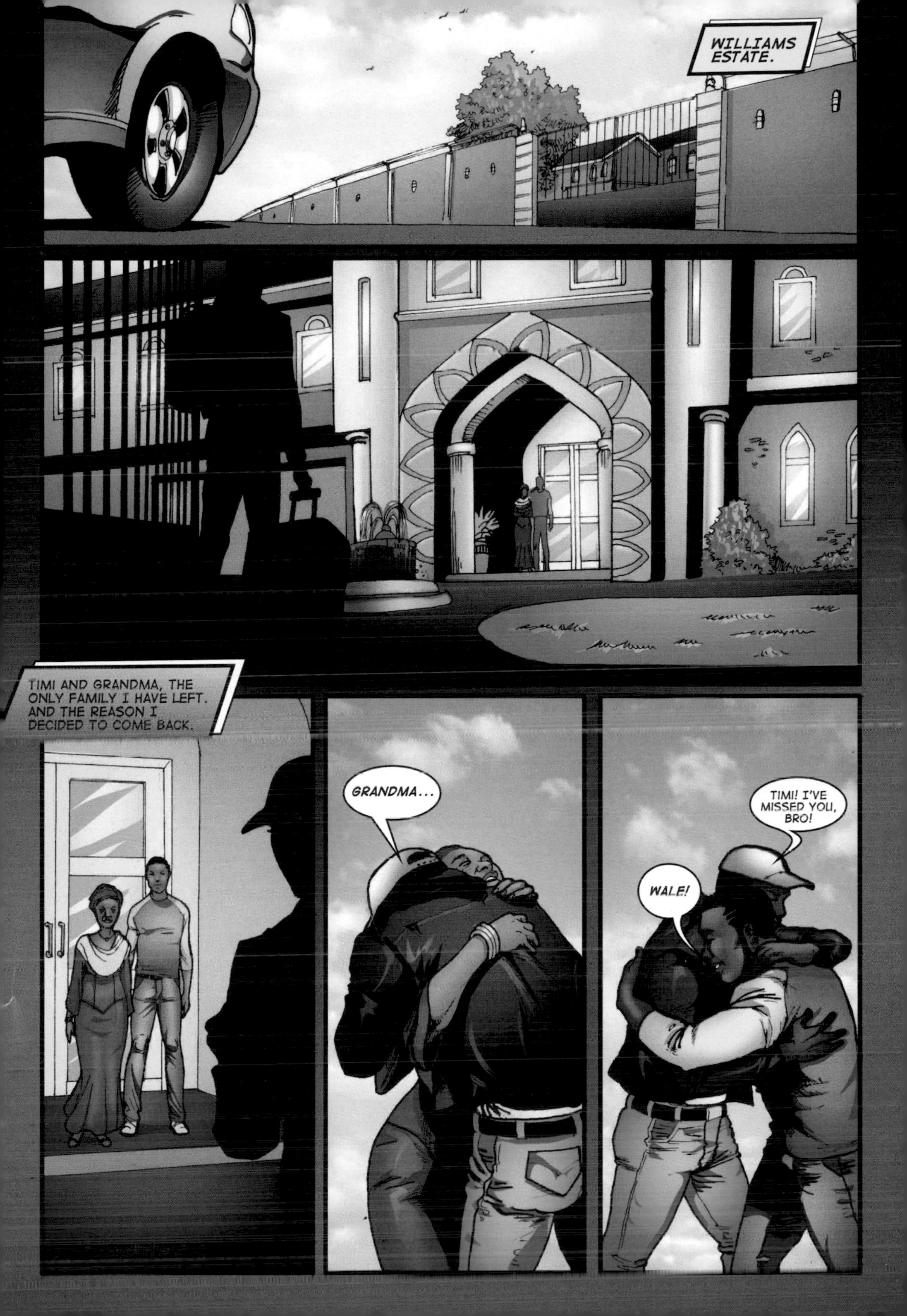
WILLIAMS ESTATE.
TIMI AND GRANDMA, THE ONLY FAMILY I HAVE LEFT. AND THE REASON I DECIDED TO COME BACK.
GRANDMA...
TIMI! I'VE MISSED YOU, BRO!
WALE!

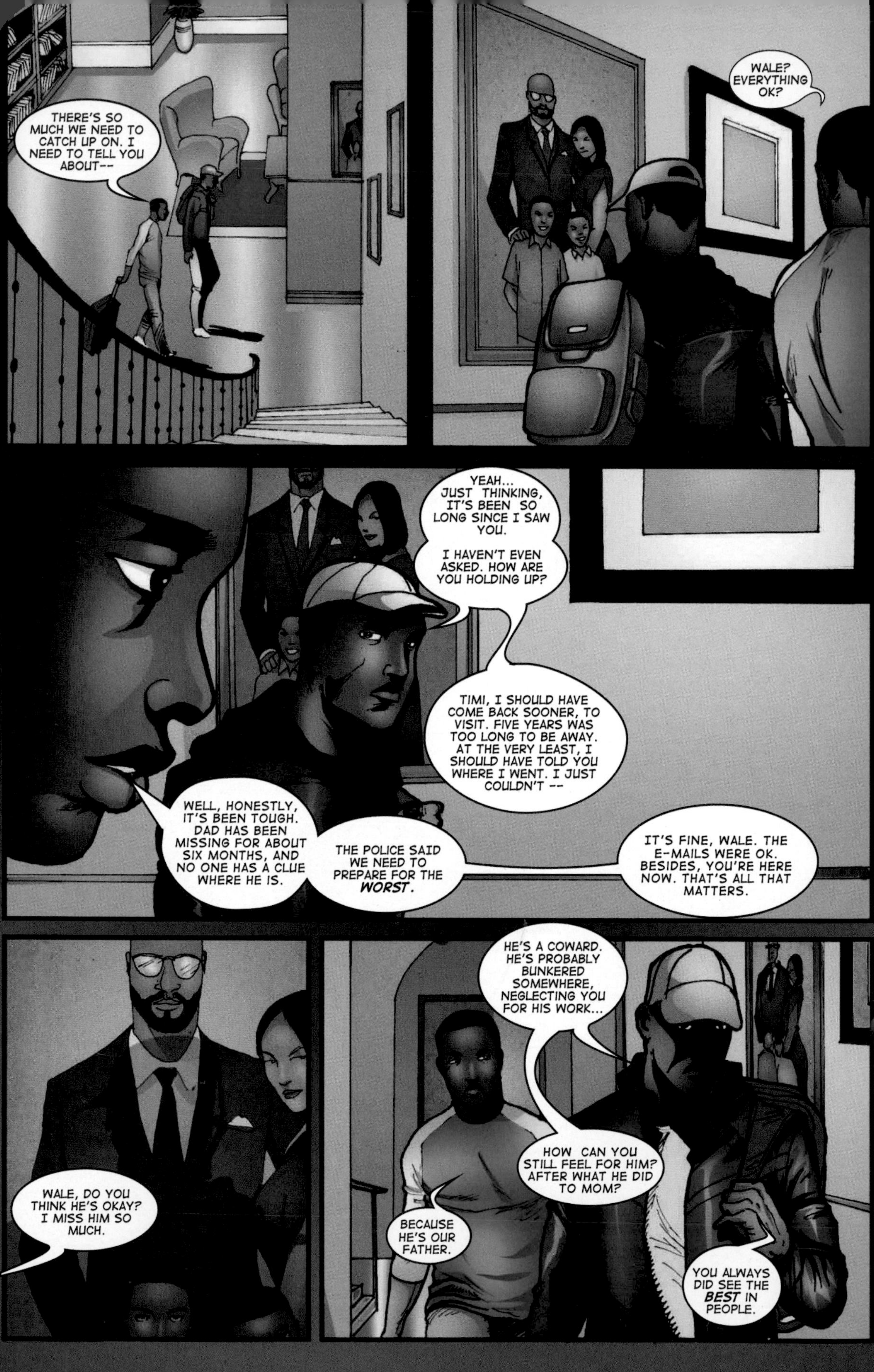
THERE'S SO MUCH WE NEED TO CATCH UP ON. I NEED TO TELL YOU ABOUT--
WALE? EVERYTHING OK?
YEAH... JUST THINKING, IT'S BEEN SO LONG SINCE I SAW YOU.
I HAVEN'T EVEN ASKED. HOW ARE YOU HOLDING UP?
TIMI, I SHOULD HAVE COME BACK SOONER, TO VISIT. FIVE YEARS WAS TOO LONG TO BE AWAY. AT THE VERY LEAST, I SHOULD HAVE TOLD YOU WHERE I WENT. I JUST COULDN'T --
WELL, HONESTLY, IT'S BEEN TOUGH. DAD HAS BEEN MISSING FOR ABOUT SIX MONTHS, AND NO ONE HAS A CLUE WHERE HE IS.
THE POLICE SAID WE NEED TO PREPARE FOR THE ***WORST***.
IT'S FINE, WALE. THE E-MAILS WERE OK. BESIDES, YOU'RE HERE NOW. THAT'S ALL THAT MATTERS.
WALE, DO YOU THINK HE'S OKAY? I MISS HIM SO MUCH.
HE'S A COWARD. HE'S PROBABLY BUNKERED SOMEWHERE, NEGLECTING YOU FOR HIS WORK...
HOW CAN YOU STILL FEEL FOR HIM? AFTER WHAT HE DID TO MOM?
BECAUSE HE'S OUR FATHER.
YOU ALWAYS DID SEE THE ***BEST*** IN PEOPLE.

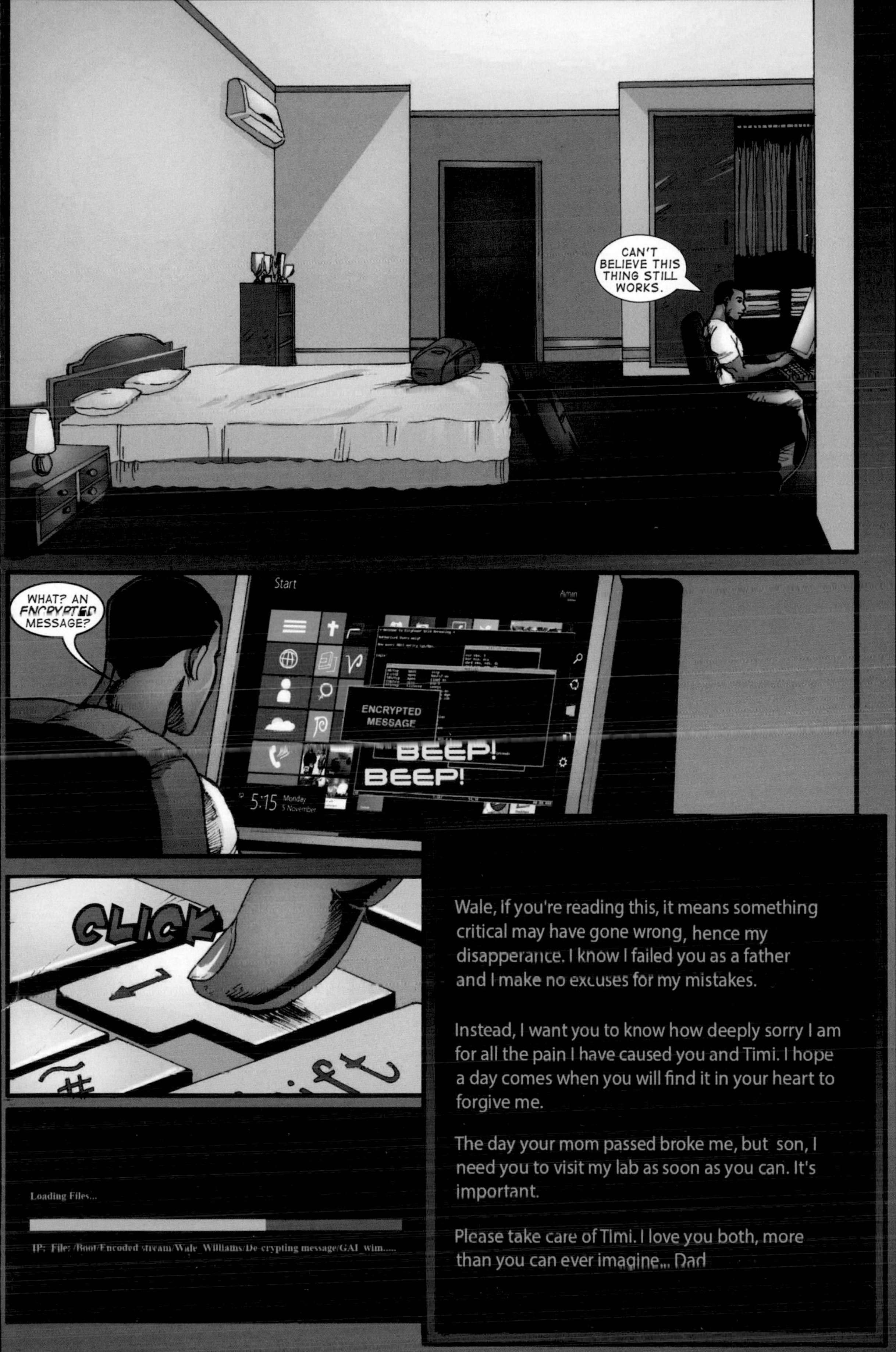
CAN'T BELIEVE THIS THING STILL WORKS.
WHAT? AN ENCRYPTED MESSAGE?
Start
ENCRYPTED MESSAGE
BEEP!
BEEP!
5:15 Monday 5 November
CLICK
Loading Files...
IP: File: /Boot/Encoded stream/Wale_Williams/De-crypting message/GAI_wim.....
Wale, If you're reading this, it means something critical may have gone wrong, hence my disapperance. I know I failed you as a father and I make no excuses for my mistakes.
Instead, I want you to know how deeply sorry I am for all the pain I have caused you and Timi. I hope a day comes when you will find it in your heart to forgive me.
The day your mom passed broke me, but son, I need you to visit my lab as soon as you can. It's important.
Please take care of Timi. I love you both, more than you can ever imagine... Dad

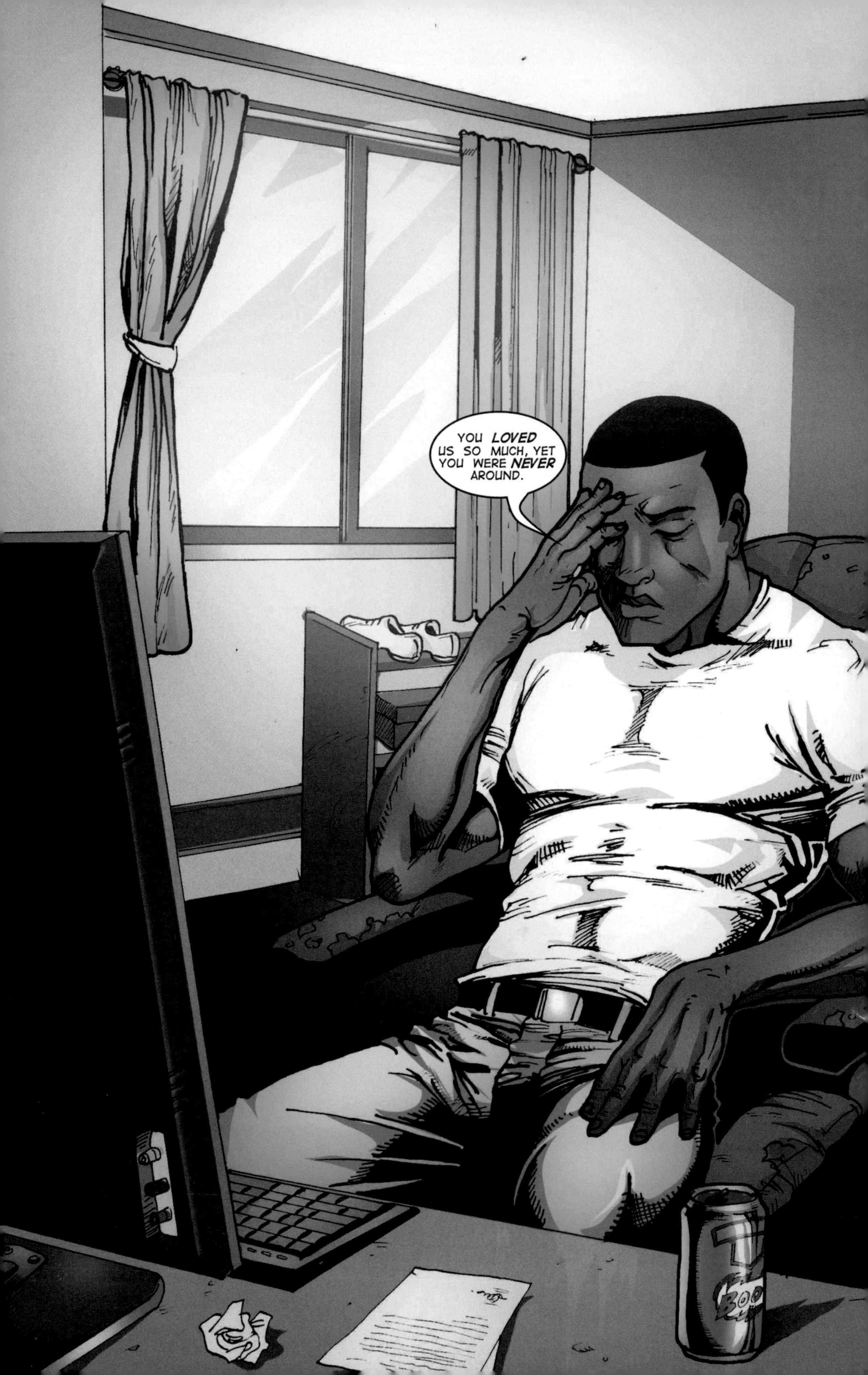
YOU LOVED US SO MUCH, YET YOU WERE NEVER AROUND.

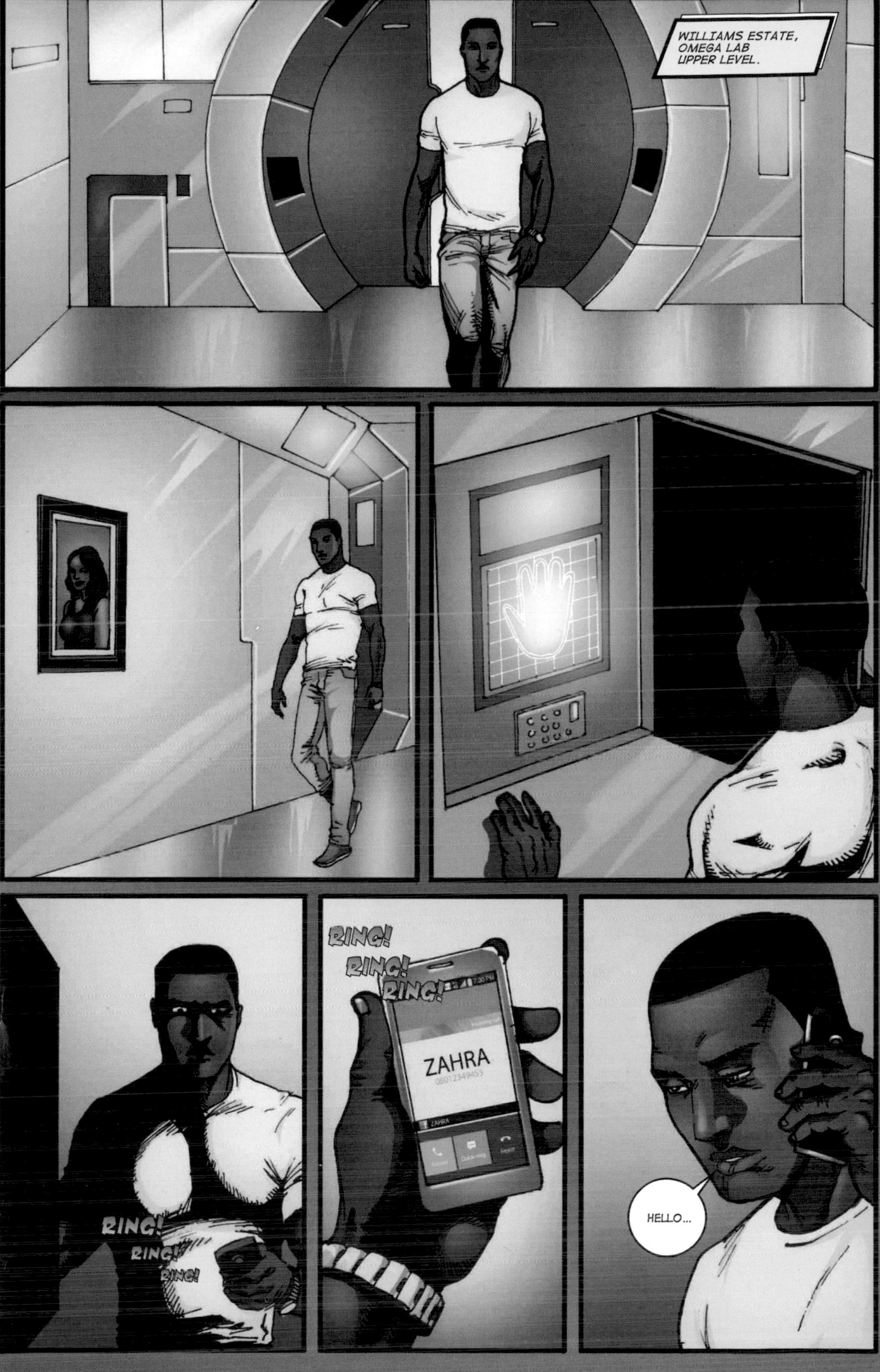
WILLIAMS ESTATE, OMEGA LAB UPPER LEVEL.
RING! RING! RING!
RING! RING! RING!
ZAHRA
08012349455
HELLO...

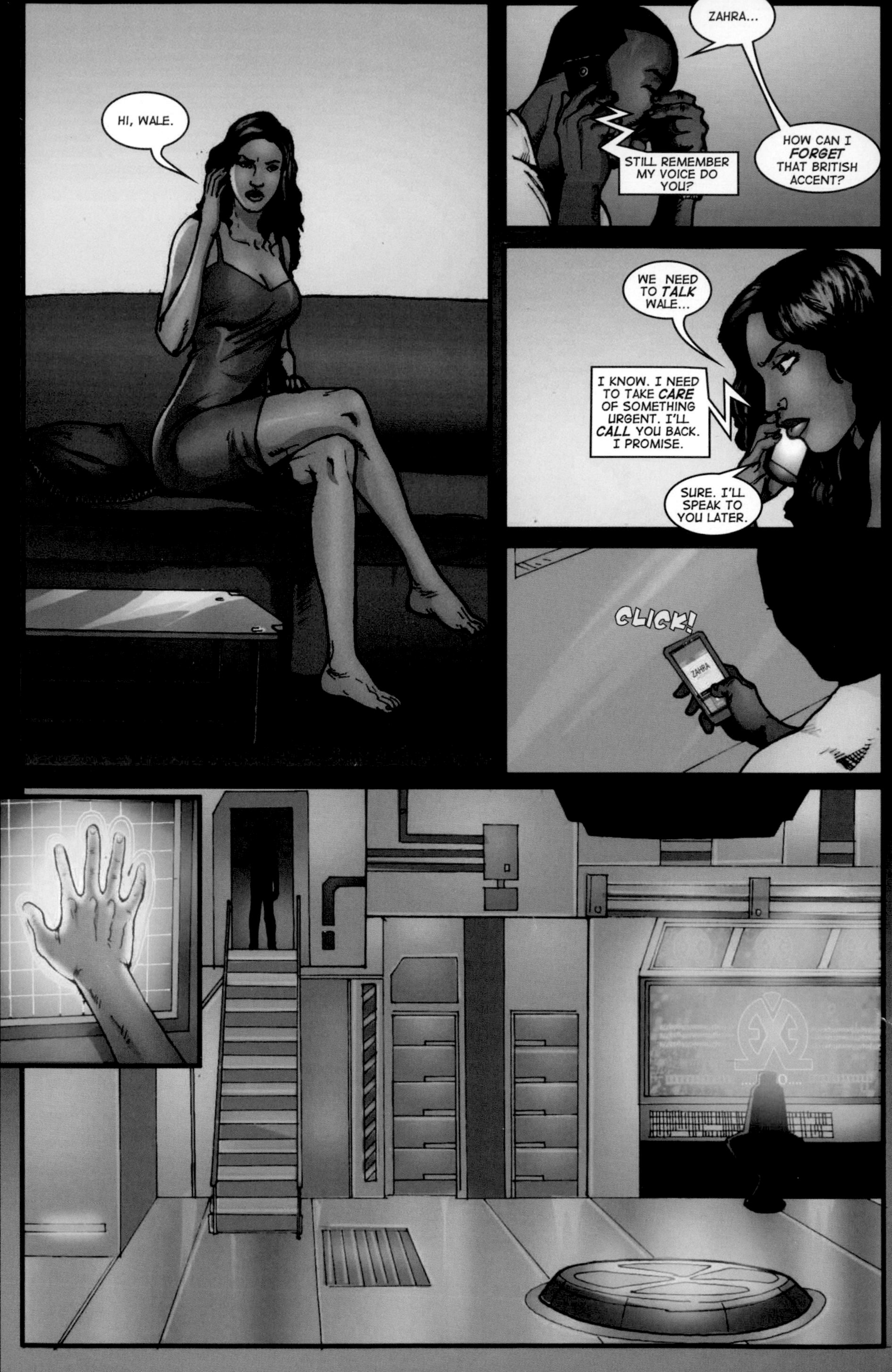
HI, WALE.
ZAHRA...
STILL REMEMBER MY VOICE DO YOU?
HOW CAN I FORGET THAT BRITISH ACCENT?
WE NEED TO TALK WALE...
I KNOW. I NEED TO TAKE CARE OF SOMETHING URGENT. I'LL CALL YOU BACK. I PROMISE.
SURE. I'LL SPEAK TO YOU LATER.
CLICK!
ZAHRA

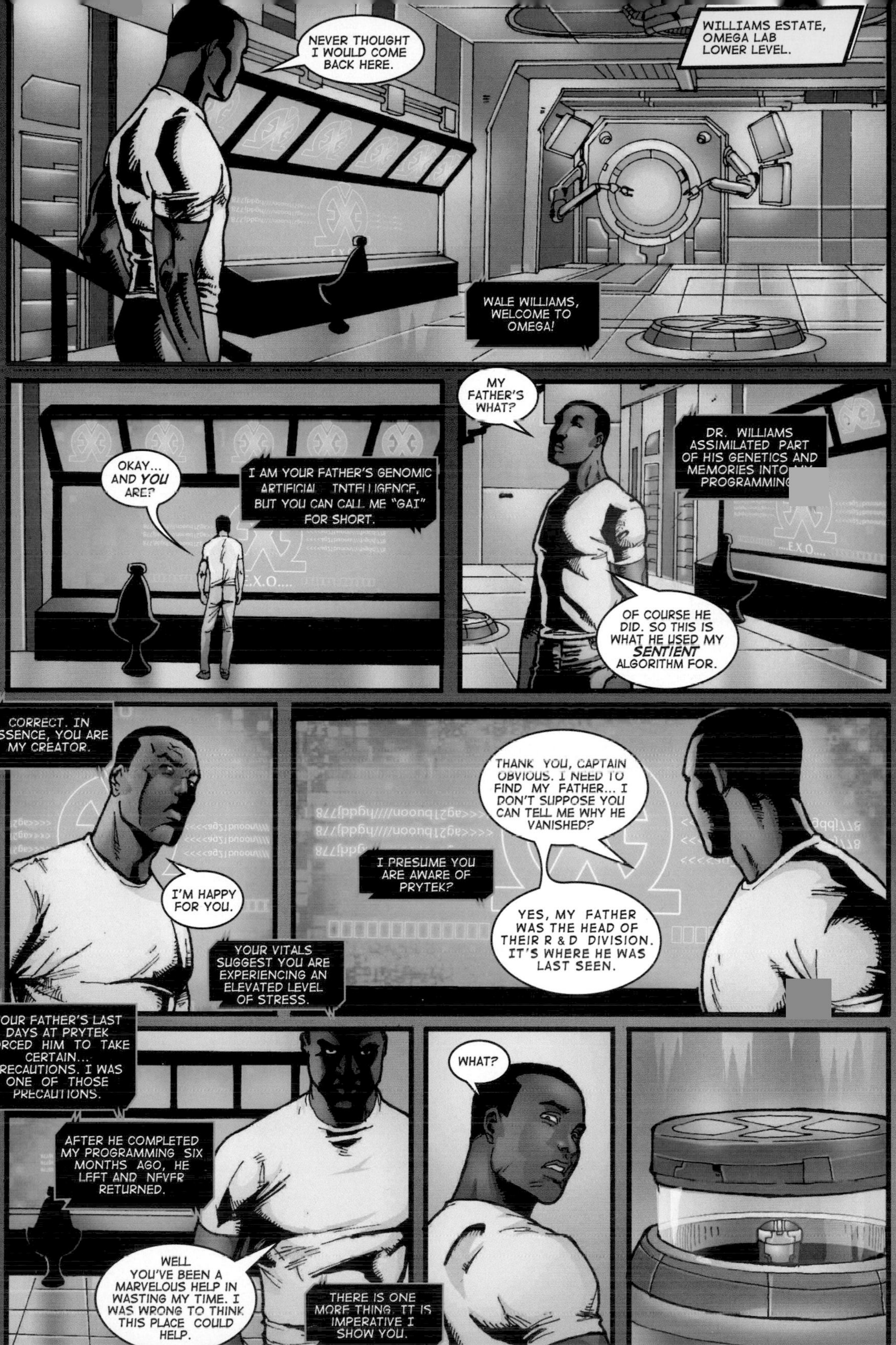
WILLIAMS ESTATE, OMEGA LAB LOWER LEVEL.
NEVER THOUGHT I WOULD COME BACK HERE.
WALE WILLIAMS, WELCOME TO OMEGA!
OKAY... AND YOU ARE?
I AM YOUR FATHER'S GENOMIC ARTIFICIAL INTELLIGENCE, BUT YOU CAN CALL ME "GAI" FOR SHORT.
MY FATHER'S WHAT?
DR. WILLIAMS ASSIMILATED PART OF HIS GENETICS AND MEMORIES INTO MY PROGRAMMING.
OF COURSE HE DID. SO THIS IS WHAT HE USED MY SENTIENT ALGORITHM FOR.
CORRECT. IN ESSENCE, YOU ARE MY CREATOR.
I'M HAPPY FOR YOU.
YOUR VITALS SUGGEST YOU ARE EXPERIENCING AN ELEVATED LEVEL OF STRESS.
THANK YOU, CAPTAIN OBVIOUS. I NEED TO FIND MY FATHER... I DON'T SUPPOSE YOU CAN TELL ME WHY HE VANISHED?
I PRESUME YOU ARE AWARE OF PRYTEK?
YES, MY FATHER WAS THE HEAD OF THEIR R & D DIVISION. IT'S WHERE HE WAS LAST SEEN.
YOUR FATHER'S LAST DAYS AT PRYTEK FORCED HIM TO TAKE CERTAIN... PRECAUTIONS. I WAS ONE OF THOSE PRECAUTIONS.
AFTER HE COMPLETED MY PROGRAMMING SIX MONTHS AGO, HE LEFT AND NEVER RETURNED.
WELL YOU'VE BEEN A MARVELOUS HELP IN WASTING MY TIME. I WAS WRONG TO THINK THIS PLACE COULD HELP.
THERE IS ONE MORE THING. IT IS IMPERATIVE I SHOW YOU.
WHAT?

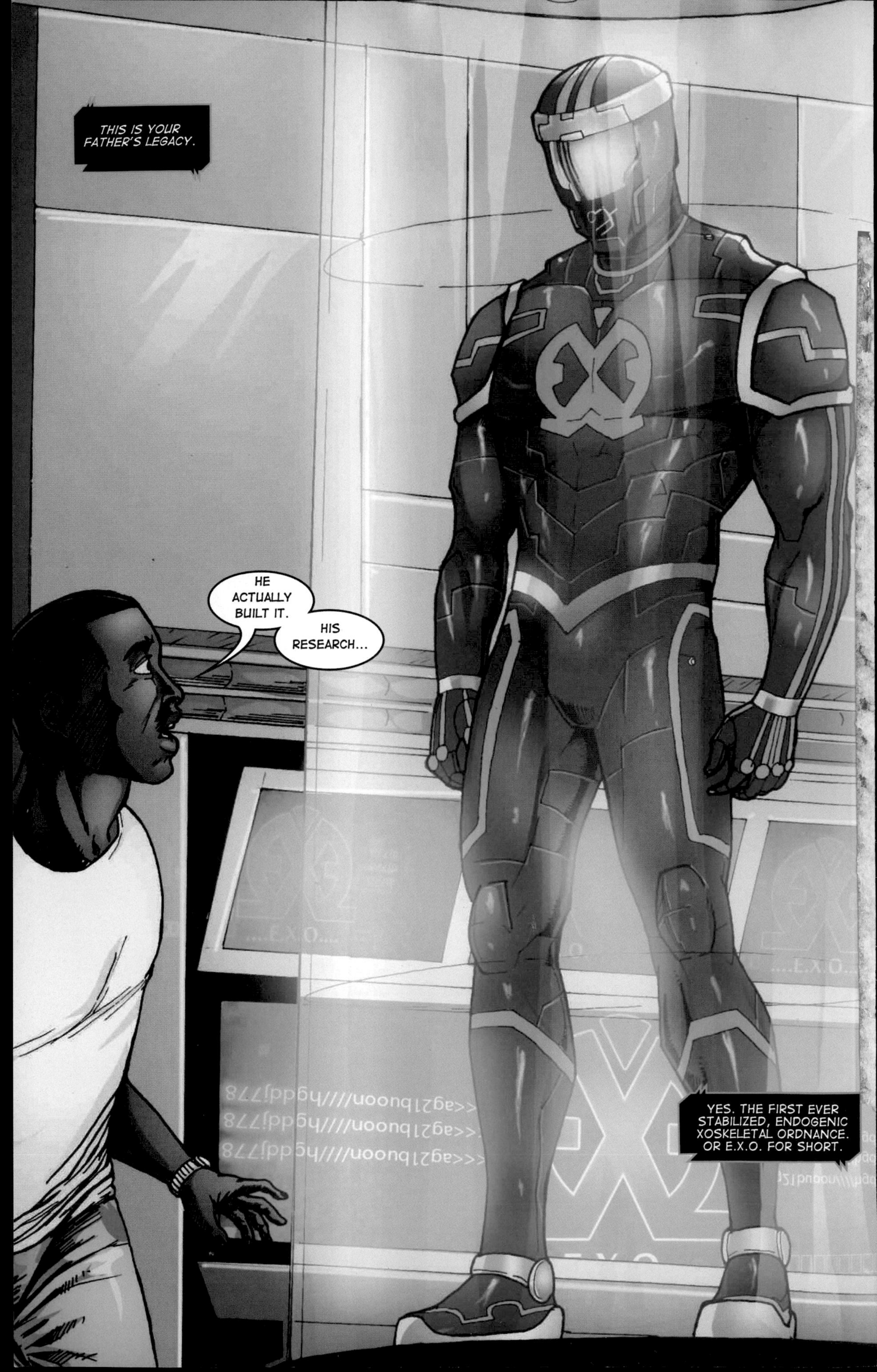
THIS IS YOUR FATHER'S LEGACY.
HE ACTUALLY BUILT IT.
HIS RESEARCH...
YES. THE FIRST EVER STABILIZED, ENDOGENIC XOSKELETAL ORDNANCE. OR E.X.O. FOR SHORT.

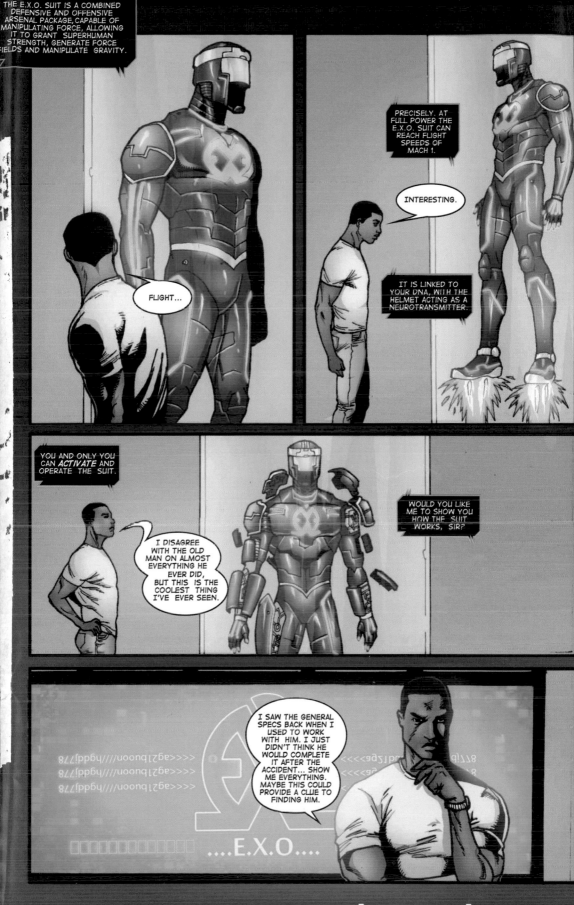

THE E.X.O. SUIT IS A COMBINED DEFENSIVE AND OFFENSIVE ARSENAL PACKAGE, CAPABLE OF MANIPULATING FORCE, ALLOWING IT TO GRANT SUPERHUMAN STRENGTH, GENERATE FORCE FIELDS AND MANIPULATE GRAVITY.

FLIGHT...

PRECISELY. AT FULL POWER THE E.X.O. SUIT CAN REACH FLIGHT SPEEDS OF MACH 1.

INTERESTING.

IT IS LINKED TO YOUR DNA, WITH THE HELMET ACTING AS A NEUROTRANSMITTER.

YOU AND ONLY YOU CAN ACTIVATE AND OPERATE THE SUIT.

I DISAGREE WITH THE OLD MAN ON ALMOST EVERYTHING HE EVER DID, BUT THIS IS THE COOLEST THING I'VE EVER SEEN.

WOULD YOU LIKE ME TO SHOW YOU HOW THE SUIT WORKS, SIR?

I SAW THE GENERAL SPECS BACK WHEN I USED TO WORK WITH HIM. I JUST DIDN'T THINK HE WOULD COMPLETE IT AFTER THE ACCIDENT... SHOW ME EVERYTHING. MAYBE THIS COULD PROVIDE A CLUE TO FINDING HIM.

....E.X.O....

# END OF CHAPTER TWO

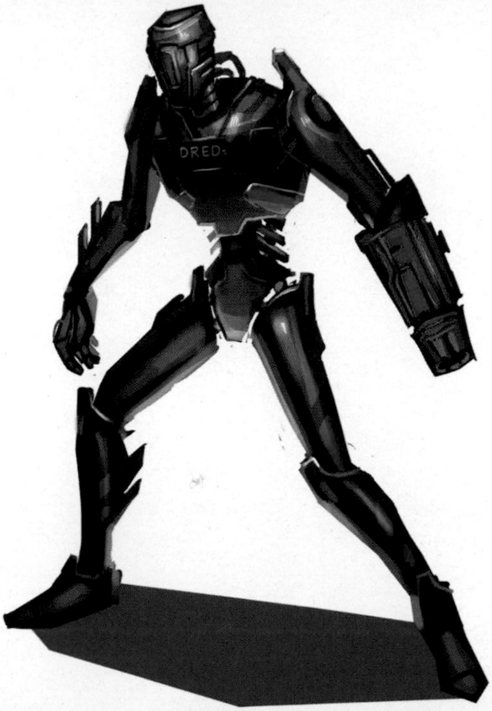
DREDs

Dominant Robotic Exoskeletal Drones.

- *DREDs*

# CHAPTER THREE

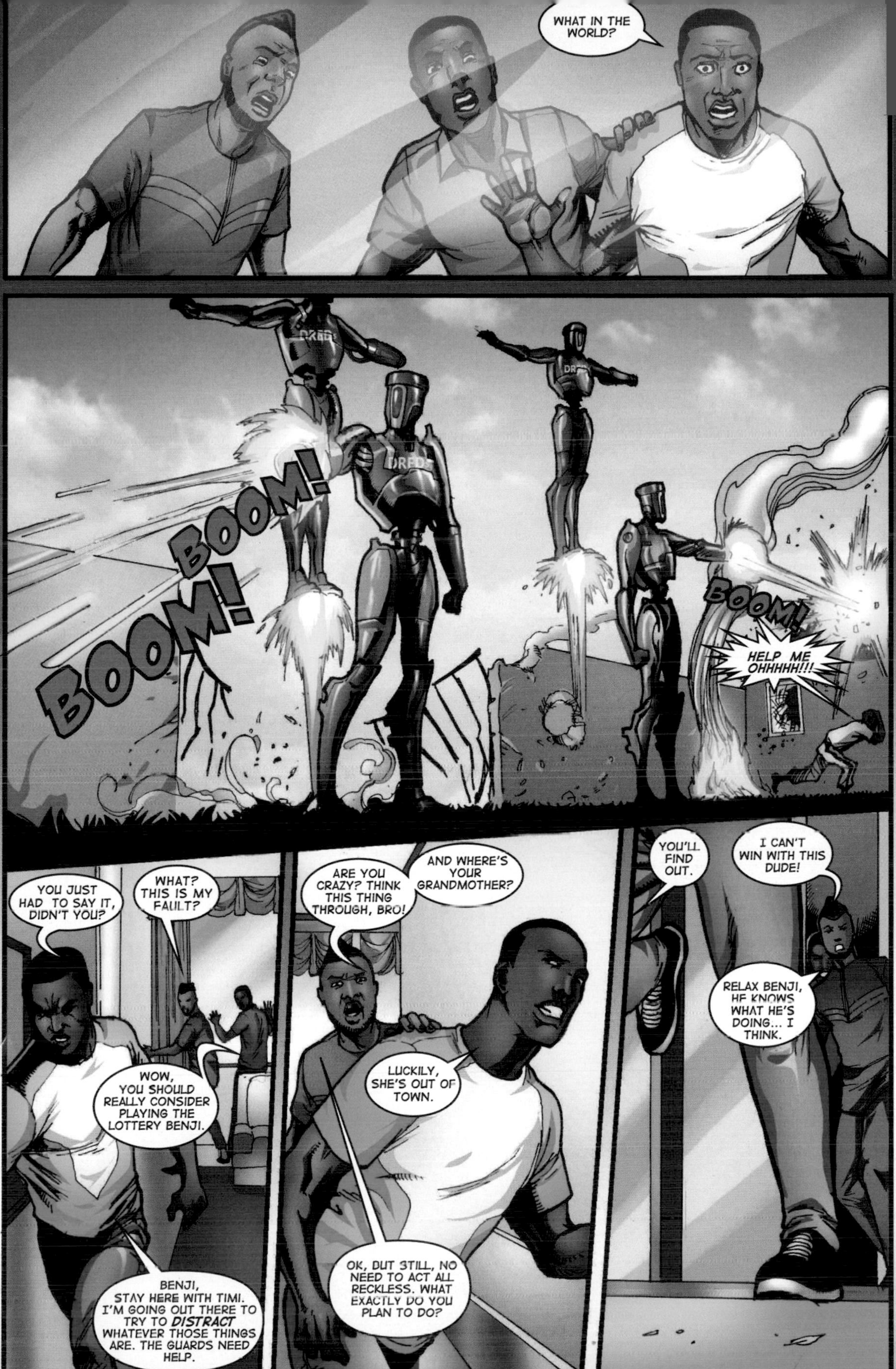
WHAT IN THE WORLD?
BOOM!
BOOM!
BOOM!
BOOM!
HELP ME OHHHHH!!!
YOU JUST HAD TO SAY IT, DIDN'T YOU?
WHAT? THIS IS MY FAULT?
WOW, YOU SHOULD REALLY CONSIDER PLAYING THE LOTTERY BENJI.
BENJI, STAY HERE WITH TIMI. I'M GOING OUT THERE TO TRY TO *DISTRACT* WHATEVER THOSE THINGS ARE. THE GUARDS NEED HELP.
ARE YOU CRAZY? THINK THIS THING THROUGH, BRO!
AND WHERE'S YOUR GRANDMOTHER?
LUCKILY, SHE'S OUT OF TOWN.
OK, BUT STILL, NO NEED TO ACT ALL RECKLESS. WHAT EXACTLY DO YOU PLAN TO DO?
YOU'LL FIND OUT.
I CAN'T WIN WITH THIS DUDE!
RELAX BENJI, HE KNOWS WHAT HE'S DOING... I THINK.

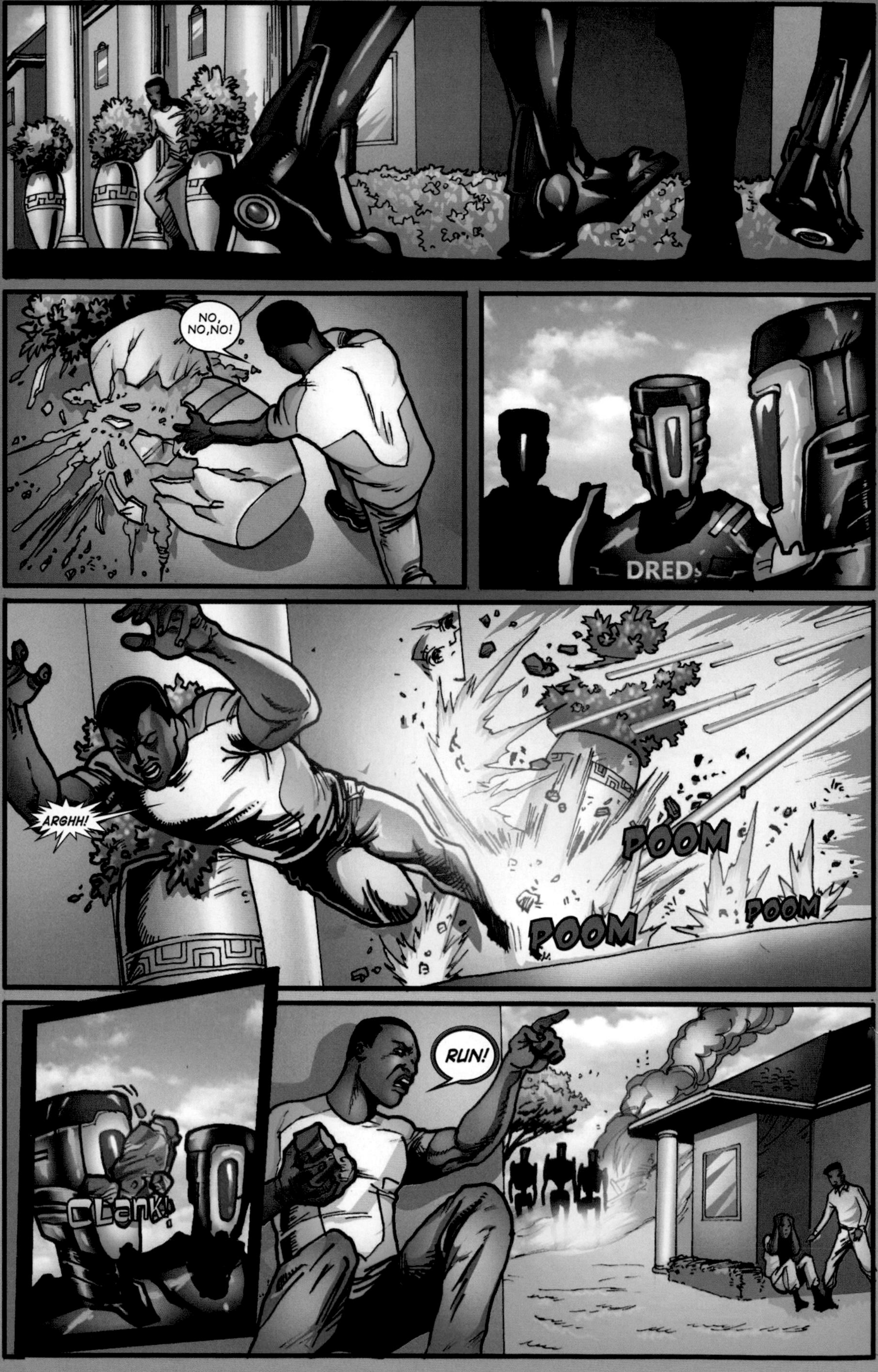
NO, NO,NO!
DREDS
ARGHH!
POOM
POOM
POOM
CLANK!
RUN!

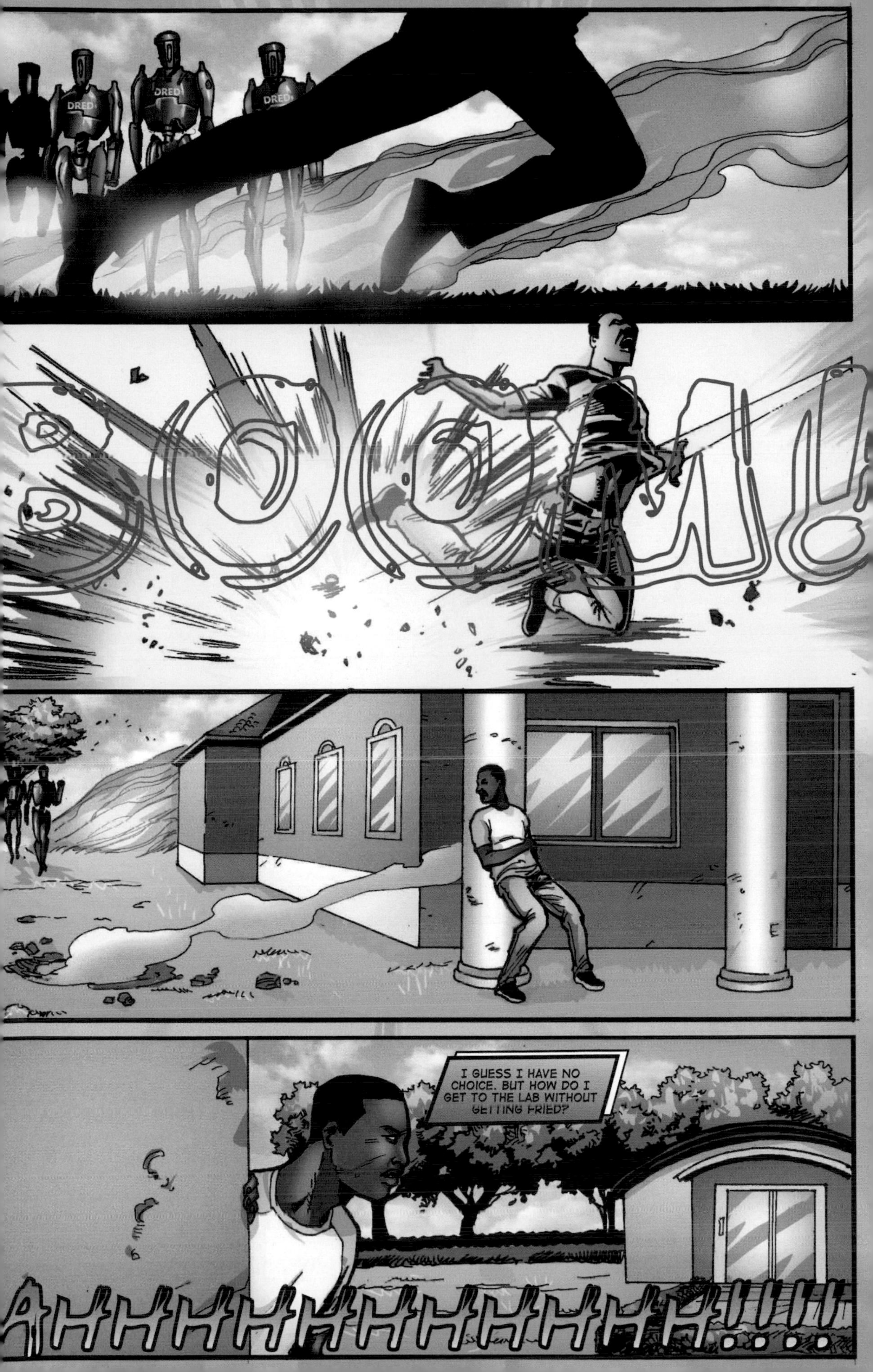
DRED
DRED
DRED
BOOM!
I GUESS I HAVE NO CHOICE. BUT HOW DO I GET TO THE LAB WITHOUT GETTING FRIED?
AHHHHHHHHHHHH!!!!!

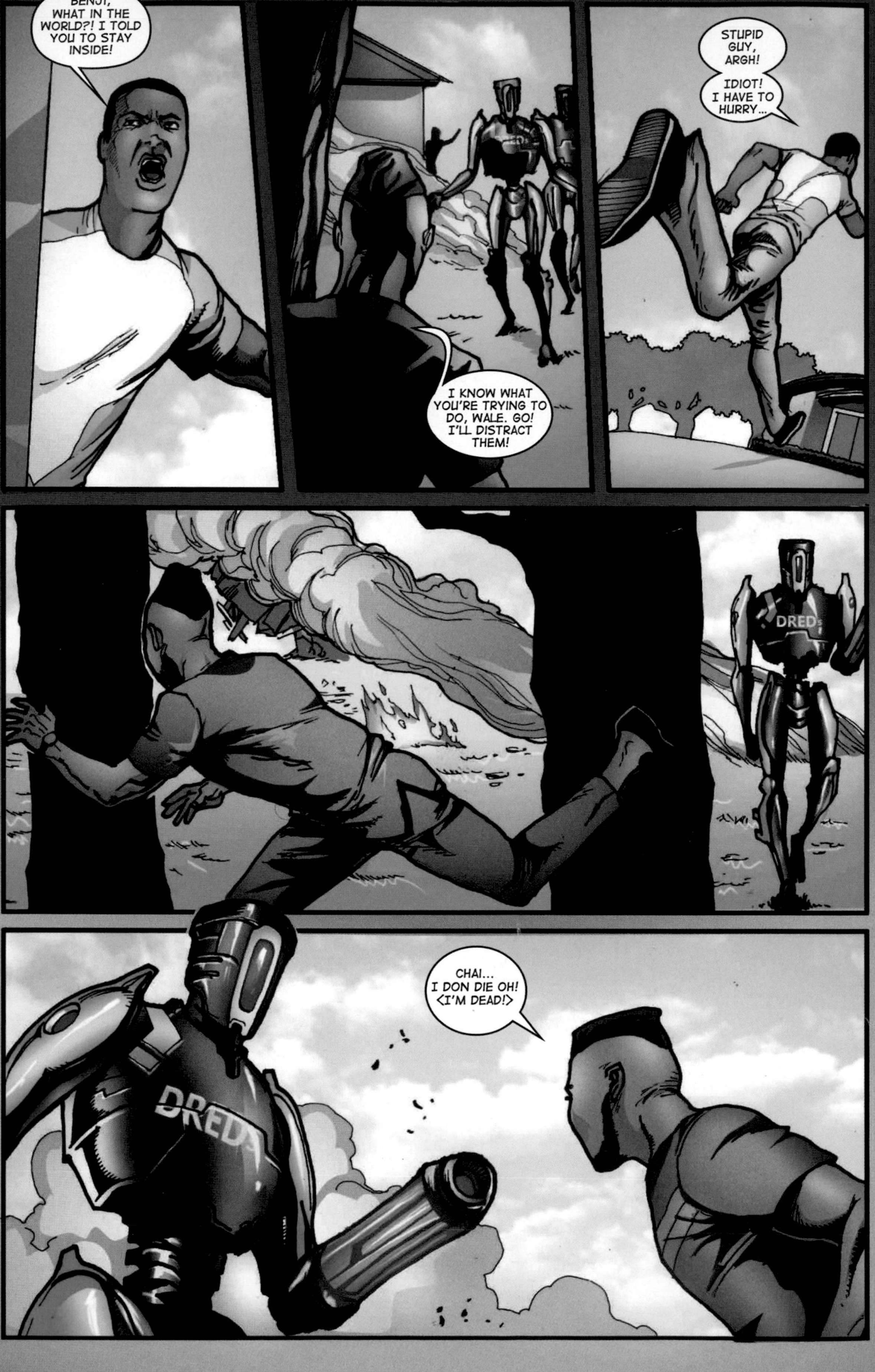
BENJI, WHAT IN THE WORLD?! I TOLD YOU TO STAY INSIDE!
I KNOW WHAT YOU'RE TRYING TO DO, WALE. GO! I'LL DISTRACT THEM!
STUPID GUY, ARGH!
IDIOT! I HAVE TO HURRY...
DREDS
CHAI... I DON DIE OH! <I'M DEAD!>
DREDS

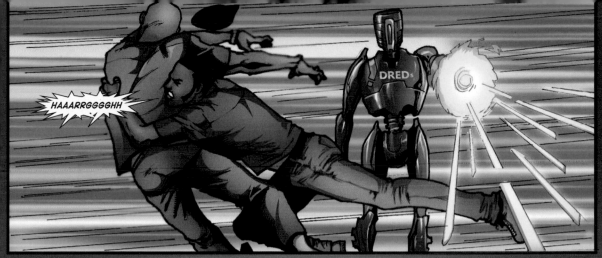

HAAARRGGGGHH

THANKS, TIMI. EVEN THOUGH ALL YOU DID WAS EXTEND MY LIFE BY AN ADDITIONAL THREE SECONDS.

IT'S NOT OVER YET...

SMASH!

WALE, IF YOU'RE GOING TO DO SOMETHING NOW WOULD BE GREAT...

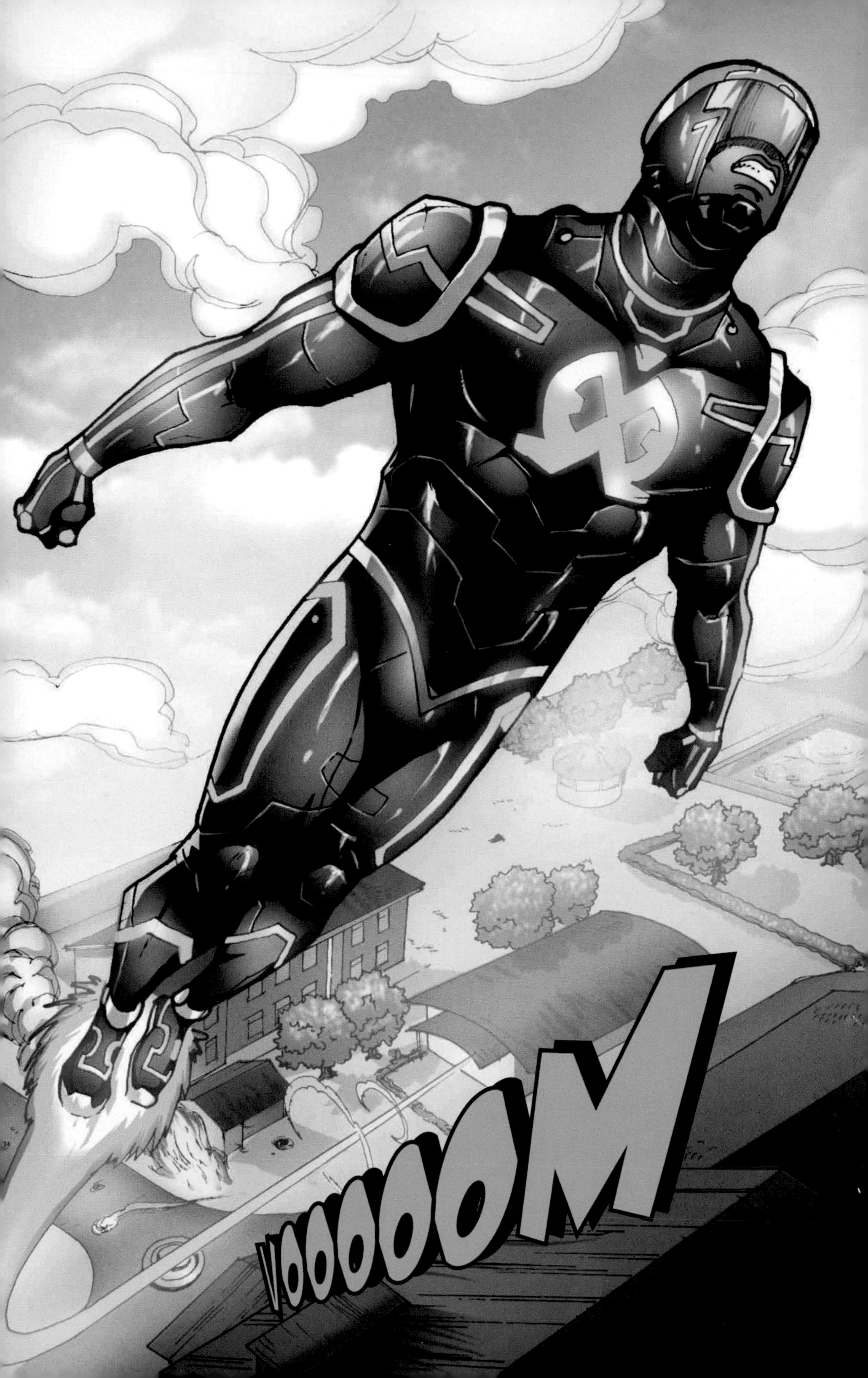
VOOOOOOM

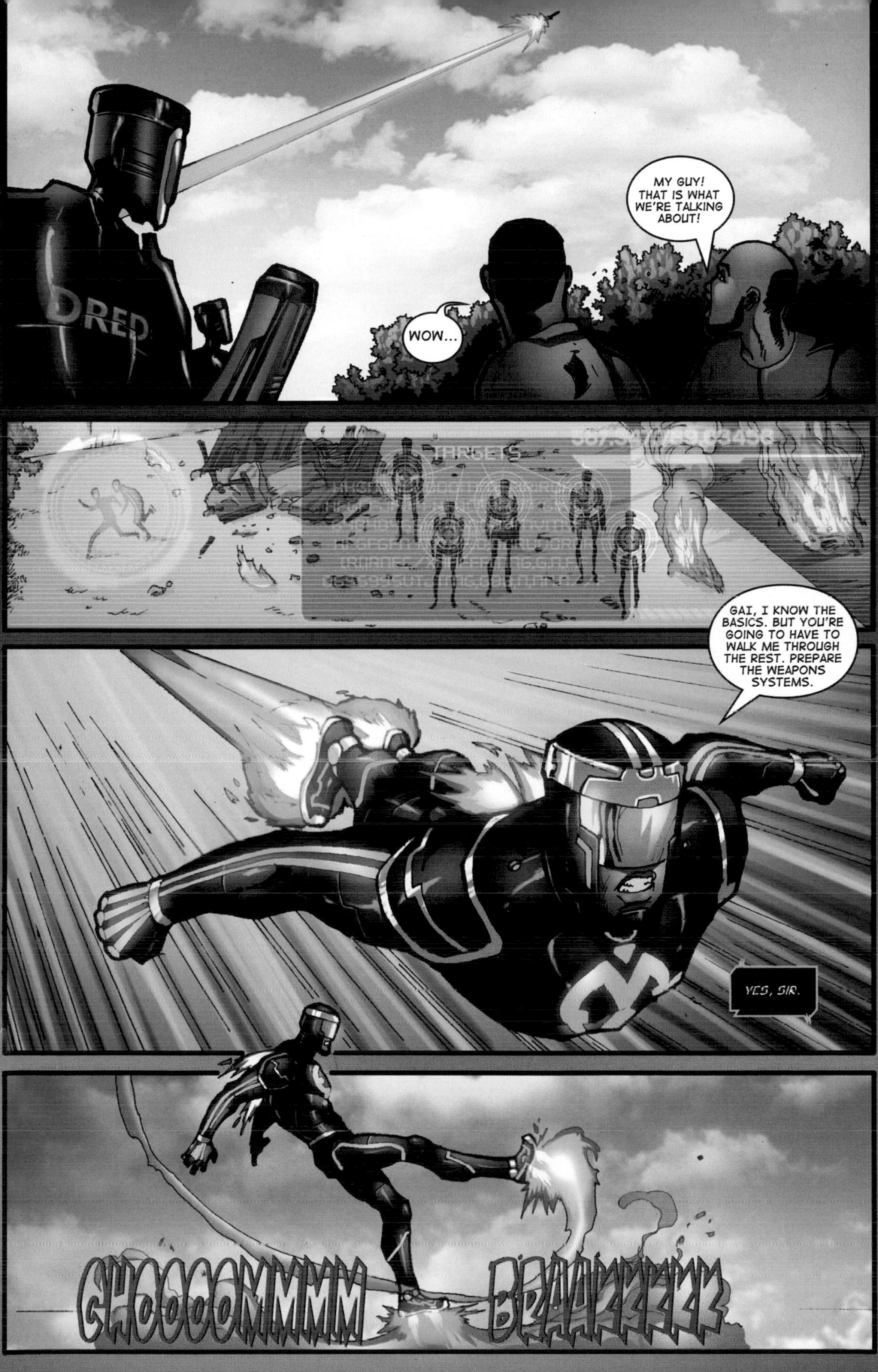
MY GUY! THAT IS WHAT WE'RE TALKING ABOUT!
WOW...
DRED
TARGETS
GAI, I KNOW THE BASICS. BUT YOU'RE GOING TO HAVE TO WALK ME THROUGH THE REST. PREPARE THE WEAPONS SYSTEMS.
YES, SIR.
CHOOOOOMMMMM

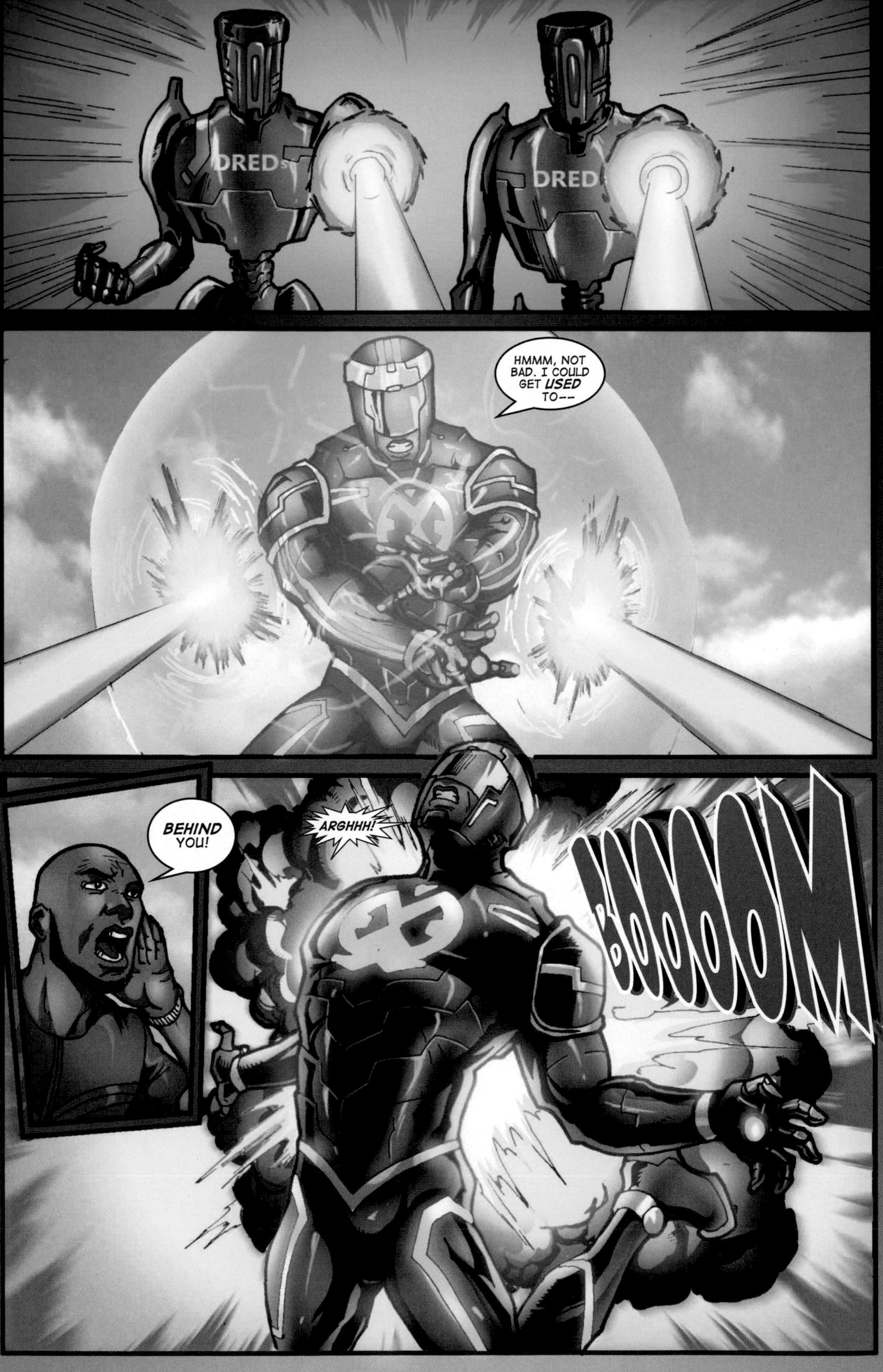
DRED
DRED
HMMM, NOT BAD. I COULD GET *USED* TO--
*BEHIND* YOU!
*ARGHHH!*
BOOOOM

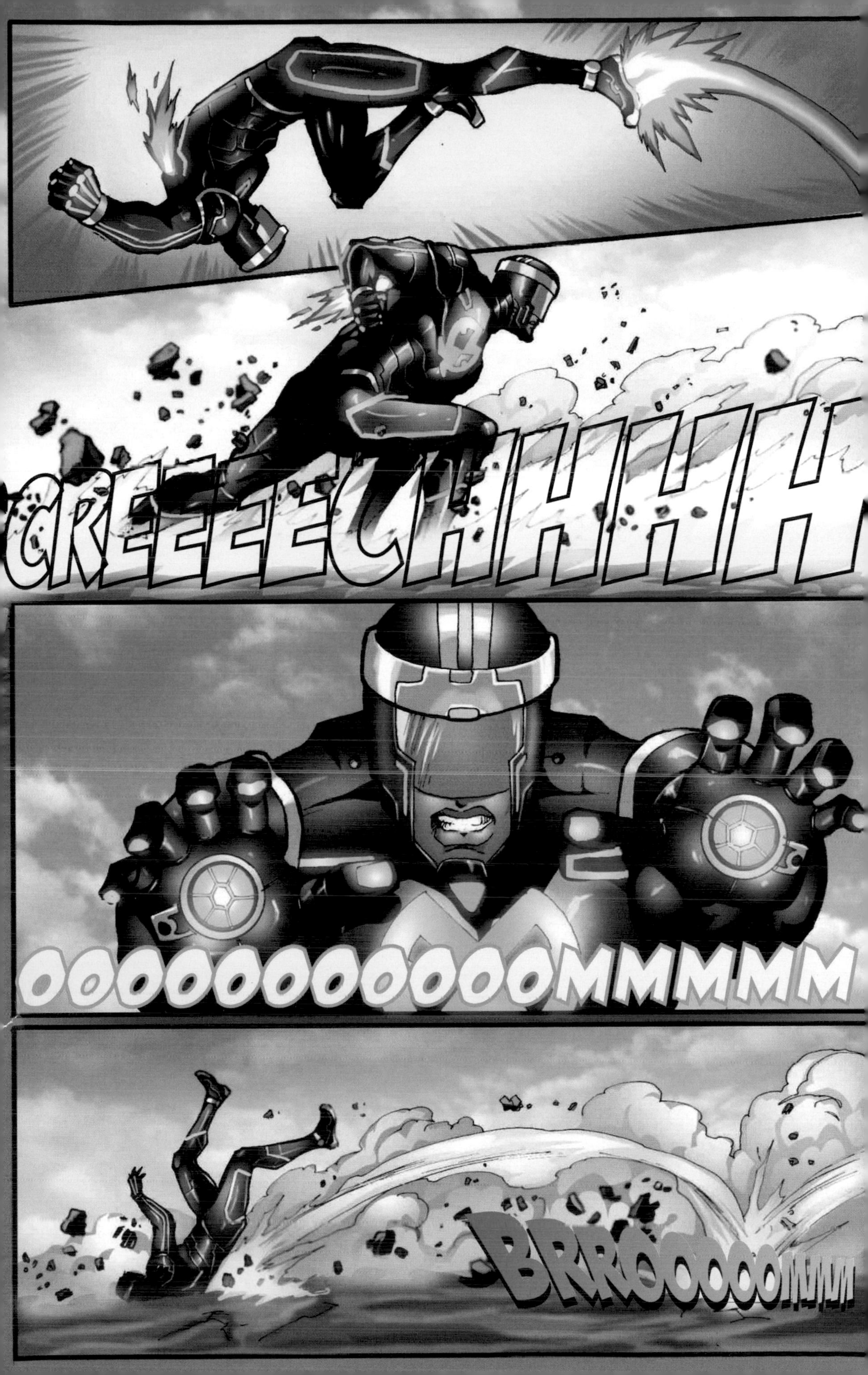
CREEEECHHHHH
OOOOOOOOOOOOMMMMMM
BRROOOOOMMM

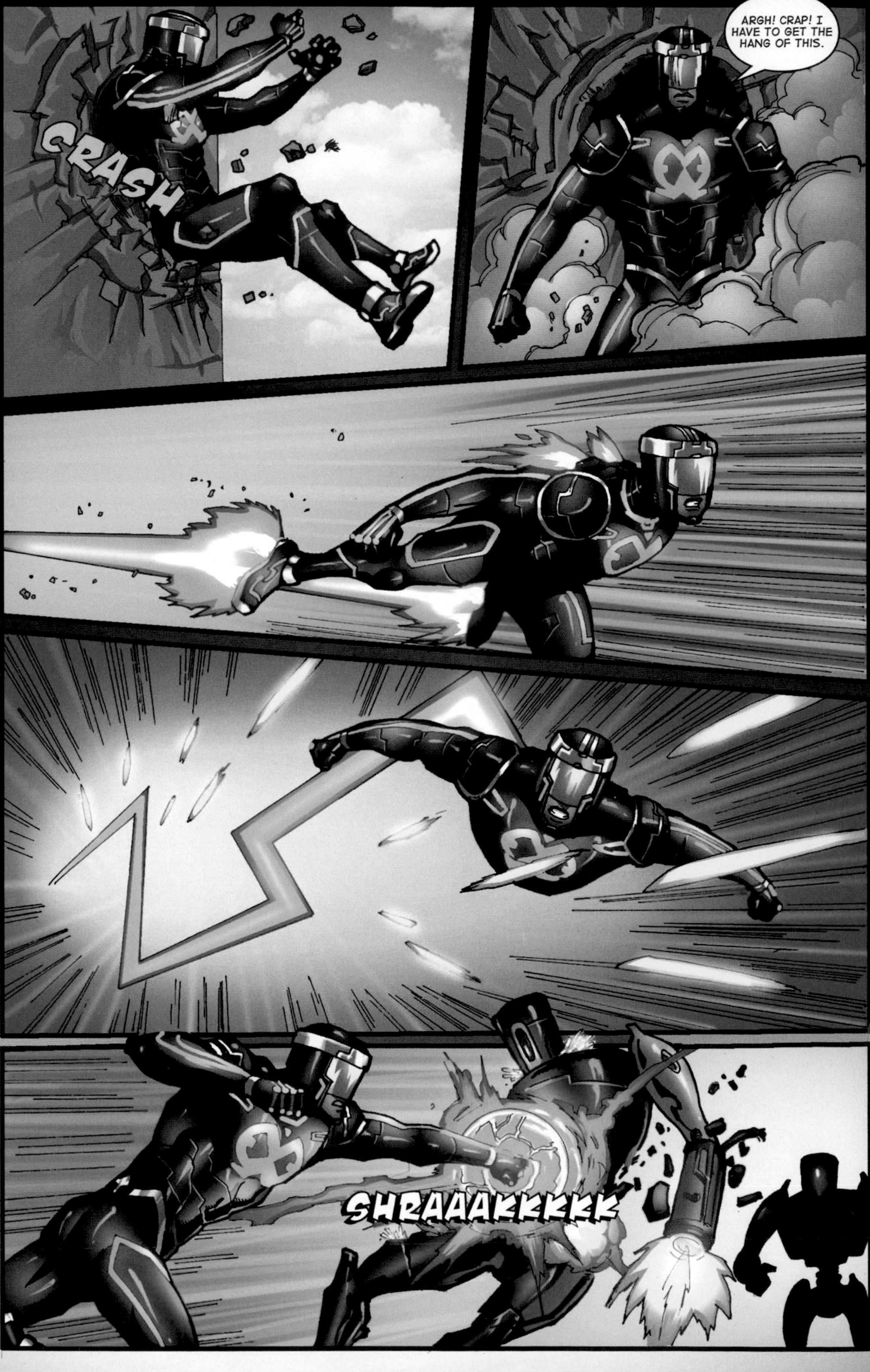
CRASH
ARGH! CRAP! I HAVE TO GET THE HANG OF THIS.
SHRAAAKKKKK

CHINK
CHINK
ARGH! WHAT NOW? GAI WHY--
ARGHH...
BROOOMMMMM

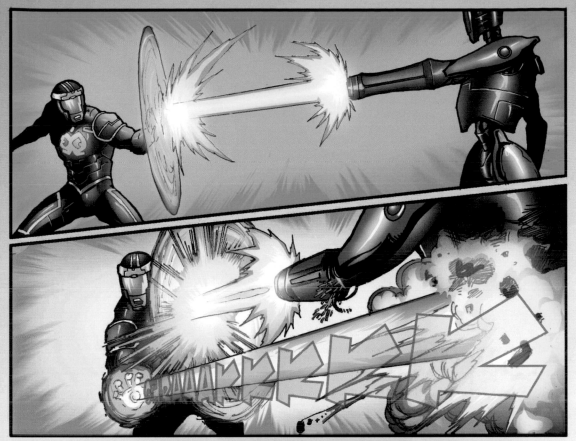

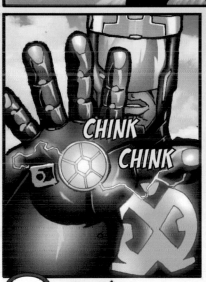

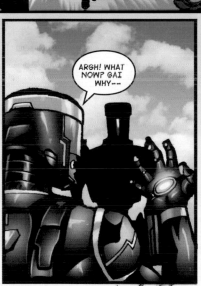

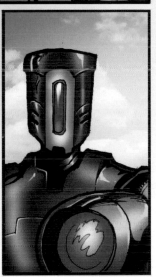

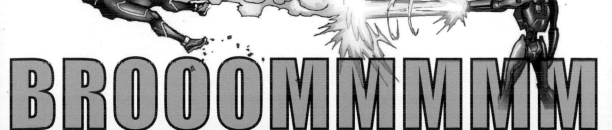

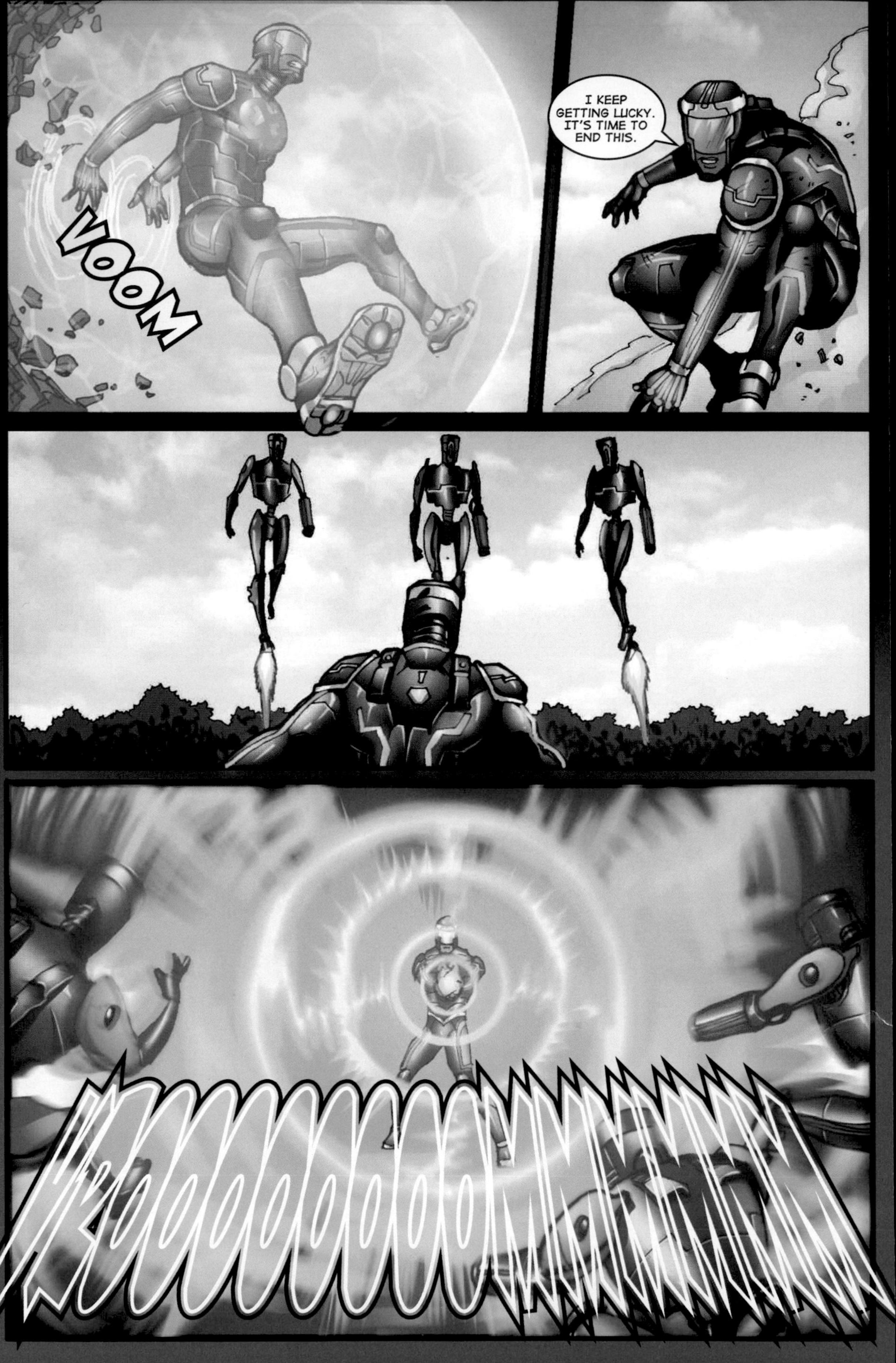
VOOM
I KEEP GETTING LUCKY. IT'S TIME TO END THIS.
KOOOOOOOOOMMMMMM

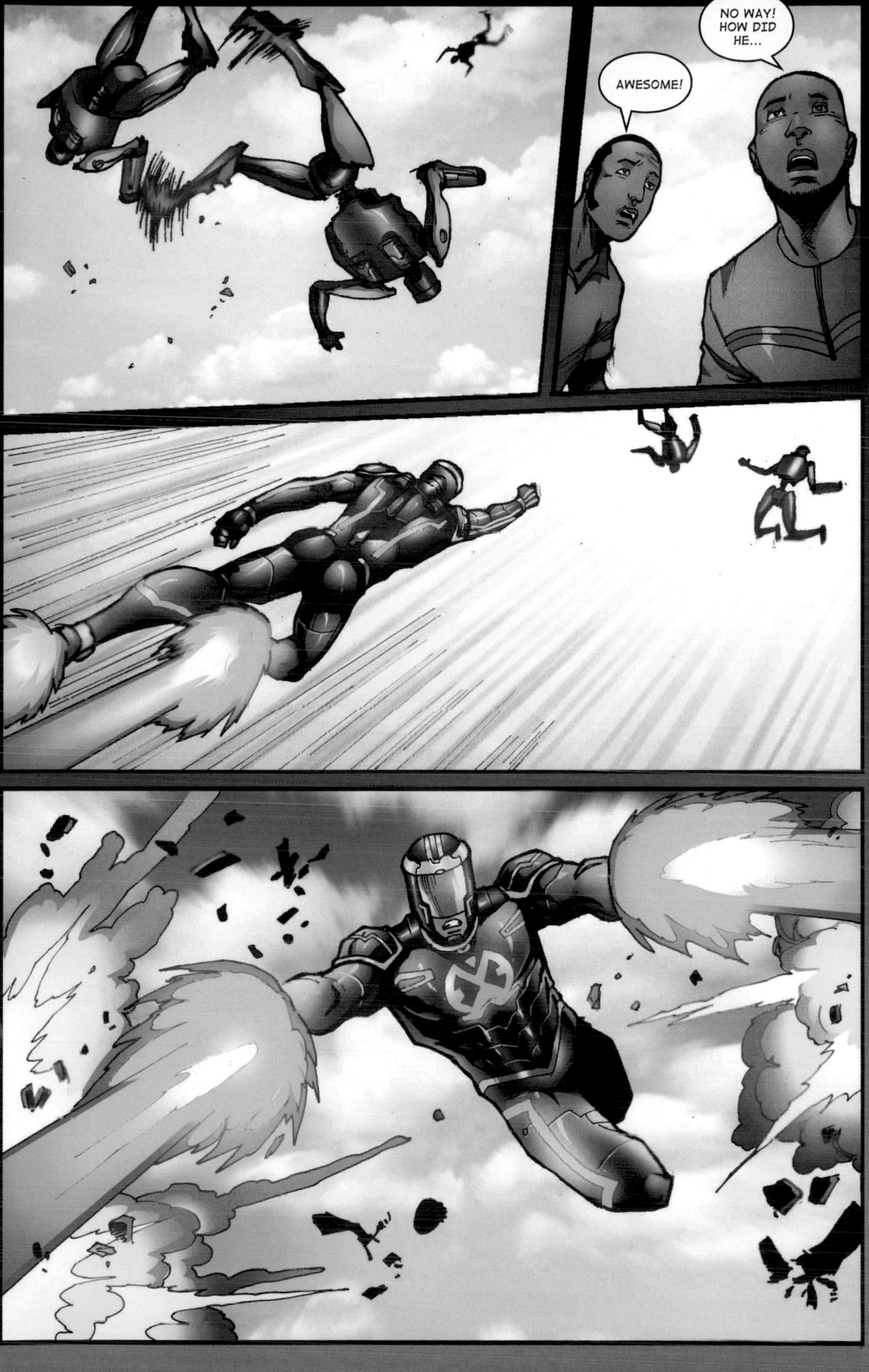
NO WAY!
HOW DID
HE...
AWESOME!

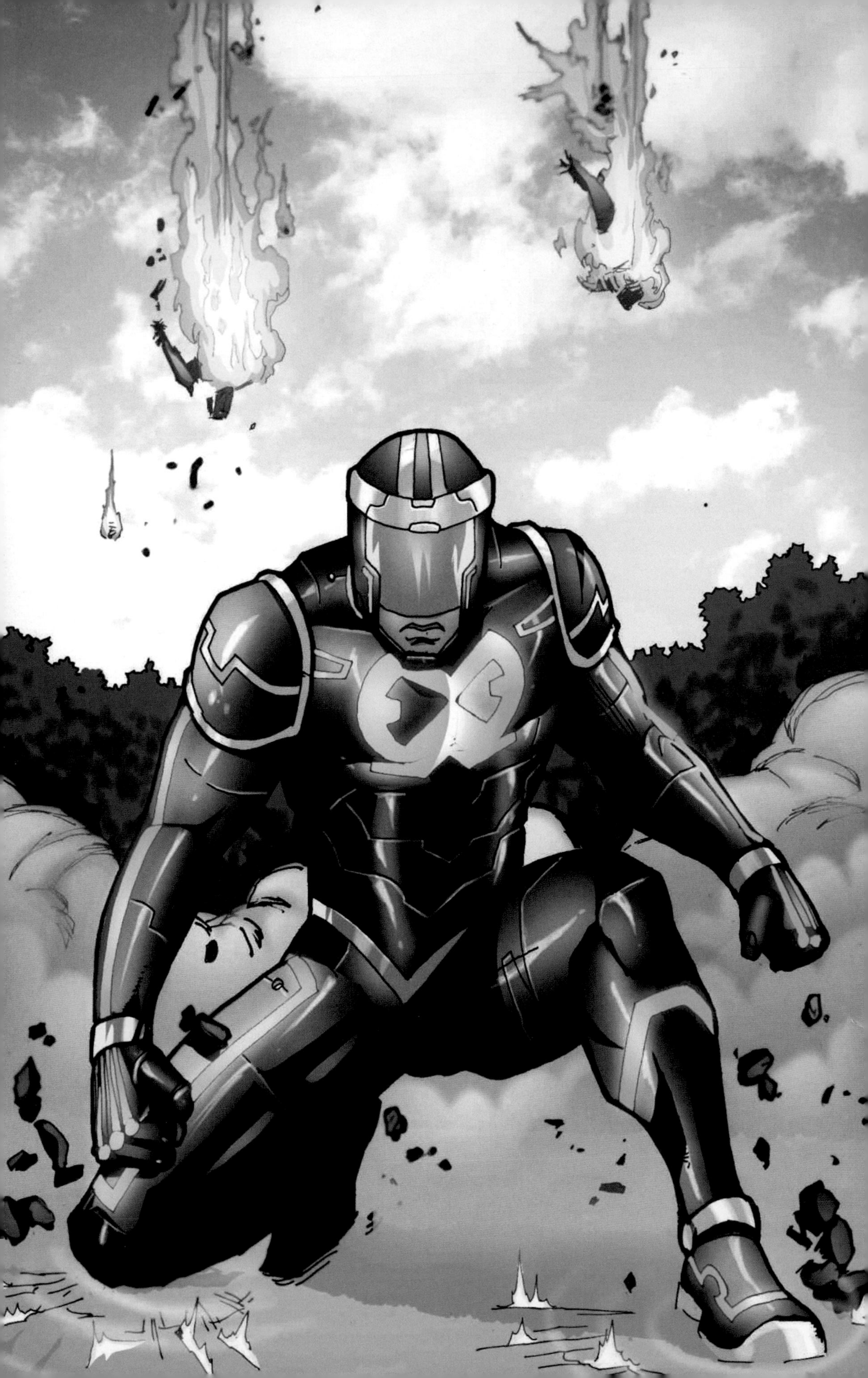

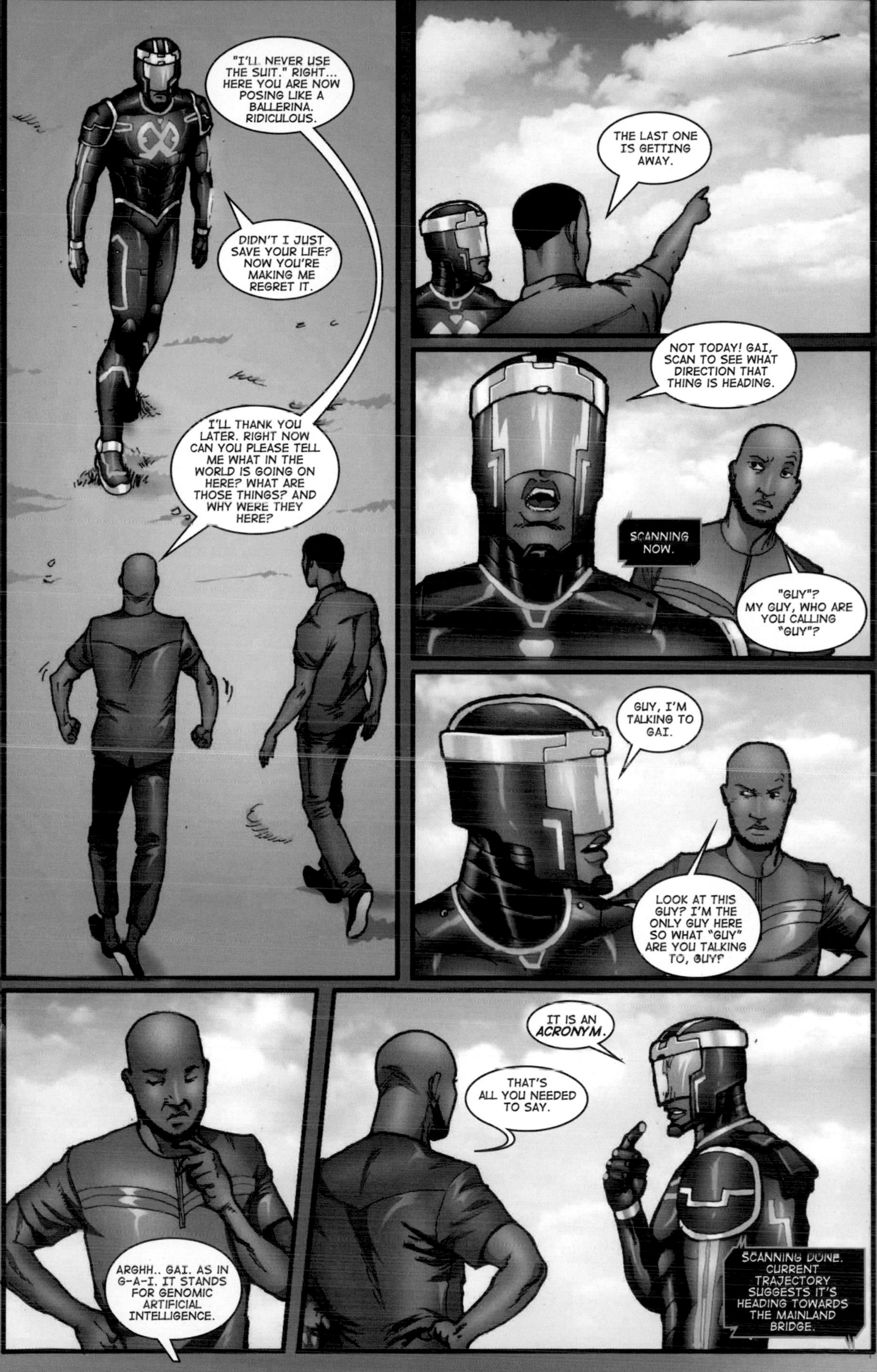
"I'LL NEVER USE THE SUIT." RIGHT... HERE YOU ARE NOW POSING LIKE A BALLERINA. RIDICULOUS.
DIDN'T I JUST SAVE YOUR LIFE? NOW YOU'RE MAKING ME REGRET IT.
I'LL THANK YOU LATER. RIGHT NOW CAN YOU PLEASE TELL ME WHAT IN THE WORLD IS GOING ON HERE? WHAT ARE THOSE THINGS? AND WHY WERE THEY HERE?
THE LAST ONE IS GETTING AWAY.
NOT TODAY! GAI, SCAN TO SEE WHAT DIRECTION THAT THING IS HEADING.
SCANNING NOW.
"GUY"? MY GUY, WHO ARE YOU CALLING "GUY"?
GUY, I'M TALKING TO GAI.
LOOK AT THIS GUY? I'M THE ONLY GUY HERE SO WHAT "GUY" ARE YOU TALKING TO, GUY?
ARGHH.. GAI. AS IN G-A-I. IT STANDS FOR GENOMIC ARTIFICIAL INTELLIGENCE.
IT IS AN *ACRONYM*.
THAT'S ALL YOU NEEDED TO SAY.
SCANNING DONE. CURRENT TRAJECTORY SUGGESTS IT'S HEADING TOWARDS THE MAINLAND BRIDGE.

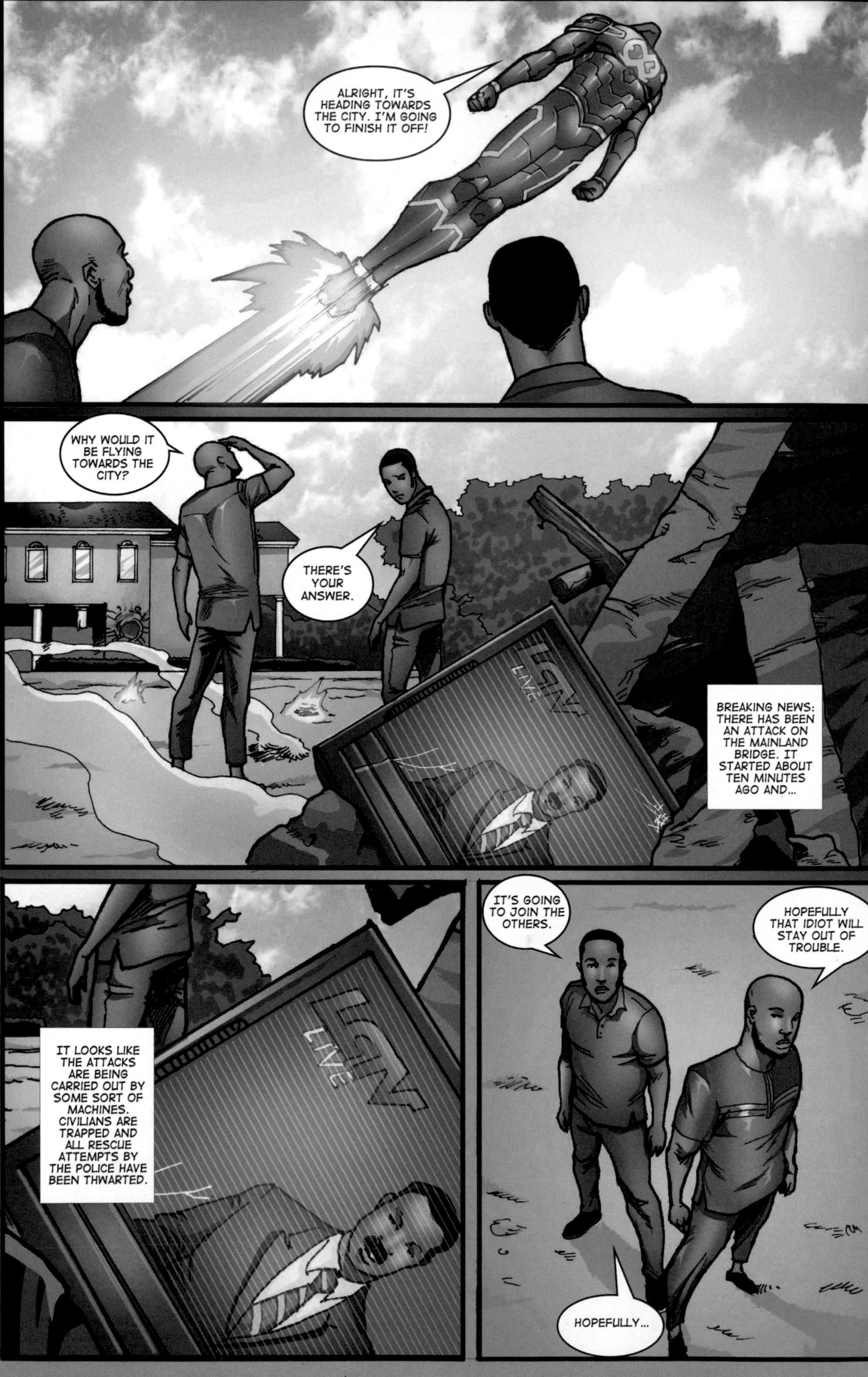
ALRIGHT, IT'S HEADING TOWARDS THE CITY. I'M GOING TO FINISH IT OFF!
WHY WOULD IT BE FLYING TOWARDS THE CITY?
THERE'S YOUR ANSWER.
LGN LIVE
BREAKING NEWS: THERE HAS BEEN AN ATTACK ON THE MAINLAND BRIDGE. IT STARTED ABOUT TEN MINUTES AGO AND...
LGN LIVE
IT LOOKS LIKE THE ATTACKS ARE BEING CARRIED OUT BY SOME SORT OF MACHINES. CIVILIANS ARE TRAPPED AND ALL RESCUE ATTEMPTS BY THE POLICE HAVE BEEN THWARTED.
IT'S GOING TO JOIN THE OTHERS.
HOPEFULLY THAT IDIOT WILL STAY OUT OF TROUBLE.
HOPEFULLY...

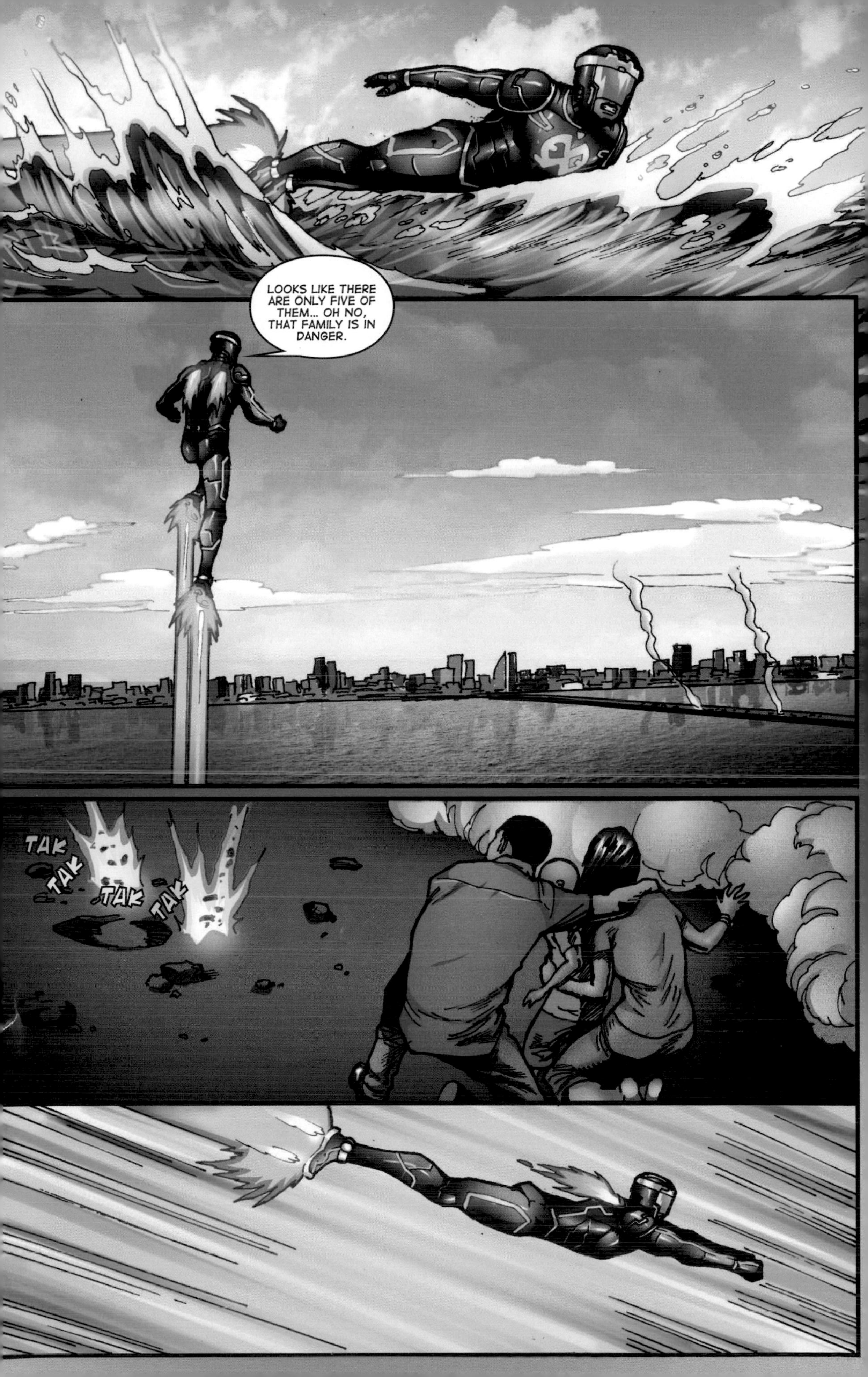
LOOKS LIKE THERE ARE ONLY FIVE OF THEM... OH NO, THAT FAMILY IS IN DANGER.
TAK
TAK
TAK
TAK

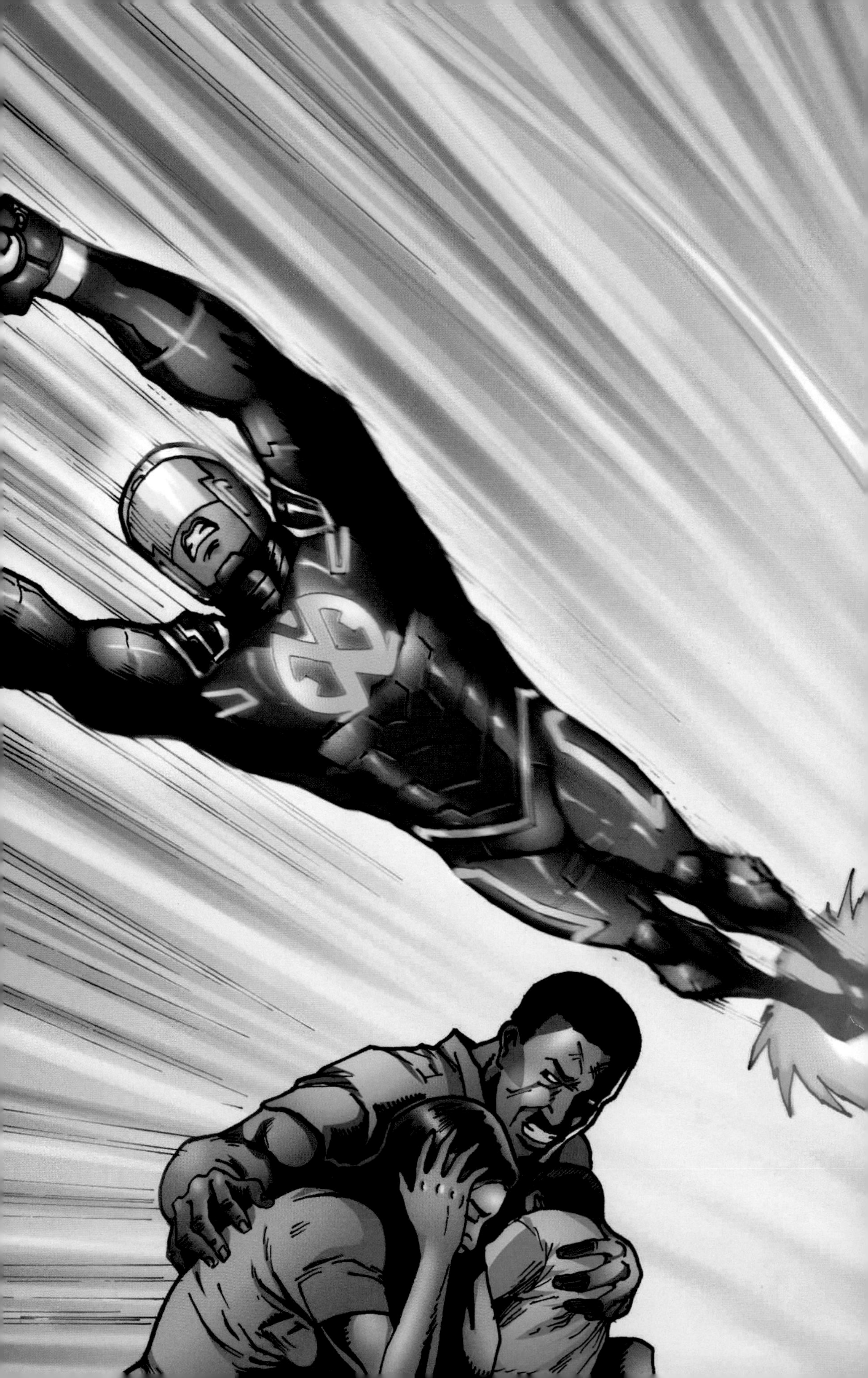

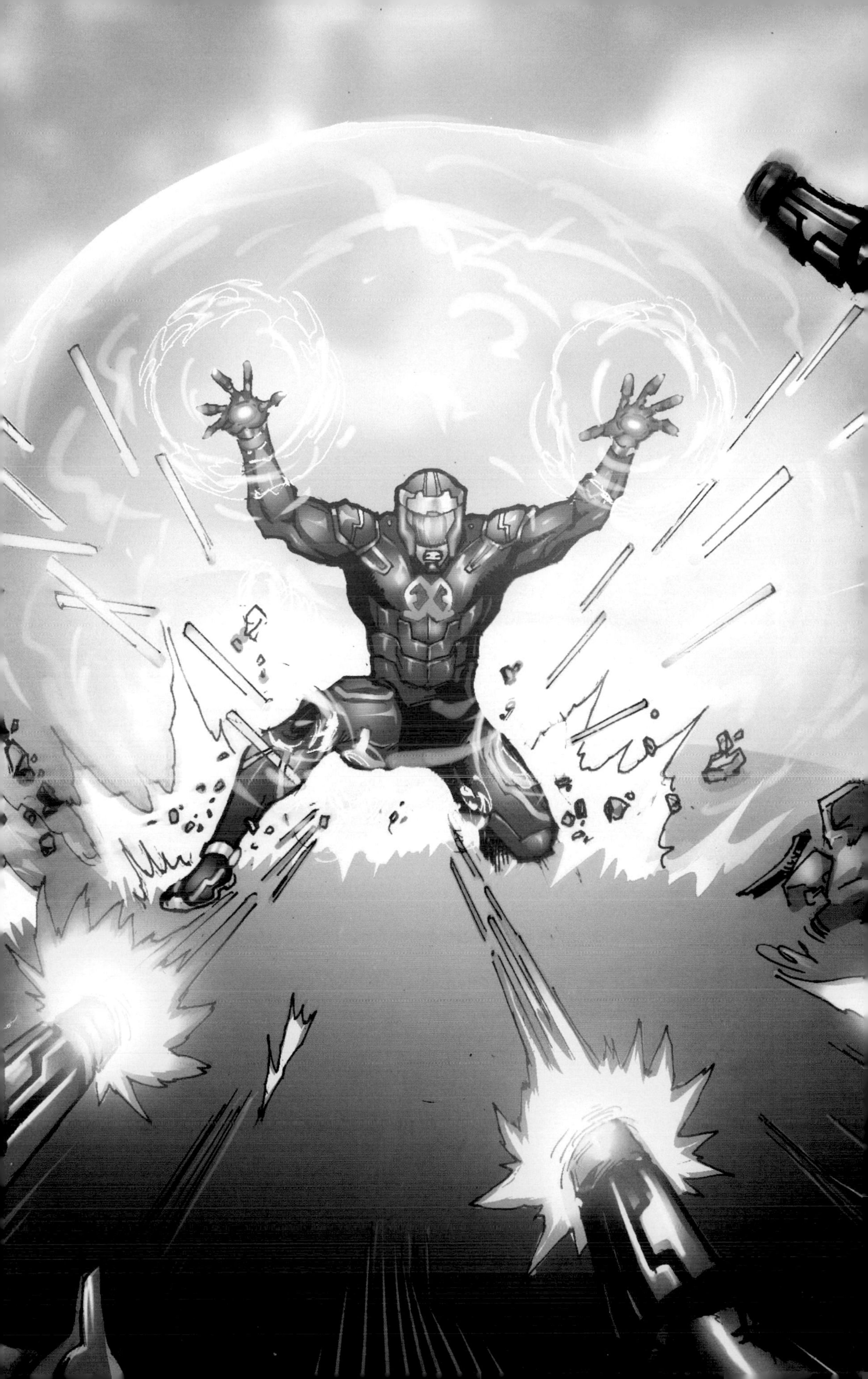

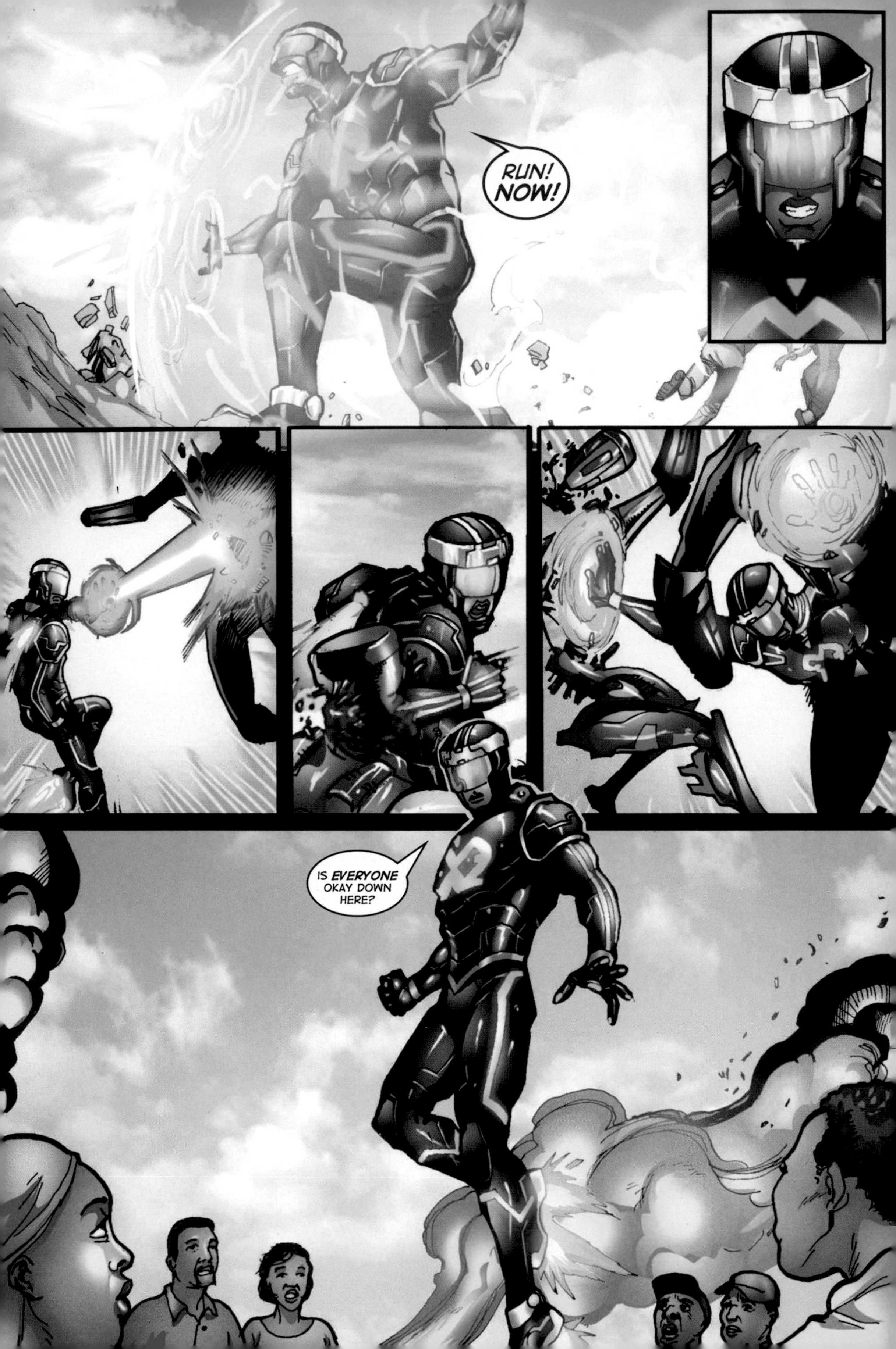
RUN! NOW!
IS EVERYONE OKAY DOWN HERE?

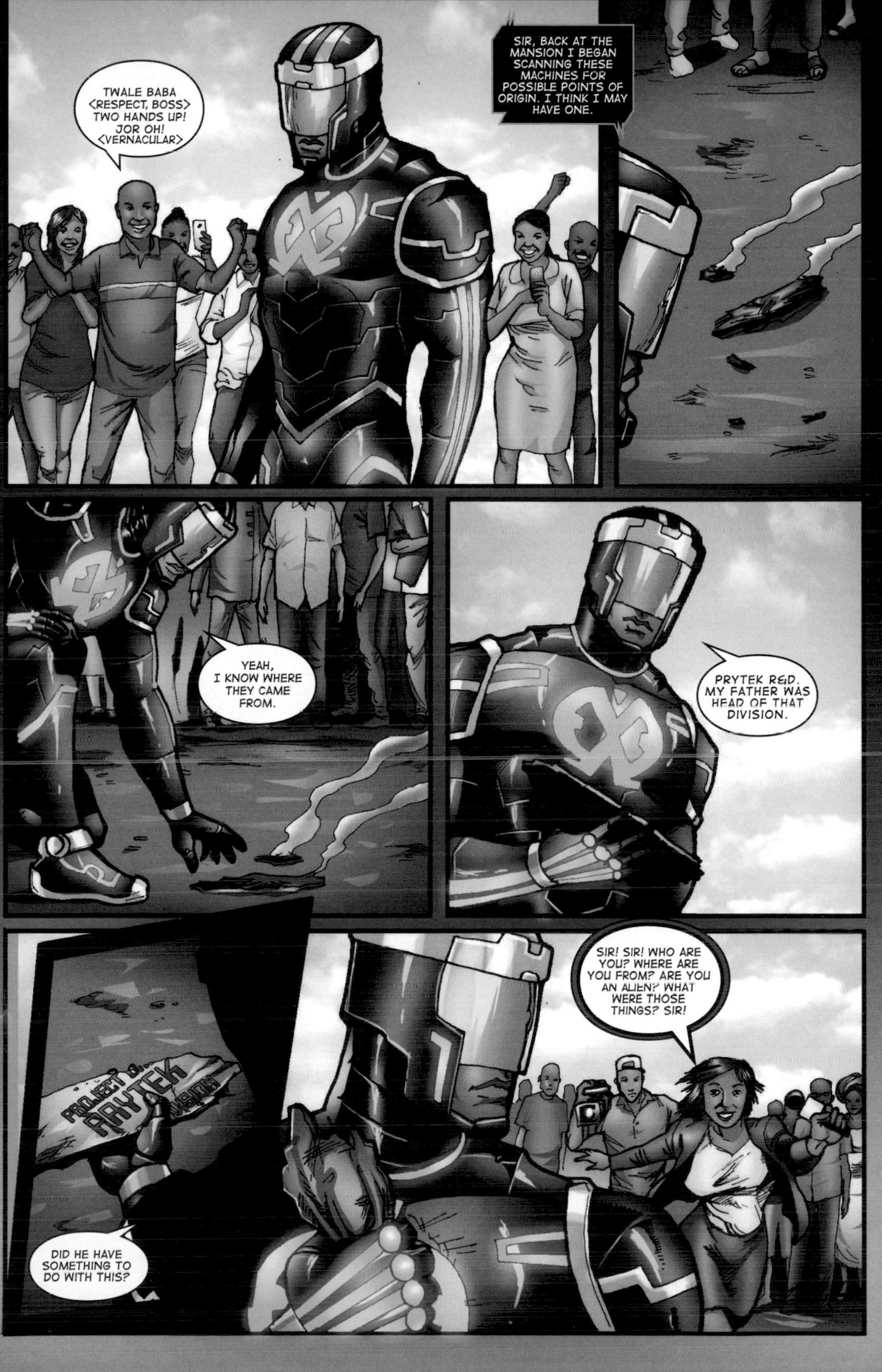
TWALE BABA <RESPECT, BOSS> TWO HANDS UP! JOR OH! <VERNACULAR>
SIR, BACK AT THE MANSION I BEGAN SCANNING THESE MACHINES FOR POSSIBLE POINTS OF ORIGIN. I THINK I MAY HAVE ONE.
YEAH, I KNOW WHERE THEY CAME FROM.
PRYTEK R&D. MY FATHER WAS HEAD OF THAT DIVISION.
RAYTEK
DID HE HAVE SOMETHING TO DO WITH THIS?
SIR! SIR! WHO ARE YOU? WHERE ARE YOU FROM? ARE YOU AN ALIEN? WHAT WERE THOSE THINGS? SIR!

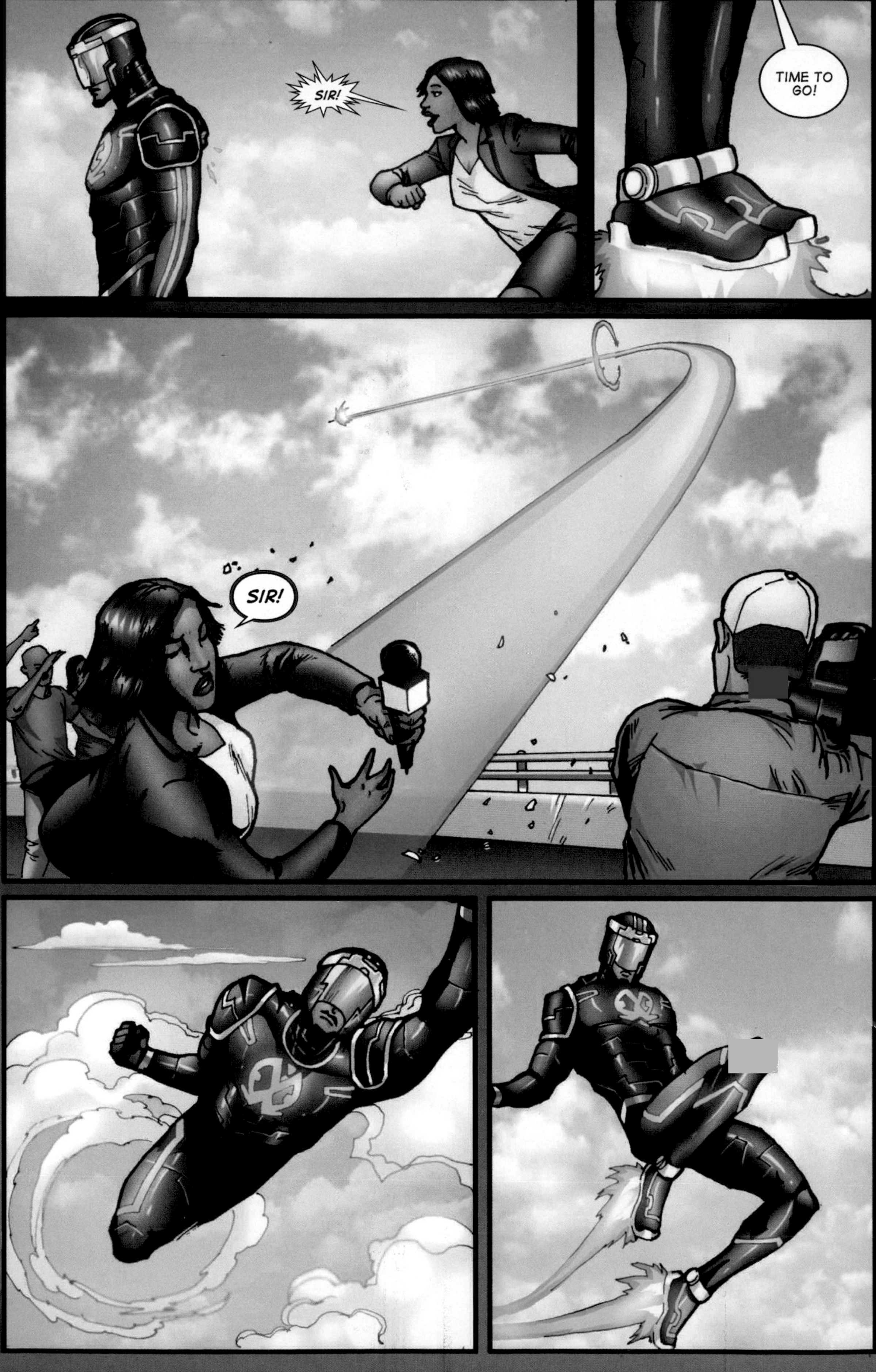
SIR!
TIME TO GO!
SIR!

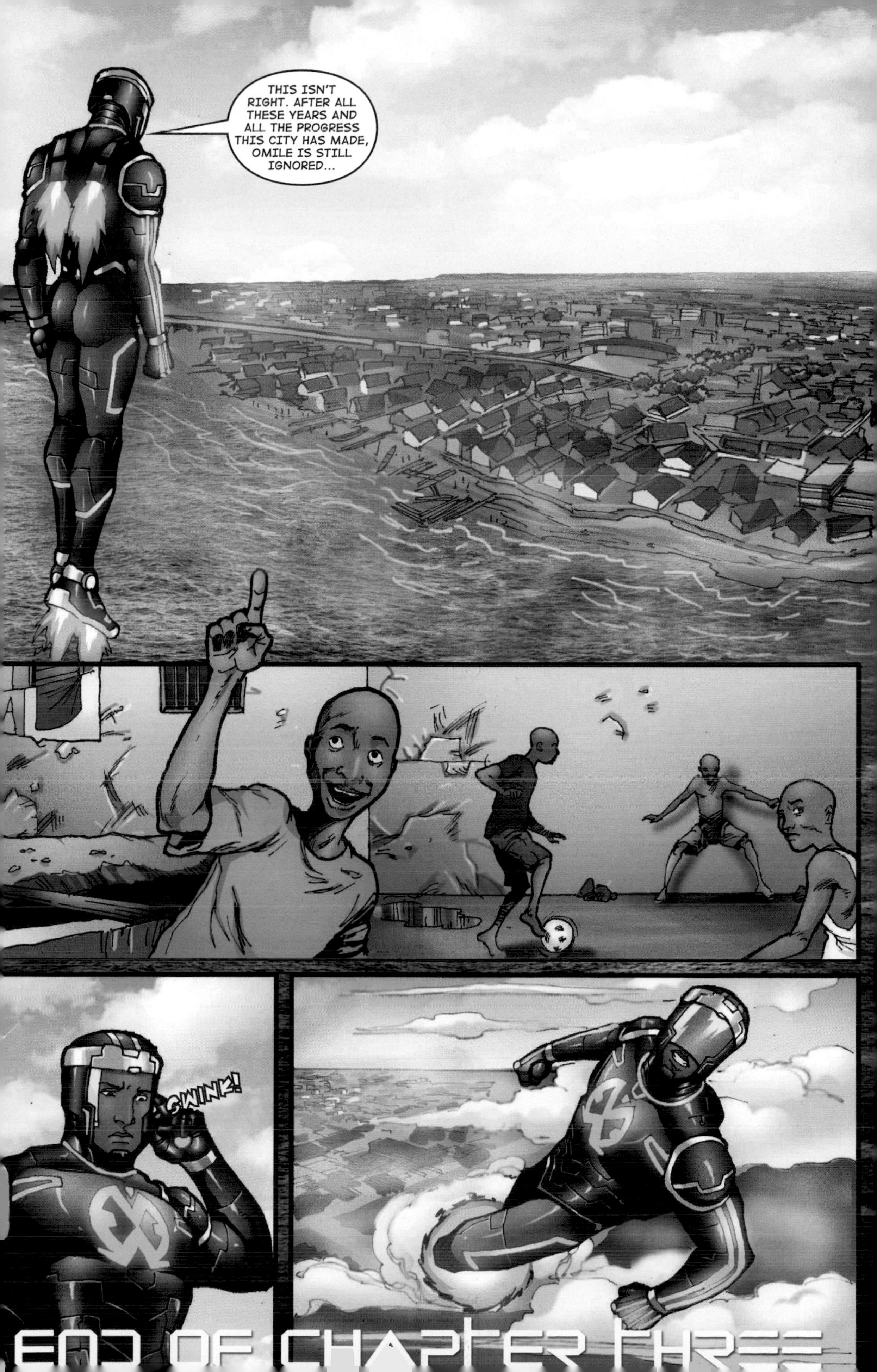
THIS ISN'T RIGHT. AFTER ALL THESE YEARS AND ALL THE PROGRESS THIS CITY HAS MADE, OMILE IS STILL IGNORED...
SWINK!
END OF CHAPTER THREE

"Their corruption and lack of discipline has given birth to a frail nation."

*- Oniku*

CHAPTER

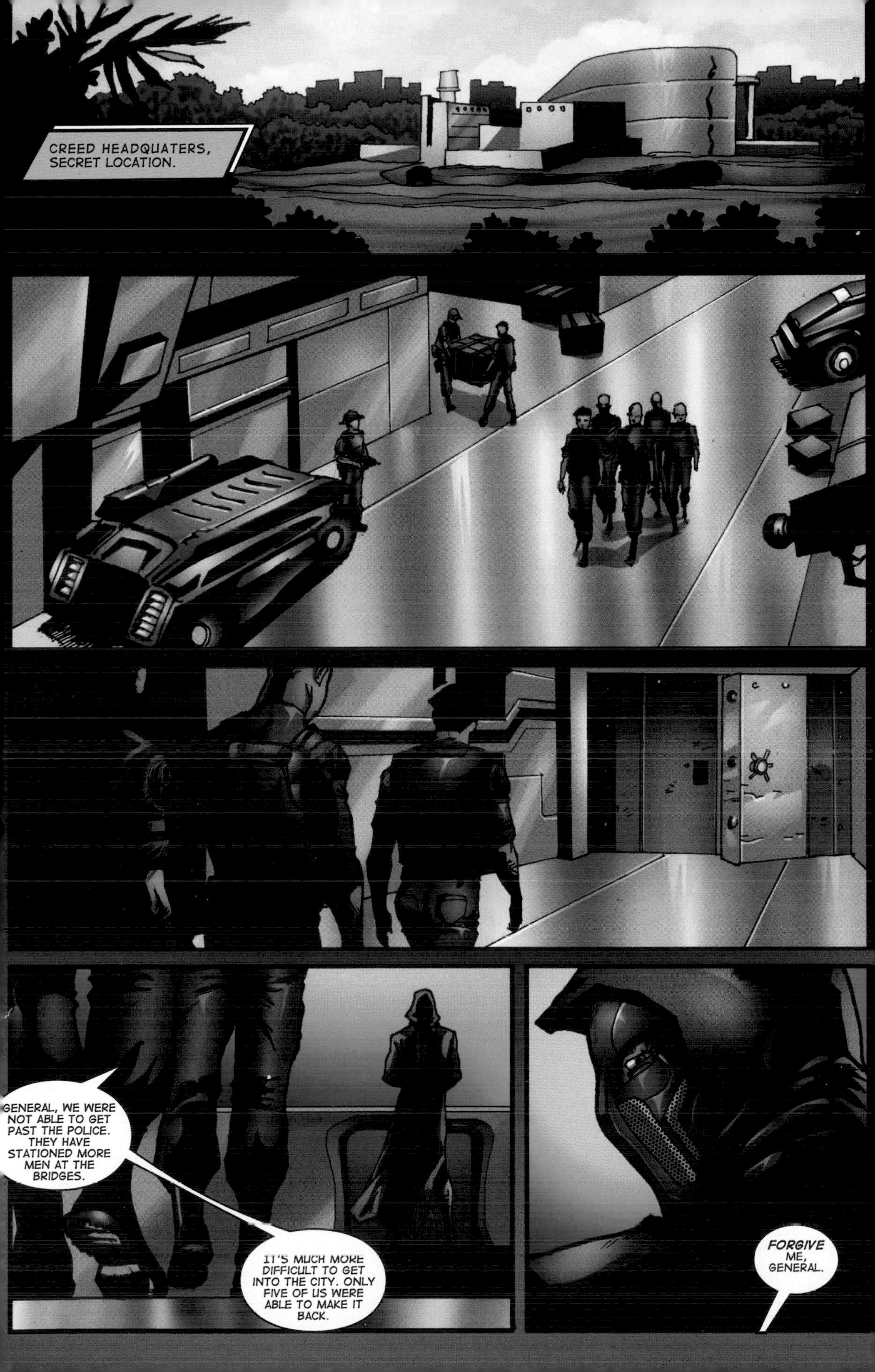
CREED HEADQUATERS, SECRET LOCATION.
GENERAL, WE WERE NOT ABLE TO GET PAST THE POLICE. THEY HAVE STATIONED MORE MEN AT THE BRIDGES.
IT'S MUCH MORE DIFFICULT TO GET INTO THE CITY. ONLY FIVE OF US WERE ABLE TO MAKE IT BACK.
FORGIVE ME, GENERAL.

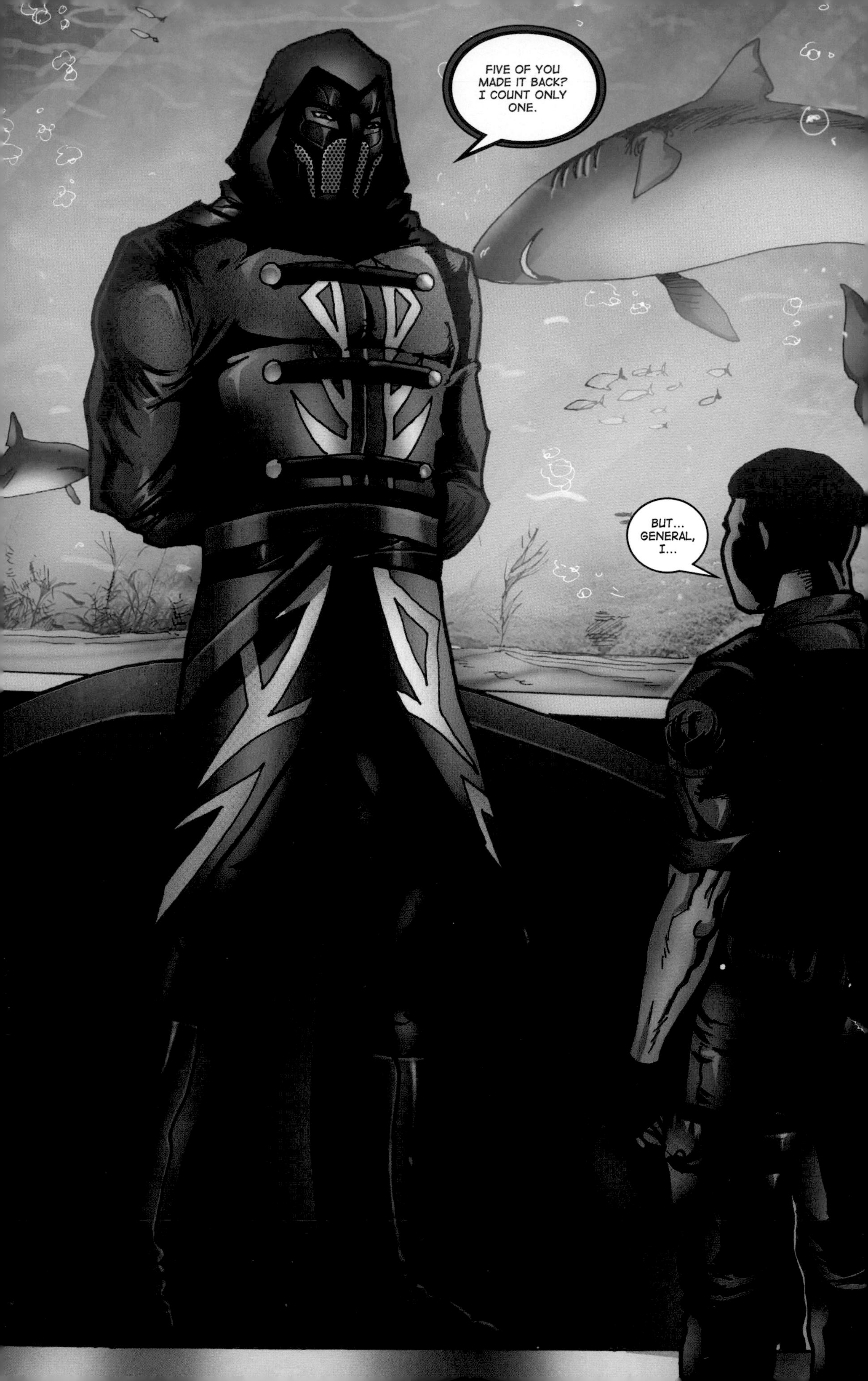
FIVE OF YOU MADE IT BACK? I COUNT ONLY ONE.
BUT... GENERAL, I...

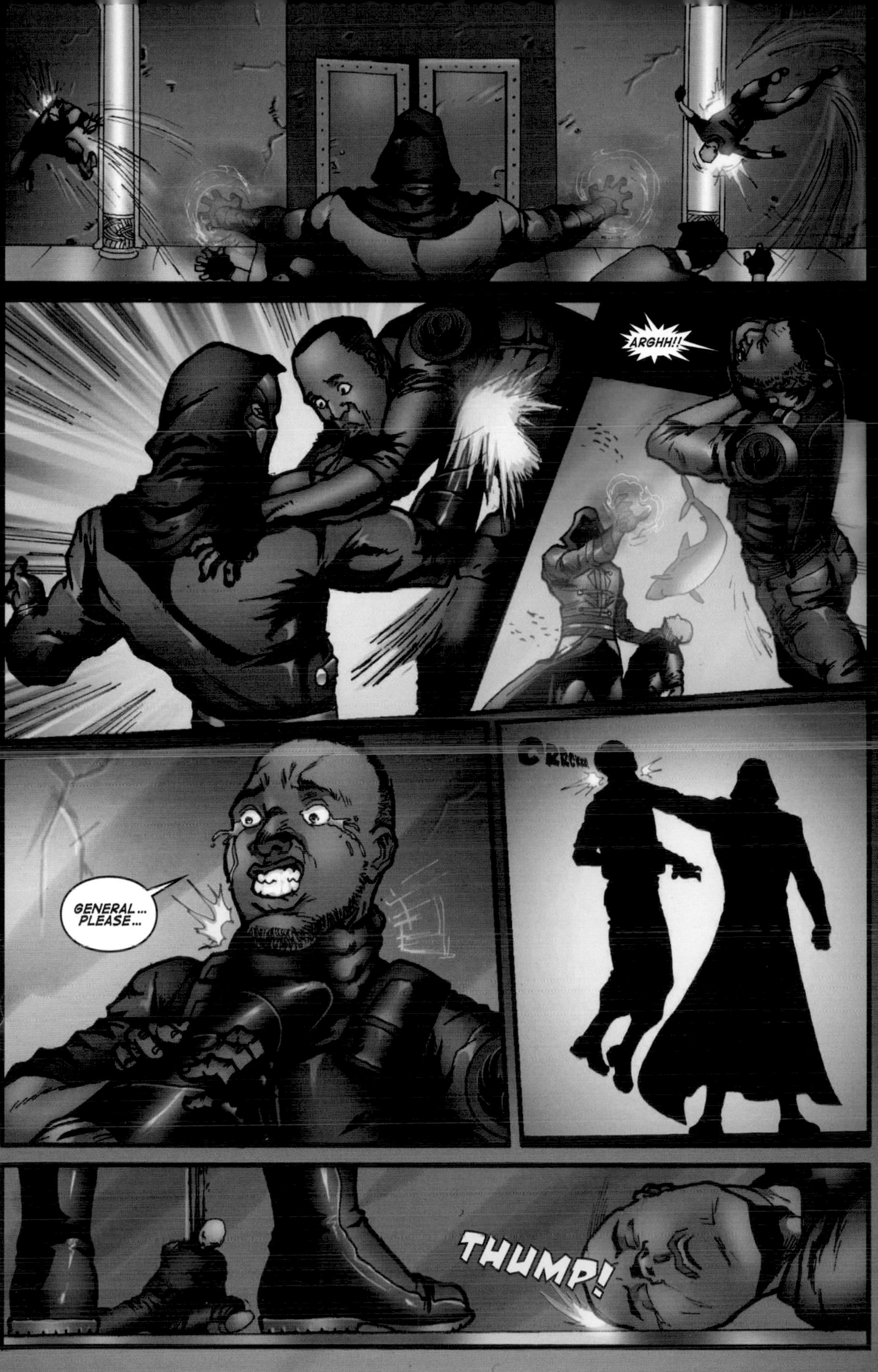
ARGHH!!
GENERAL... PLEASE...
THUMP!

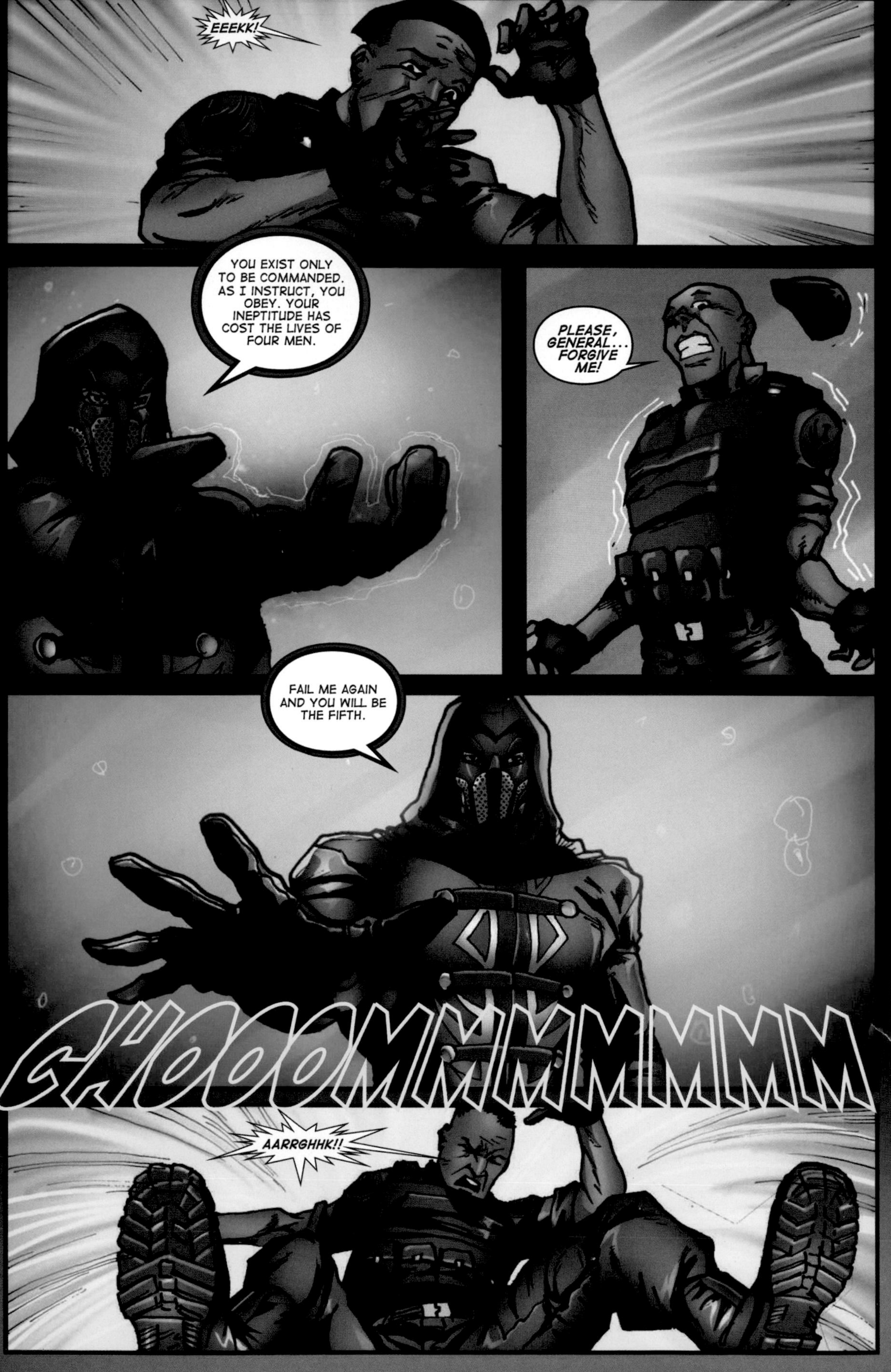
EEEKK!
YOU EXIST ONLY TO BE COMMANDED. AS I INSTRUCT, YOU OBEY. YOUR INEPTITUDE HAS COST THE LIVES OF FOUR MEN.
PLEASE, GENERAL... FORGIVE ME!
FAIL ME AGAIN AND YOU WILL BE THE FIFTH.
CHOOOOMMMMMMMM
AARRGHHK!!

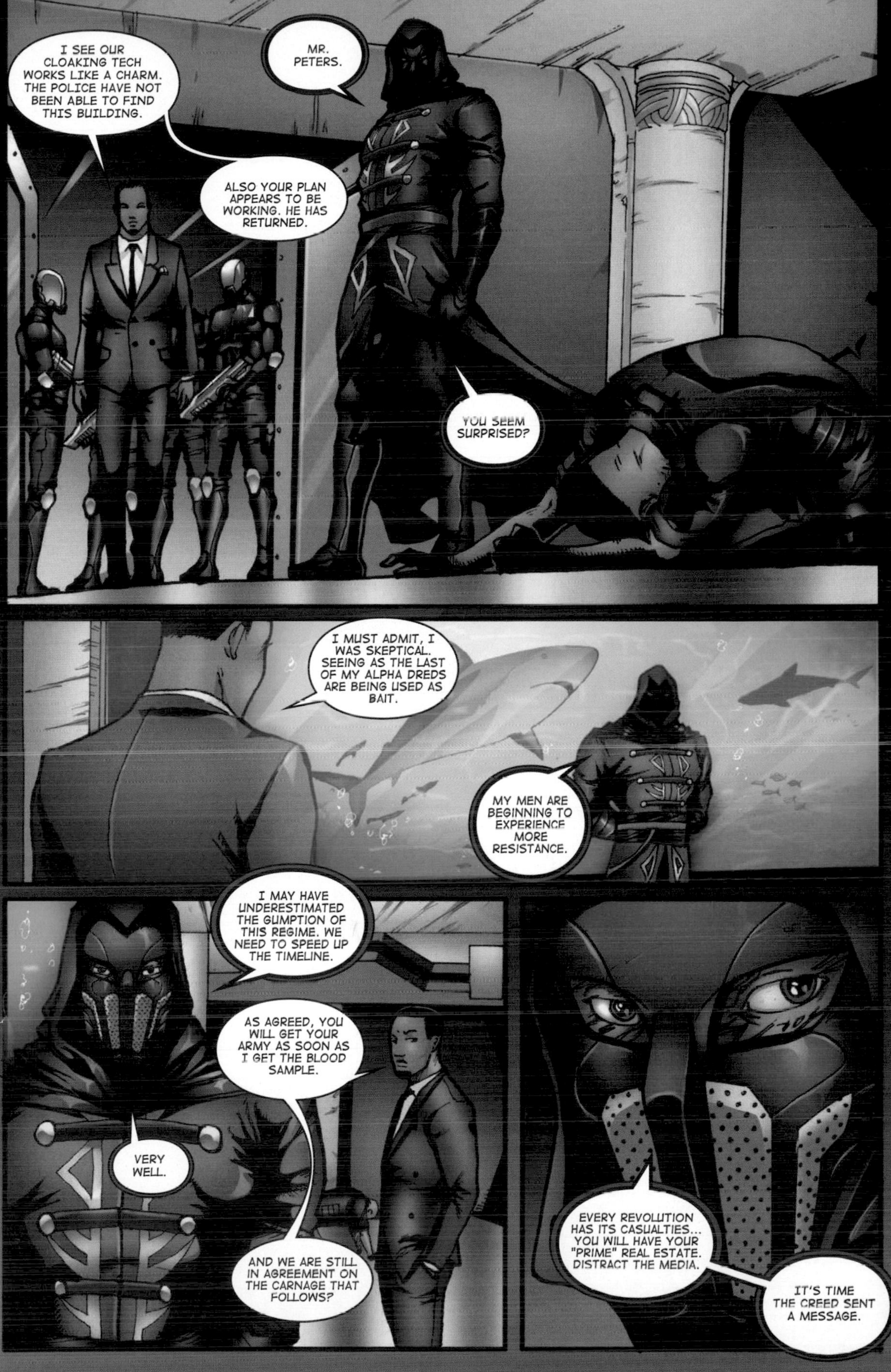
I SEE OUR CLOAKING TECH WORKS LIKE A CHARM. THE POLICE HAVE NOT BEEN ABLE TO FIND THIS BUILDING.
MR. PETERS.
ALSO YOUR PLAN APPEARS TO BE WORKING. HE HAS RETURNED.
YOU SEEM SURPRISED?
I MUST ADMIT, I WAS SKEPTICAL. SEEING AS THE LAST OF MY ALPHA DREDS ARE BEING USED AS BAIT.
MY MEN ARE BEGINNING TO EXPERIENCE MORE RESISTANCE.
I MAY HAVE UNDERESTIMATED THE GUMPTION OF THIS REGIME. WE NEED TO SPEED UP THE TIMELINE.
AS AGREED, YOU WILL GET YOUR ARMY AS SOON AS I GET THE BLOOD SAMPLE.
VERY WELL.
AND WE ARE STILL IN AGREEMENT ON THE CARNAGE THAT FOLLOWS?
EVERY REVOLUTION HAS ITS CASUALTIES... YOU WILL HAVE YOUR "PRIME" REAL ESTATE. DISTRACT THE MEDIA.
IT'S TIME THE CREED SENT A MESSAGE.

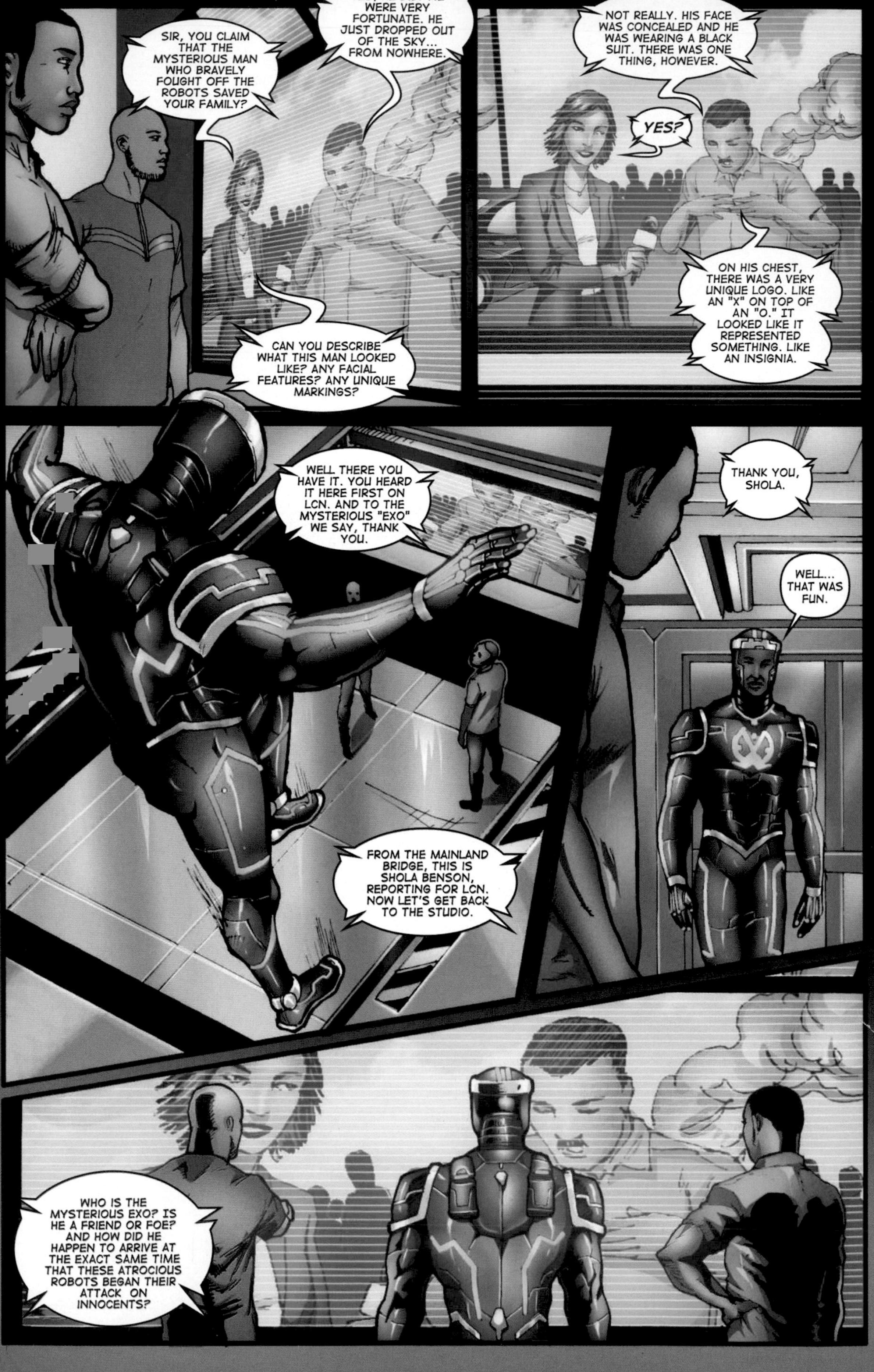
SIR, YOU CLAIM THAT THE MYSTERIOUS MAN WHO BRAVELY FOUGHT OFF THE ROBOTS SAVED YOUR FAMILY?
YES, HE DID. WE WERE VERY FORTUNATE. HE JUST DROPPED OUT OF THE SKY... FROM NOWHERE.
CAN YOU DESCRIBE WHAT THIS MAN LOOKED LIKE? ANY FACIAL FEATURES? ANY UNIQUE MARKINGS?
NOT REALLY. HIS FACE WAS CONCEALED AND HE WAS WEARING A BLACK SUIT. THERE WAS ONE THING, HOWEVER.
YES?
ON HIS CHEST, THERE WAS A VERY UNIQUE LOGO. LIKE AN "X" ON TOP OF AN "O." IT LOOKED LIKE IT REPRESENTED SOMETHING. LIKE AN INSIGNIA.
WELL THERE YOU HAVE IT. YOU HEARD IT HERE FIRST ON LCN. AND TO THE MYSTERIOUS "EXO" WE SAY, THANK YOU.
FROM THE MAINLAND BRIDGE, THIS IS SHOLA BENSON, REPORTING FOR LCN. NOW LET'S GET BACK TO THE STUDIO.
THANK YOU, SHOLA.
WELL... THAT WAS FUN.
WHO IS THE MYSTERIOUS EXO? IS HE A FRIEND OR FOE? AND HOW DID HE HAPPEN TO ARRIVE AT THE EXACT SAME TIME THAT THESE ATROCIOUS ROBOTS BEGAN THEIR ATTACK ON INNOCENTS?

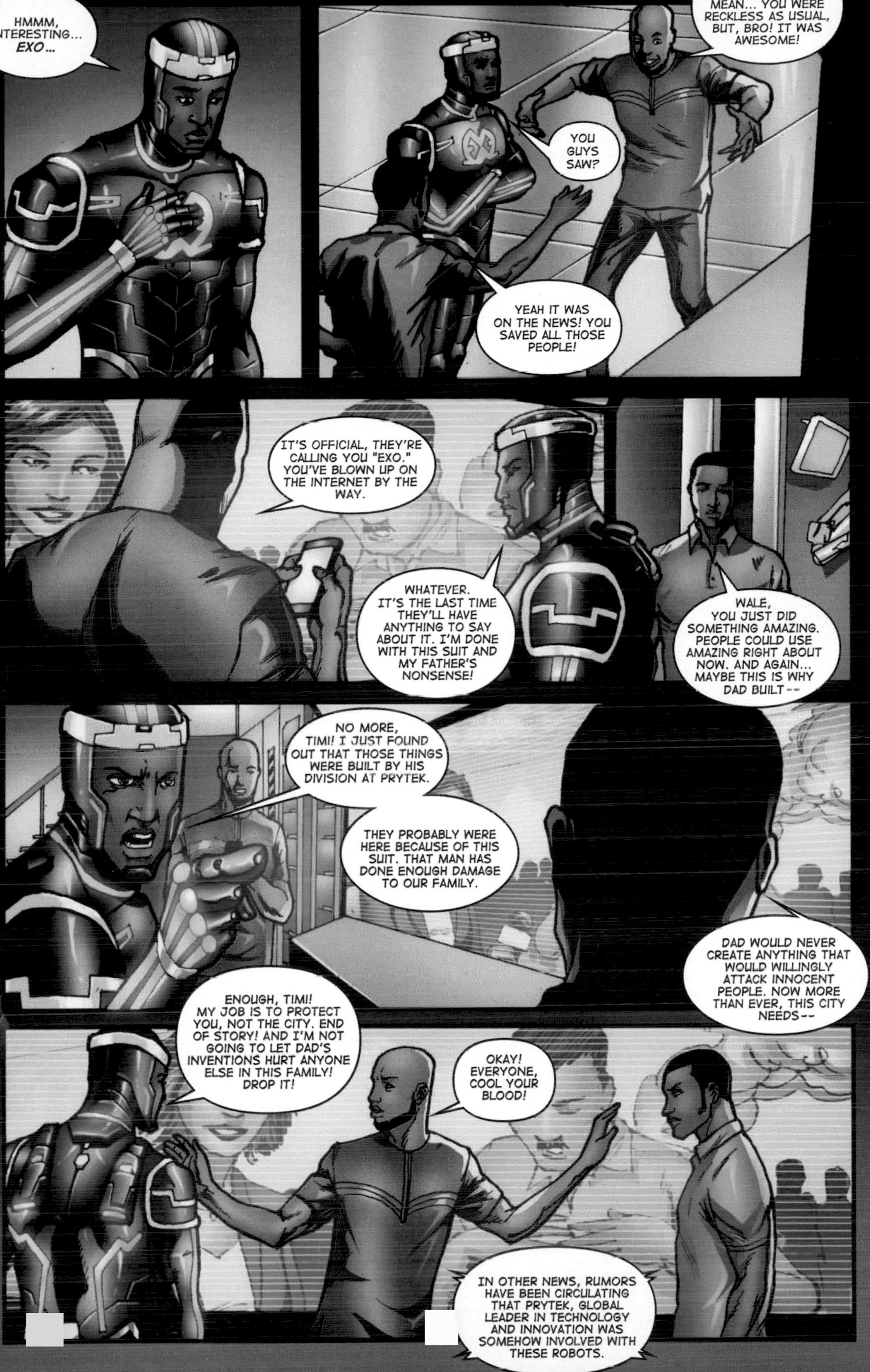
HMMM, INTERESTING... EXO...
GEN GEN <VERNACULAR>! THE HERO OF LC. I MEAN... YOU WERE RECKLESS AS USUAL, BUT, BRO! IT WAS AWESOME!
YOU GUYS SAW?
YEAH IT WAS ON THE NEWS! YOU SAVED ALL THOSE PEOPLE!
IT'S OFFICIAL, THEY'RE CALLING YOU "EXO." YOU'VE BLOWN UP ON THE INTERNET BY THE WAY.
WHATEVER. IT'S THE LAST TIME THEY'LL HAVE ANYTHING TO SAY ABOUT IT. I'M DONE WITH THIS SUIT AND MY FATHER'S NONSENSE!
WALE, YOU JUST DID SOMETHING AMAZING. PEOPLE COULD USE AMAZING RIGHT ABOUT NOW. AND AGAIN... MAYBE THIS IS WHY DAD BUILT--
NO MORE, TIMI! I JUST FOUND OUT THAT THOSE THINGS WERE BUILT BY HIS DIVISION AT PRYTEK.
THEY PROBABLY WERE HERE BECAUSE OF THIS SUIT. THAT MAN HAS DONE ENOUGH DAMAGE TO OUR FAMILY.
DAD WOULD NEVER CREATE ANYTHING THAT WOULD WILLINGLY ATTACK INNOCENT PEOPLE. NOW MORE THAN EVER, THIS CITY NEEDS--
ENOUGH, TIMI! MY JOB IS TO PROTECT YOU, NOT THE CITY. END OF STORY! AND I'M NOT GOING TO LET DAD'S INVENTIONS HURT ANYONE ELSE IN THIS FAMILY! DROP IT!
OKAY! EVERYONE, COOL YOUR BLOOD!
IN OTHER NEWS, RUMORS HAVE BEEN CIRCULATING THAT PRYTEK, GLOBAL LEADER IN TECHNOLOGY AND INNOVATION WAS SOMEHOW INVOLVED WITH THESE ROBOTS.

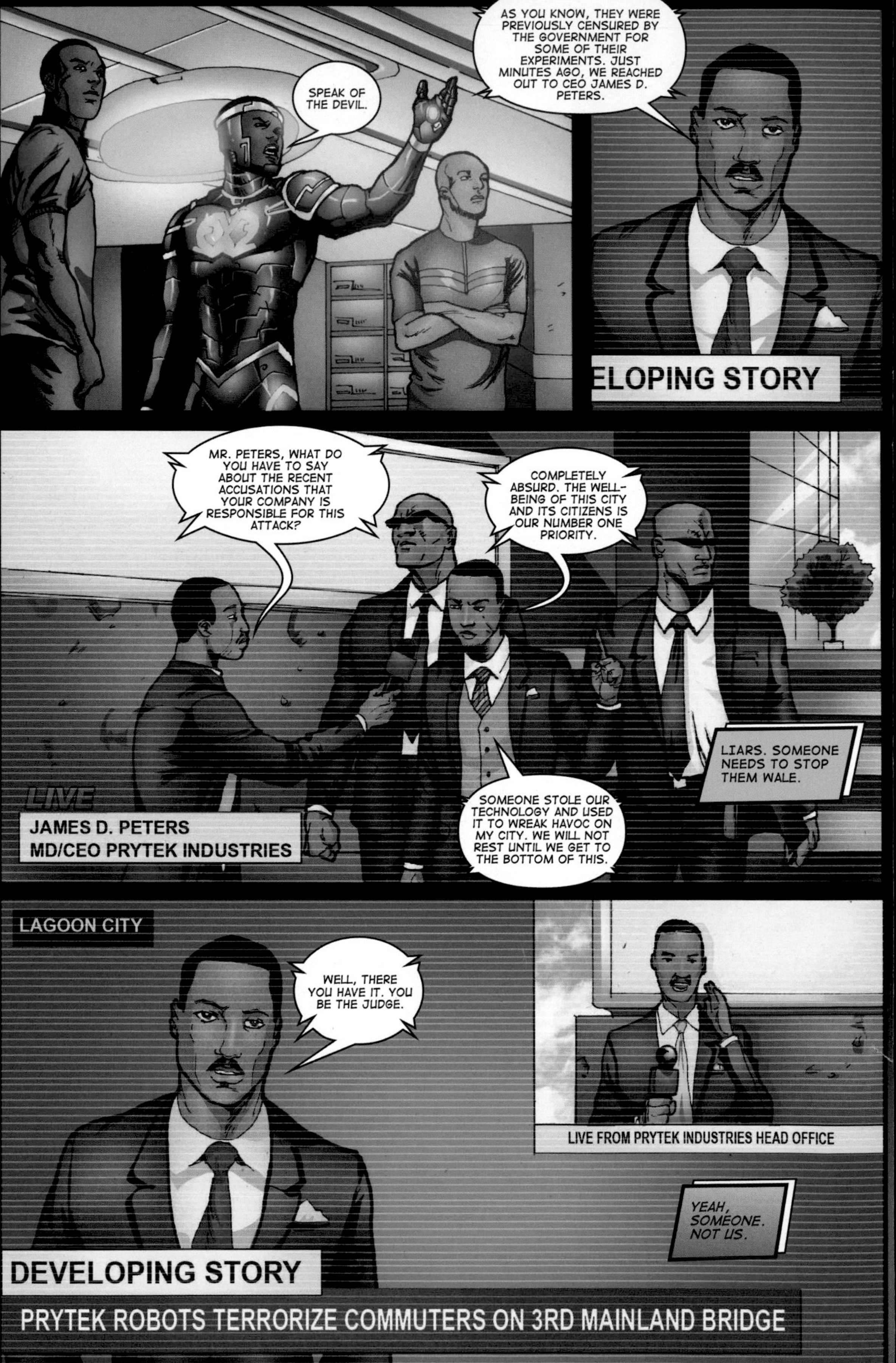
SPEAK OF THE DEVIL.
AS YOU KNOW, THEY WERE PREVIOUSLY CENSURED BY THE GOVERNMENT FOR SOME OF THEIR EXPERIMENTS. JUST MINUTES AGO, WE REACHED OUT TO CEO JAMES D. PETERS.
ELOPING STORY
MR. PETERS, WHAT DO YOU HAVE TO SAY ABOUT THE RECENT ACCUSATIONS THAT YOUR COMPANY IS RESPONSIBLE FOR THIS ATTACK?
COMPLETELY ABSURD. THE WELL-BEING OF THIS CITY AND ITS CITIZENS IS OUR NUMBER ONE PRIORITY.
SOMEONE STOLE OUR TECHNOLOGY AND USED IT TO WREAK HAVOC ON MY CITY. WE WILL NOT REST UNTIL WE GET TO THE BOTTOM OF THIS.
LIARS. SOMEONE NEEDS TO STOP THEM WALE.
LIVE
JAMES D. PETERS
MD/CEO PRYTEK INDUSTRIES
LAGOON CITY
WELL, THERE YOU HAVE IT. YOU BE THE JUDGE.
LIVE FROM PRYTEK INDUSTRIES HEAD OFFICE
YEAH, SOMEONE. NOT US.
DEVELOPING STORY
PRYTEK ROBOTS TERRORIZE COMMUTERS ON 3RD MAINLAND BRIDGE

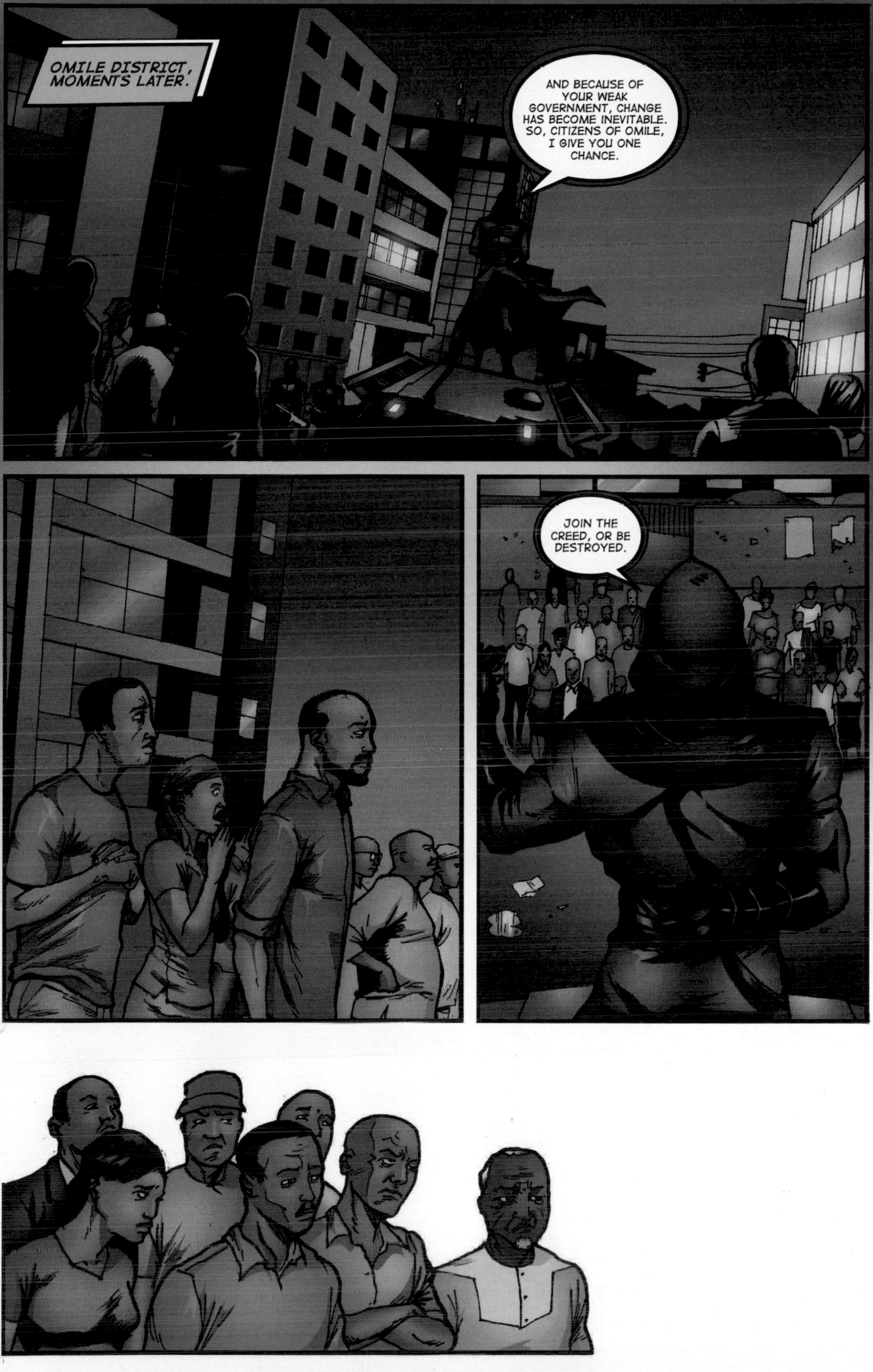
OMILE DISTRICT, MOMENTS LATER.
AND BECAUSE OF YOUR WEAK GOVERNMENT, CHANGE HAS BECOME INEVITABLE. SO, CITIZENS OF OMILE, I GIVE YOU ONE CHANCE.
JOIN THE CREED, OR BE DESTROYED.

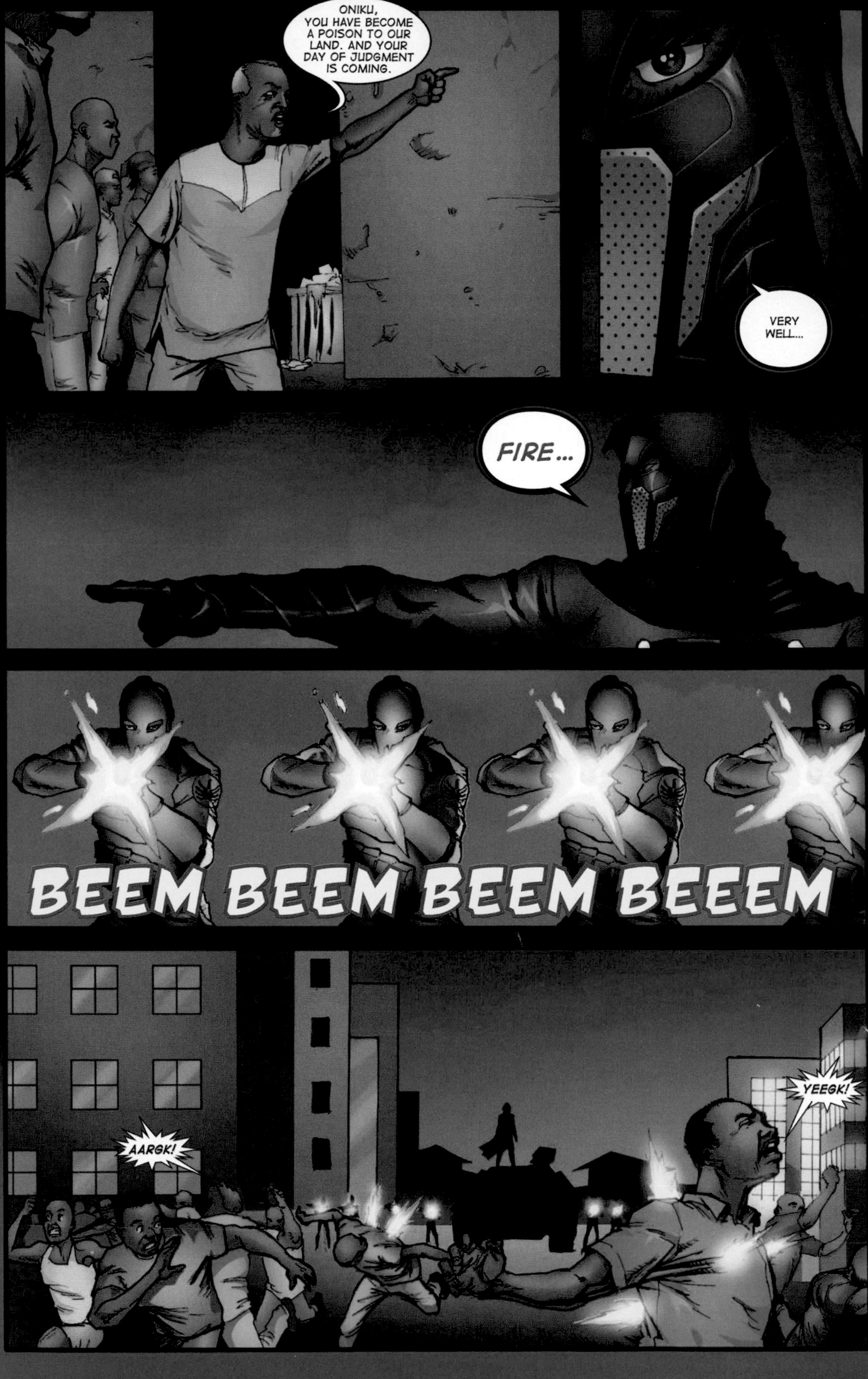
ONIKU, YOU HAVE BECOME A POISON TO OUR LAND. AND YOUR DAY OF JUDGMENT IS COMING.
VERY WELL...
FIRE...
BEEM BEEM BEEM BEEEM
AARGK!
YEEGK!

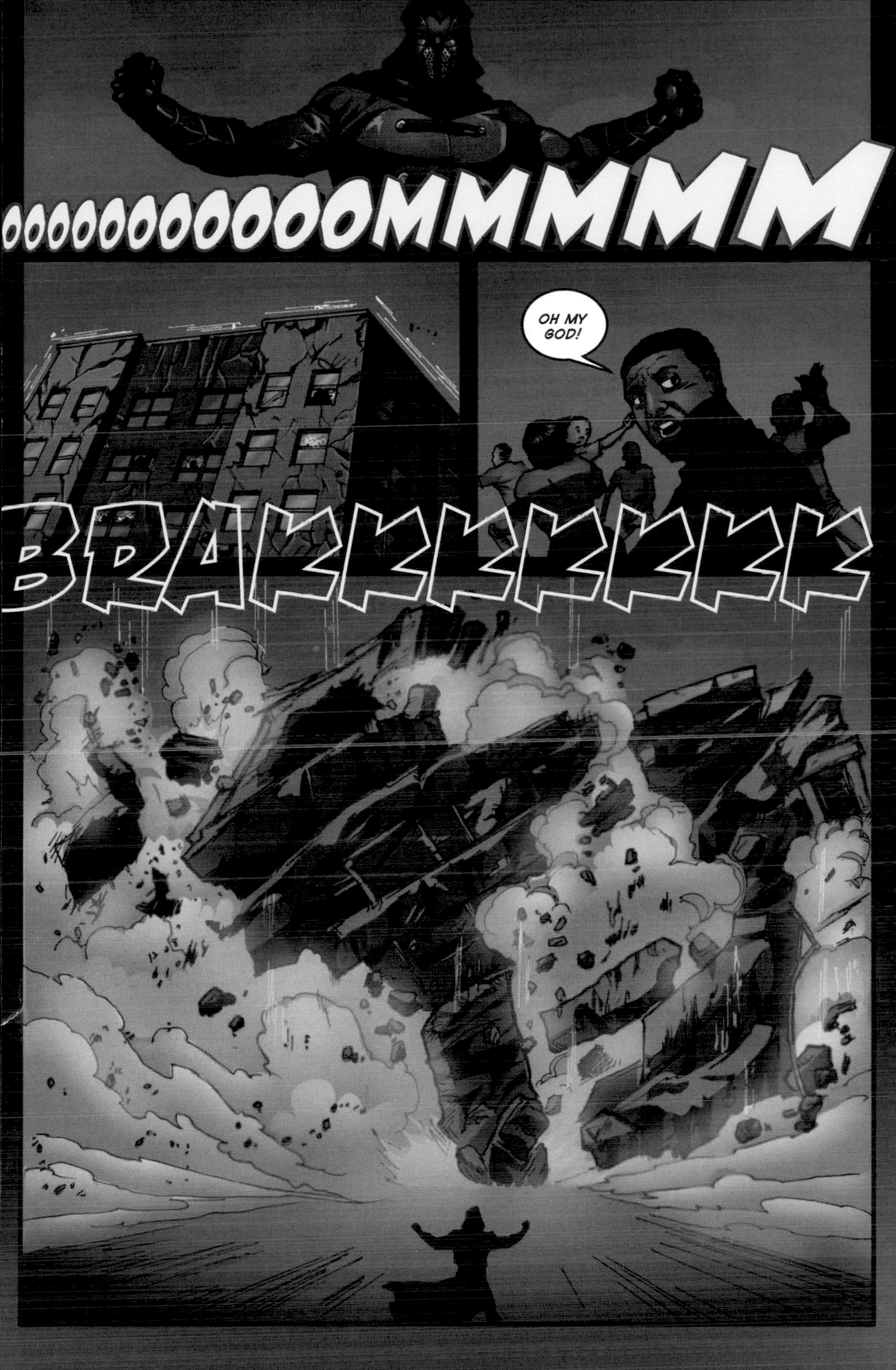
OOOOOOOOOOOOMMMMMM
OH MY GOD!
BRAKKKKKKK

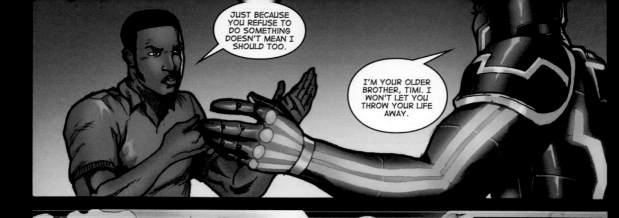

JUST BECAUSE YOU REFUSE TO DO SOMETHING DOESN'T MEAN I SHOULD TOO.

I'M YOUR OLDER BROTHER, TIMI. I WON'T LET YOU THROW YOUR LIFE AWAY.

BREAKING NEWS: THERE HAS BEEN A CREED ATTACK IN OMILE, RESULTING IN SEVERAL CIVILIAN CASUALTIES.

THIS WOULD MAKE THE THIRD ATTACK IN FOUR MONTHS. IT WOULD SEEM THAT THE CREED, ORIGINALLY ASSUMED TO BE A SMALL GROUP OF EXTREMISTS BASED IN OMILE, ARE A MORE STRUCTURED AND WELL-EQUIPPED ORGANIZATION.

THIS IS AN UNSETTLING REVELATION, GIVEN THAT THE CREED ONLY EMERGED IN THE PAST YEAR.

**BREAKING NEWS**

THE CREED DESTROYS APARTMENT COMPLEX AT OMILE. HUNDREDS FEARED DEAD.

DOWNLOAD THE LAGOON TV MOBILE APP TO SHARE IMAGES.   SENATE ADVOCATES STATE OF EMERGENCY FOR LAGO

LAGOON CITY

AT THIS POINT, IT'S SAFE TO ASSUME THE CREED HAS TAKEN ALL BUT TOTAL CONTROL OF OMILE, LAGOON CITY'S POOREST DISTRICT.

THE POLICE HAVE ASSURED US THAT THE SEARCH FOR ONIKU, THE LEADER OF THE CREED, HAS BEEN RELENTLESS.

THE CREED DESTROYS APARTMENT COMPLEX AT OMILE. HUNDREDS FEARED DEAD.

HOWEVER, THESE RAIDS HAVE BEEN FUTILE, DUE TO HUGE NUMBERS OF CREED INSURGENTS IN OMILE.

THE GOVERNMENT HAS BEEN RELUCTANT TO SEND IN MILITARY FORCES FOR FEAR OF IGNITING A CIVIL WAR.

WE NOW GO LIVE TO MAYOR OJO AT CITY HALL.

**BREAKING NEWS**

THE CREED DESTROYS APARTMENT COMPLEX AT OMILE. HUNDREDS FEARED DEAD.

OCATES STATE OF EMERGENCY FOR LAGOON CITY.   OIL PRICE INDEX DROPS BY 0.5%.   SUPER EAGL

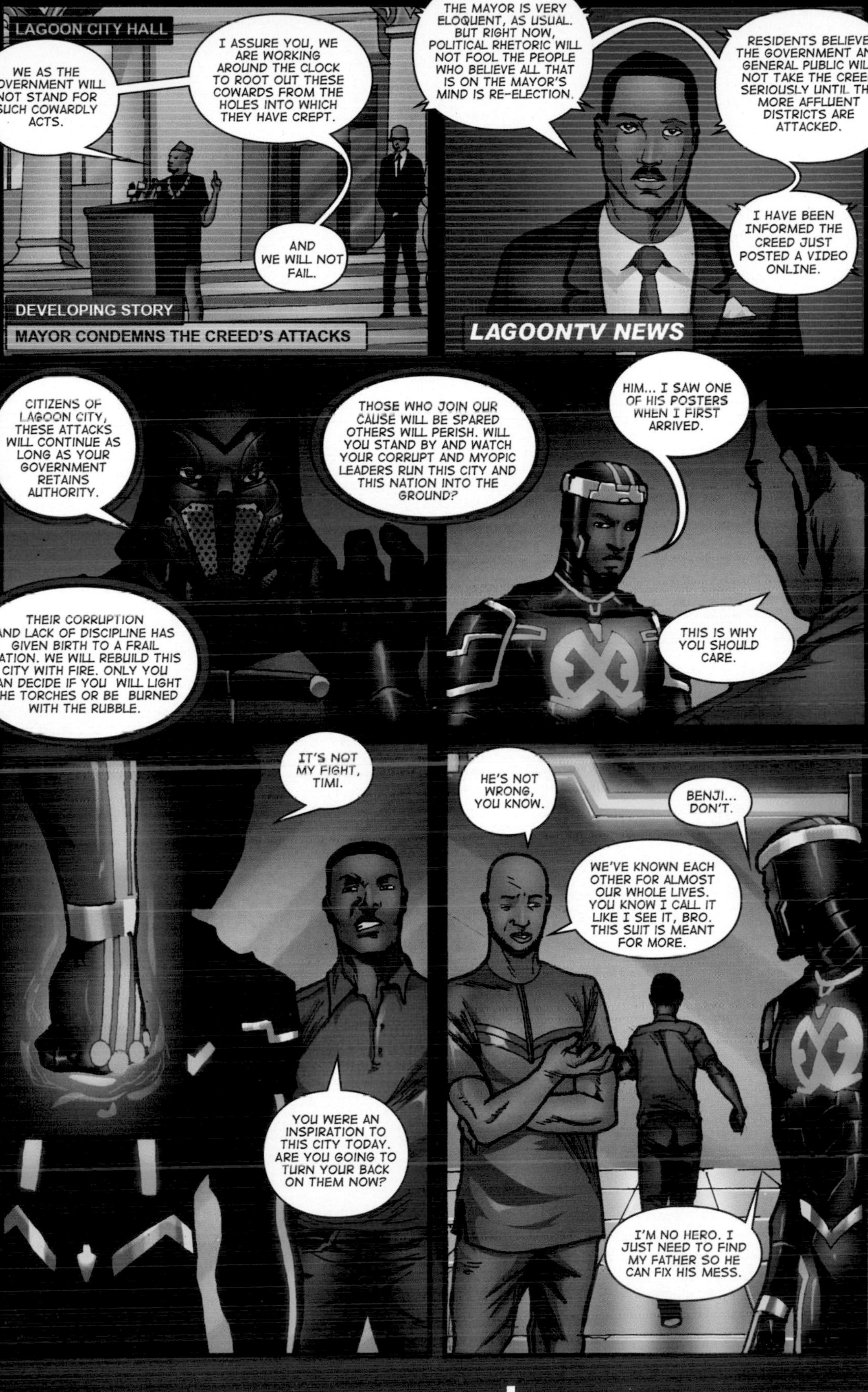
LAGOON CITY HALL
WE AS THE GOVERNMENT WILL NOT STAND FOR SUCH COWARDLY ACTS.
I ASSURE YOU, WE ARE WORKING AROUND THE CLOCK TO ROOT OUT THESE COWARDS FROM THE HOLES INTO WHICH THEY HAVE CREPT.
AND WE WILL NOT FAIL.
DEVELOPING STORY
MAYOR CONDEMNS THE CREED'S ATTACKS
THE MAYOR IS VERY ELOQUENT, AS USUAL. BUT RIGHT NOW, POLITICAL RHETORIC WILL NOT FOOL THE PEOPLE WHO BELIEVE ALL THAT IS ON THE MAYOR'S MIND IS RE-ELECTION.
RESIDENTS BELIEVE THE GOVERNMENT AND GENERAL PUBLIC WILL NOT TAKE THE CREED SERIOUSLY UNTIL THE MORE AFFLUENT DISTRICTS ARE ATTACKED.
I HAVE BEEN INFORMED THE CREED JUST POSTED A VIDEO ONLINE.
LAGOONTV NEWS
CITIZENS OF LAGOON CITY, THESE ATTACKS WILL CONTINUE AS LONG AS YOUR GOVERNMENT RETAINS AUTHORITY.
THOSE WHO JOIN OUR CAUSE WILL BE SPARED OTHERS WILL PERISH. WILL YOU STAND BY AND WATCH YOUR CORRUPT AND MYOPIC LEADERS RUN THIS CITY AND THIS NATION INTO THE GROUND?
THEIR CORRUPTION AND LACK OF DISCIPLINE HAS GIVEN BIRTH TO A FRAIL NATION. WE WILL REBUILD THIS CITY WITH FIRE. ONLY YOU CAN DECIDE IF YOU WILL LIGHT THE TORCHES OR BE BURNED WITH THE RUBBLE.
HIM... I SAW ONE OF HIS POSTERS WHEN I FIRST ARRIVED.
THIS IS WHY YOU SHOULD CARE.
IT'S NOT MY FIGHT, TIMI.
YOU WERE AN INSPIRATION TO THIS CITY TODAY. ARE YOU GOING TO TURN YOUR BACK ON THEM NOW?
HE'S NOT WRONG, YOU KNOW.
BENJI... DON'T.
WE'VE KNOWN EACH OTHER FOR ALMOST OUR WHOLE LIVES. YOU KNOW I CALL IT LIKE I SEE IT, BRO. THIS SUIT IS MEANT FOR MORE.
I'M NO HERO. I JUST NEED TO FIND MY FATHER SO HE CAN FIX HIS MESS.

# END OF CHAPTER FOUR

"The CREED is all that matters. It is all and I am none."

- *Twoshots*

CHAPTER
# FIVE

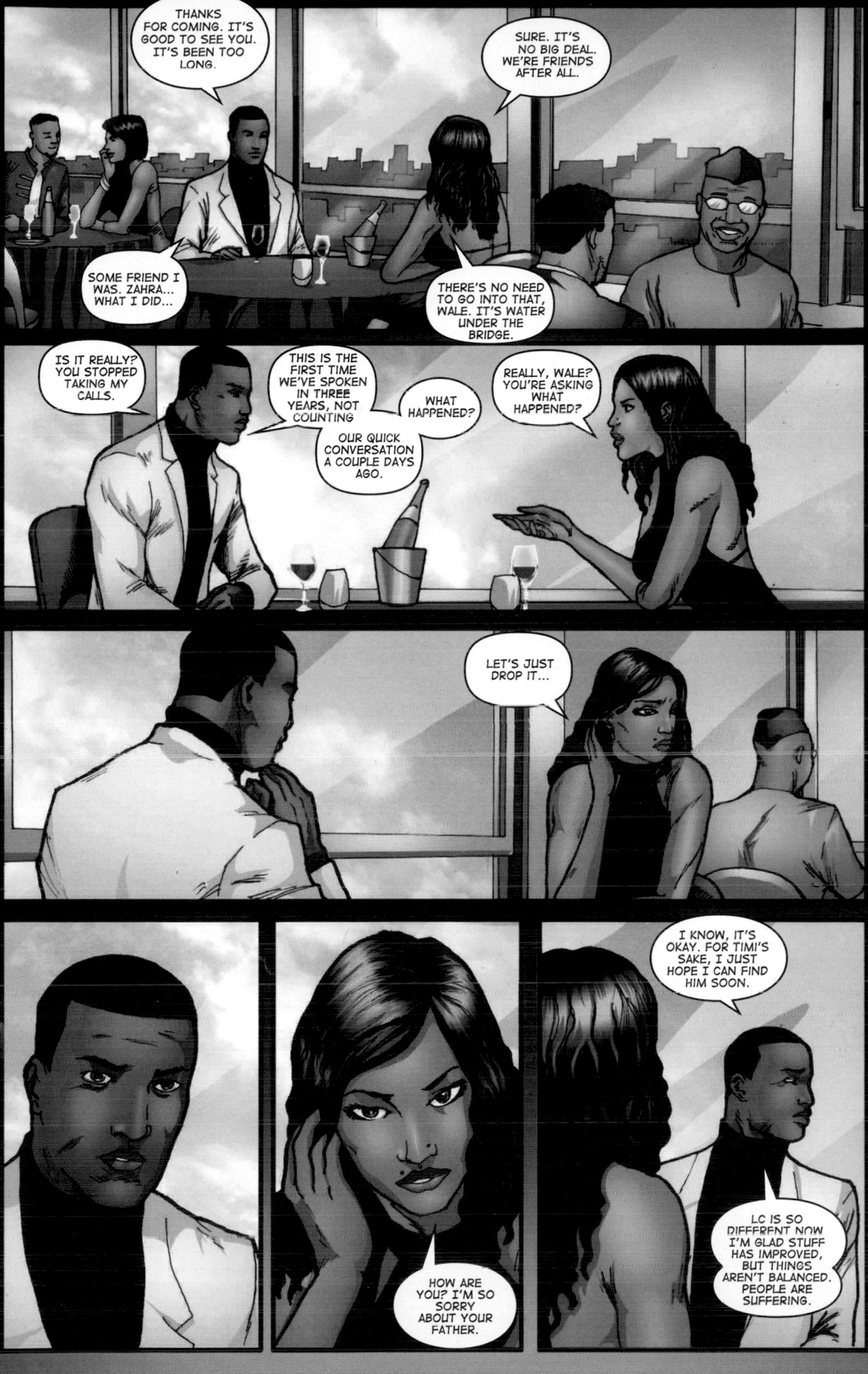
THANKS FOR COMING. IT'S GOOD TO SEE YOU. IT'S BEEN TOO LONG.
SURE. IT'S NO BIG DEAL. WE'RE FRIENDS AFTER ALL.
SOME FRIEND I WAS. ZAHRA... WHAT I DID...
THERE'S NO NEED TO GO INTO THAT, WALE. IT'S WATER UNDER THE BRIDGE.
IS IT REALLY? YOU STOPPED TAKING MY CALLS.
THIS IS THE FIRST TIME WE'VE SPOKEN IN THREE YEARS, NOT COUNTING
OUR QUICK CONVERSATION A COUPLE DAYS AGO.
WHAT HAPPENED?
REALLY, WALE? YOU'RE ASKING WHAT HAPPENED?
LET'S JUST DROP IT...
HOW ARE YOU? I'M SO SORRY ABOUT YOUR FATHER.
I KNOW, IT'S OKAY. FOR TIMI'S SAKE, I JUST HOPE I CAN FIND HIM SOON.
LC IS SO DIFFERENT NOW. I'M GLAD STUFF HAS IMPROVED, BUT THINGS AREN'T BALANCED. PEOPLE ARE SUFFERING.

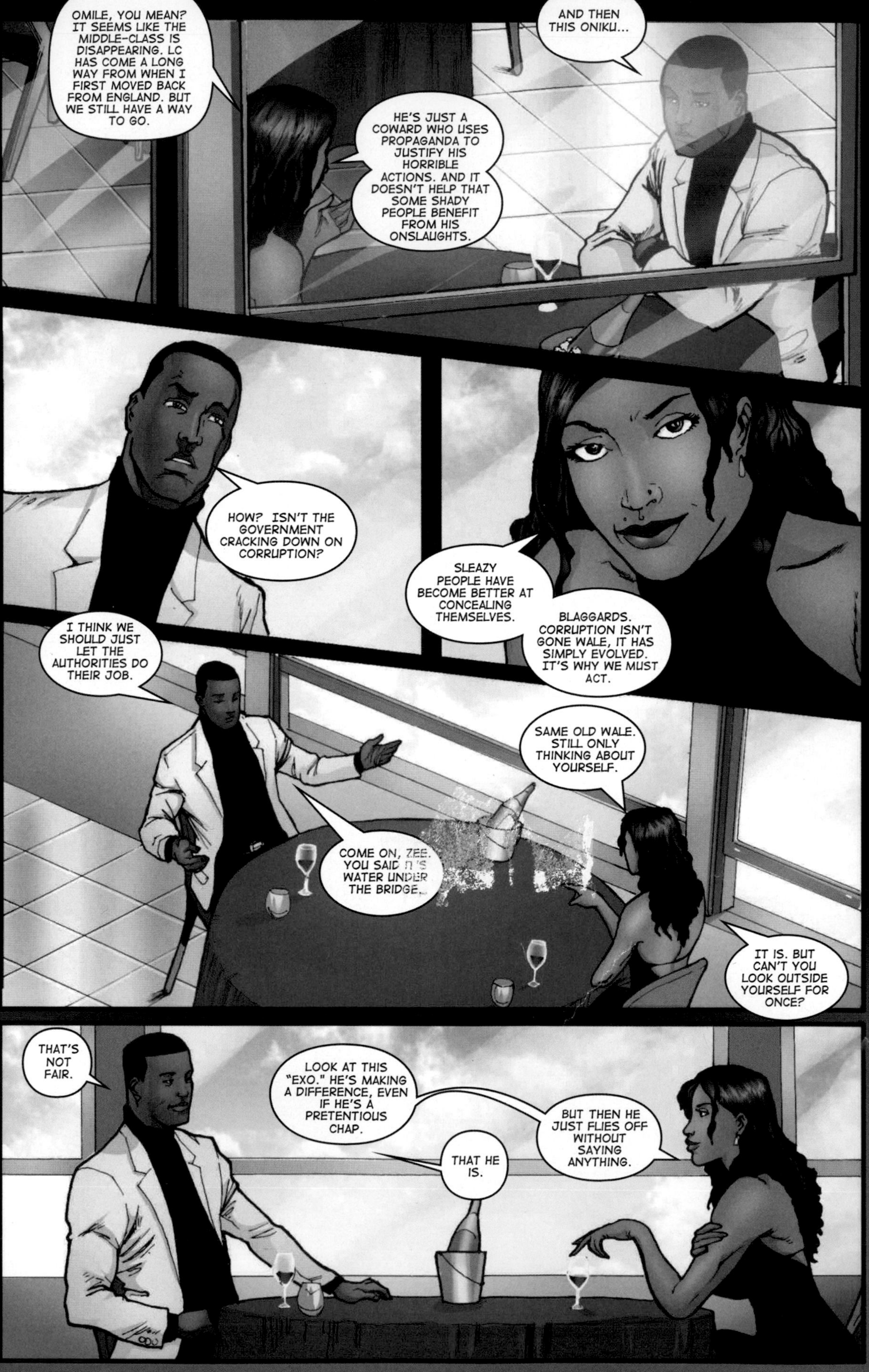
OMILE, YOU MEAN? IT SEEMS LIKE THE MIDDLE-CLASS IS DISAPPEARING. LC HAS COME A LONG WAY FROM WHEN I FIRST MOVED BACK FROM ENGLAND. BUT WE STILL HAVE A WAY TO GO.
AND THEN THIS ONIKU...
HE'S JUST A COWARD WHO USES PROPAGANDA TO JUSTIFY HIS HORRIBLE ACTIONS. AND IT DOESN'T HELP THAT SOME SHADY PEOPLE BENEFIT FROM HIS ONSLAUGHTS.
HOW? ISN'T THE GOVERNMENT CRACKING DOWN ON CORRUPTION?
SLEAZY PEOPLE HAVE BECOME BETTER AT CONCEALING THEMSELVES.
BLAGGARDS. CORRUPTION ISN'T GONE WALE, IT HAS SIMPLY EVOLVED. IT'S WHY WE MUST ACT.
I THINK WE SHOULD JUST LET THE AUTHORITIES DO THEIR JOB.
SAME OLD WALE. STILL ONLY THINKING ABOUT YOURSELF.
COME ON, ZEE. YOU SAID IT'S WATER UNDER THE BRIDGE.
IT IS. BUT CAN'T YOU LOOK OUTSIDE YOURSELF FOR ONCE?
THAT'S NOT FAIR.
LOOK AT THIS "EXO." HE'S MAKING A DIFFERENCE, EVEN IF HE'S A PRETENTIOUS CHAP.
THAT HE IS.
BUT THEN HE JUST FLIES OFF WITHOUT SAYING ANYTHING.

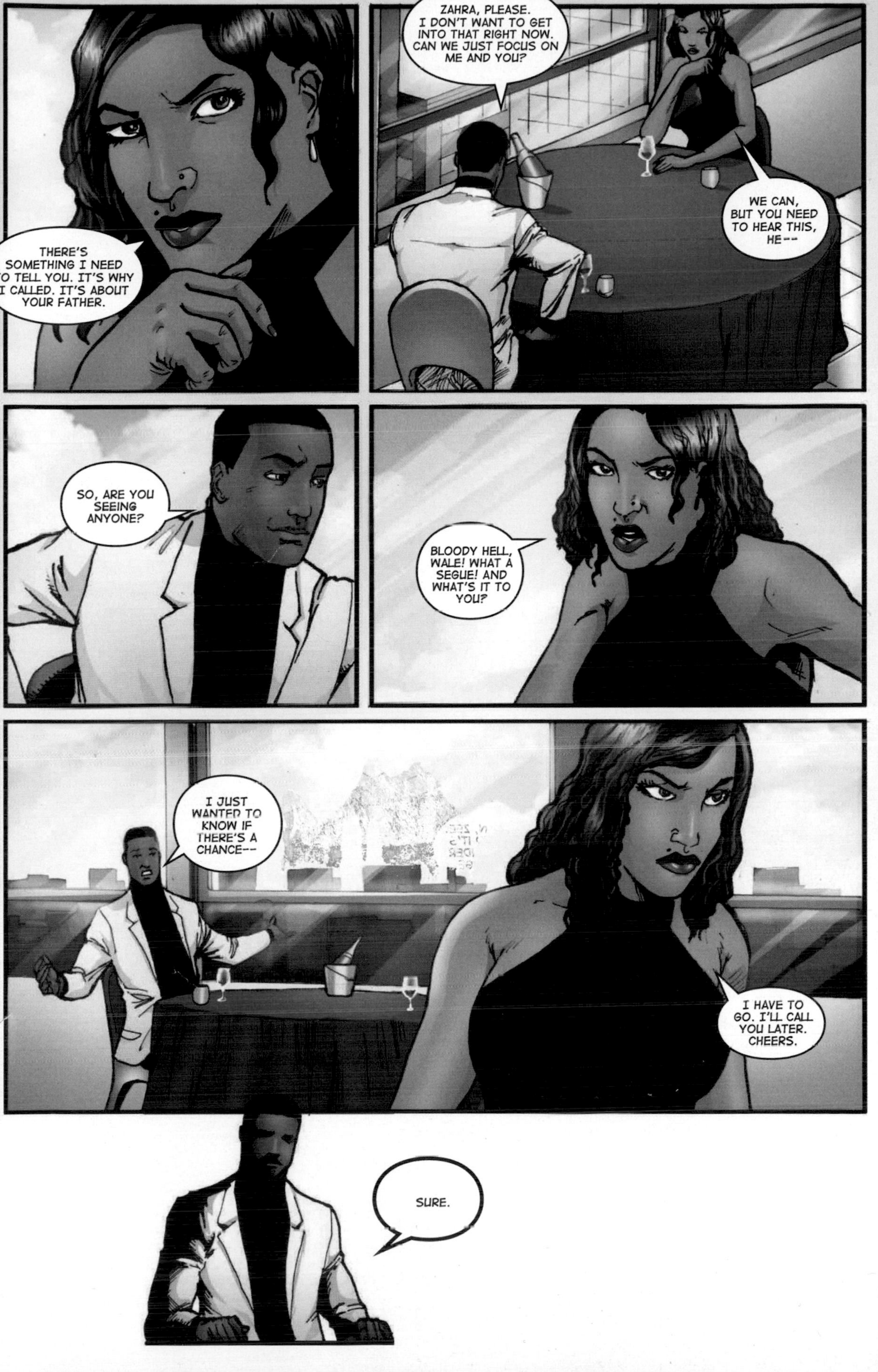
THERE'S SOMETHING I NEED TO TELL YOU. IT'S WHY I CALLED. IT'S ABOUT YOUR FATHER.
ZAHRA, PLEASE. I DON'T WANT TO GET INTO THAT RIGHT NOW. CAN WE JUST FOCUS ON ME AND YOU?
WE CAN, BUT YOU NEED TO HEAR THIS, HE--
SO, ARE YOU SEEING ANYONE?
BLOODY HELL, WALE! WHAT A SEGUE! AND WHAT'S IT TO YOU?
I JUST WANTED TO KNOW IF THERE'S A CHANCE--
I HAVE TO GO. I'LL CALL YOU LATER. CHEERS.
SURE.

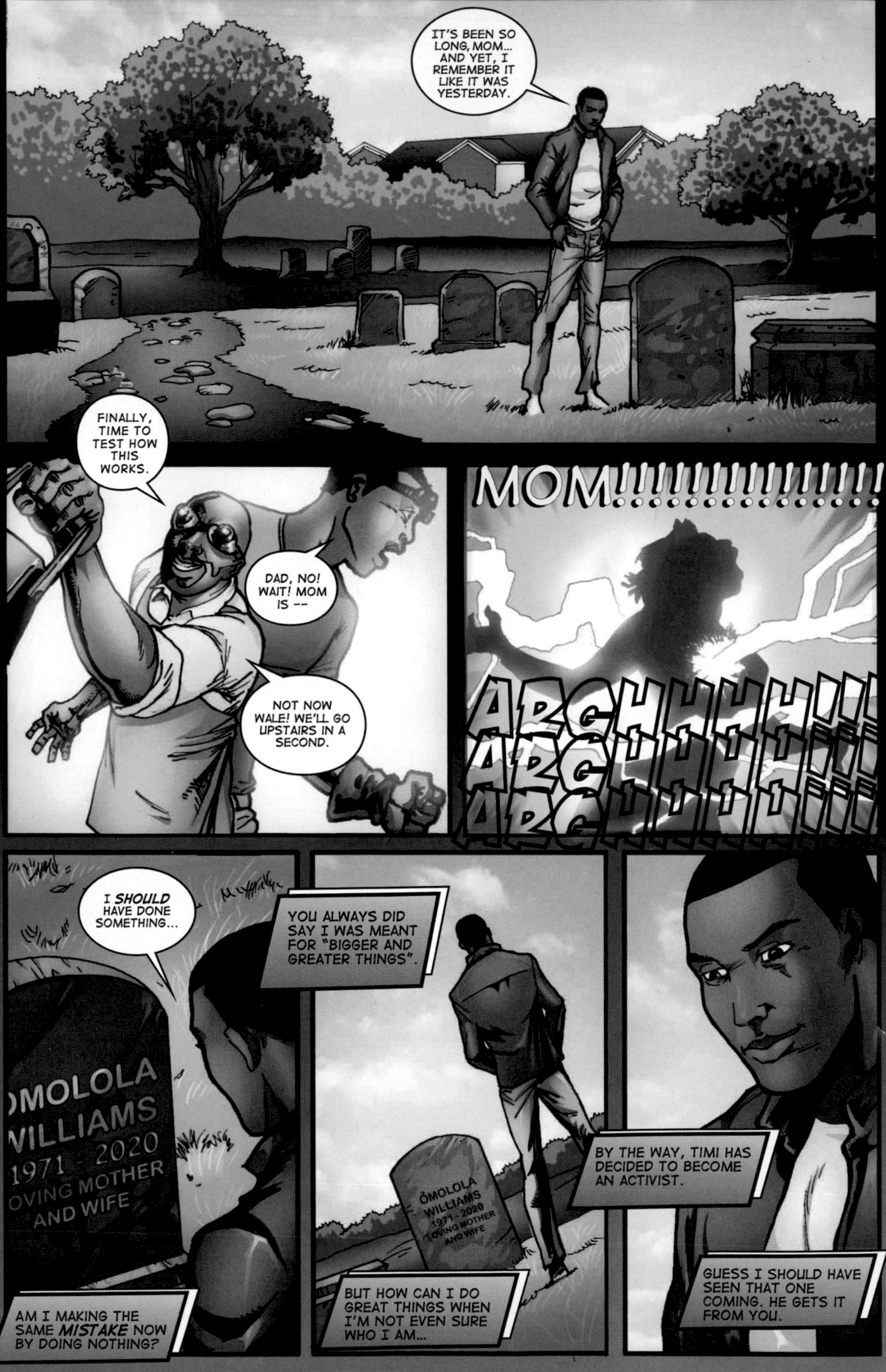
IT'S BEEN SO LONG, MOM... AND YET, I REMEMBER IT LIKE IT WAS YESTERDAY.
FINALLY, TIME TO TEST HOW THIS WORKS.
DAD, NO! WAIT! MOM IS --
NOT NOW WALE! WE'LL GO UPSTAIRS IN A SECOND.
MOM!!!!!!!!!!!!!!
ARGHHHH!!!
ARGHHHH!!!
ARGHHHH!!!
I SHOULD HAVE DONE SOMETHING...
OMOLOLA WILLIAMS 1971 - 2020 LOVING MOTHER AND WIFE
AM I MAKING THE SAME MISTAKE NOW BY DOING NOTHING?
YOU ALWAYS DID SAY I WAS MEANT FOR "BIGGER AND GREATER THINGS".
OMOLOLA WILLIAMS 1971 - 2020 LOVING MOTHER AND WIFE
BUT HOW CAN I DO GREAT THINGS WHEN I'M NOT EVEN SURE WHO I AM...
BY THE WAY, TIMI HAS DECIDED TO BECOME AN ACTIVIST.
GUESS I SHOULD HAVE SEEN THAT ONE COMING. HE GETS IT FROM YOU.

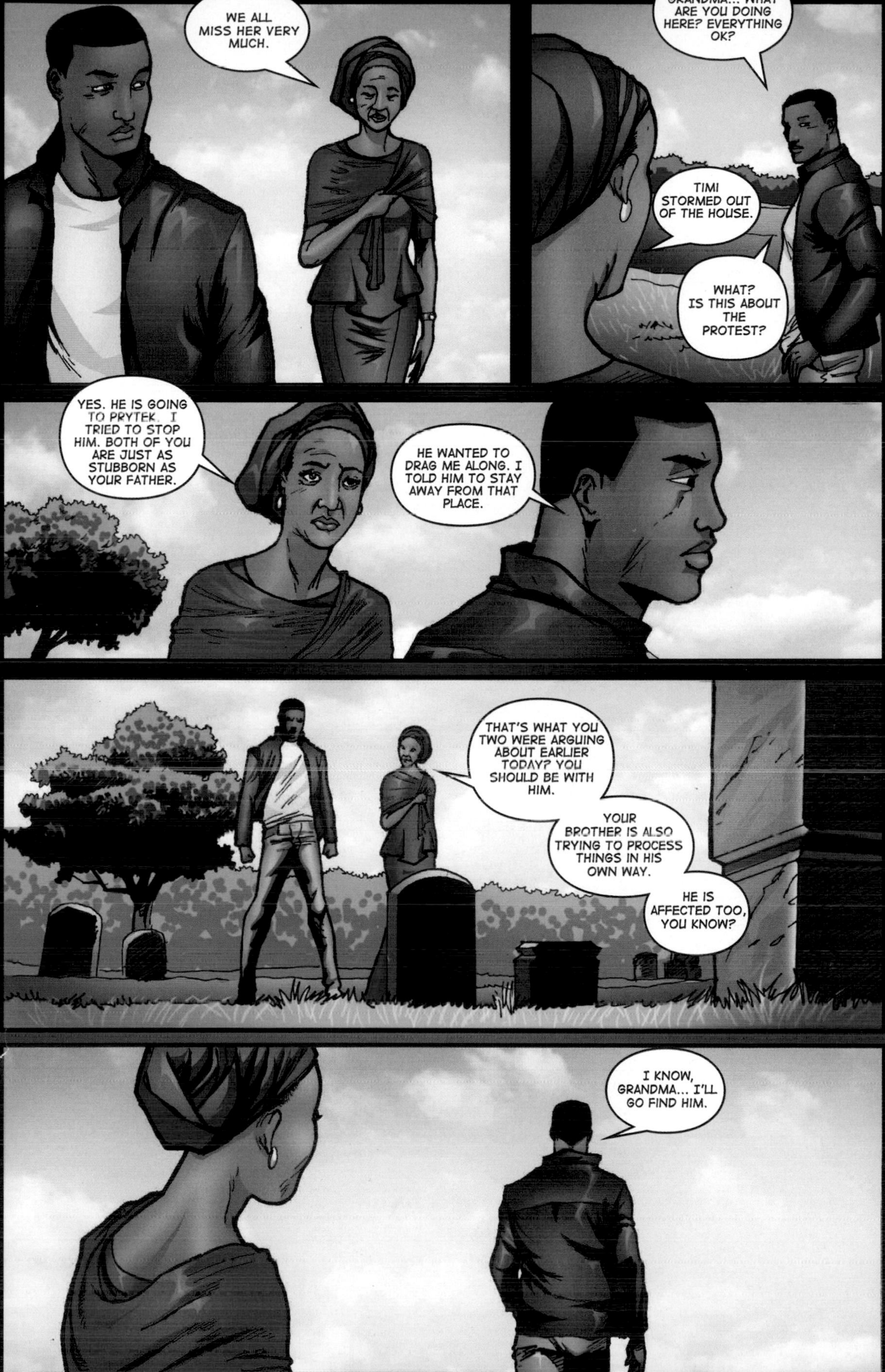
WE ALL MISS HER VERY MUCH.
GRANDMA... WHAT ARE YOU DOING HERE? EVERYTHING OK?
TIMI STORMED OUT OF THE HOUSE.
WHAT? IS THIS ABOUT THE PROTEST?
YES. HE IS GOING TO PRYTEK. I TRIED TO STOP HIM. BOTH OF YOU ARE JUST AS STUBBORN AS YOUR FATHER.
HE WANTED TO DRAG ME ALONG. I TOLD HIM TO STAY AWAY FROM THAT PLACE.
THAT'S WHAT YOU TWO WERE ARGUING ABOUT EARLIER TODAY? YOU SHOULD BE WITH HIM.
YOUR BROTHER IS ALSO TRYING TO PROCESS THINGS IN HIS OWN WAY.
HE IS AFFECTED TOO, YOU KNOW?
I KNOW, GRANDMA... I'LL GO FIND HIM.

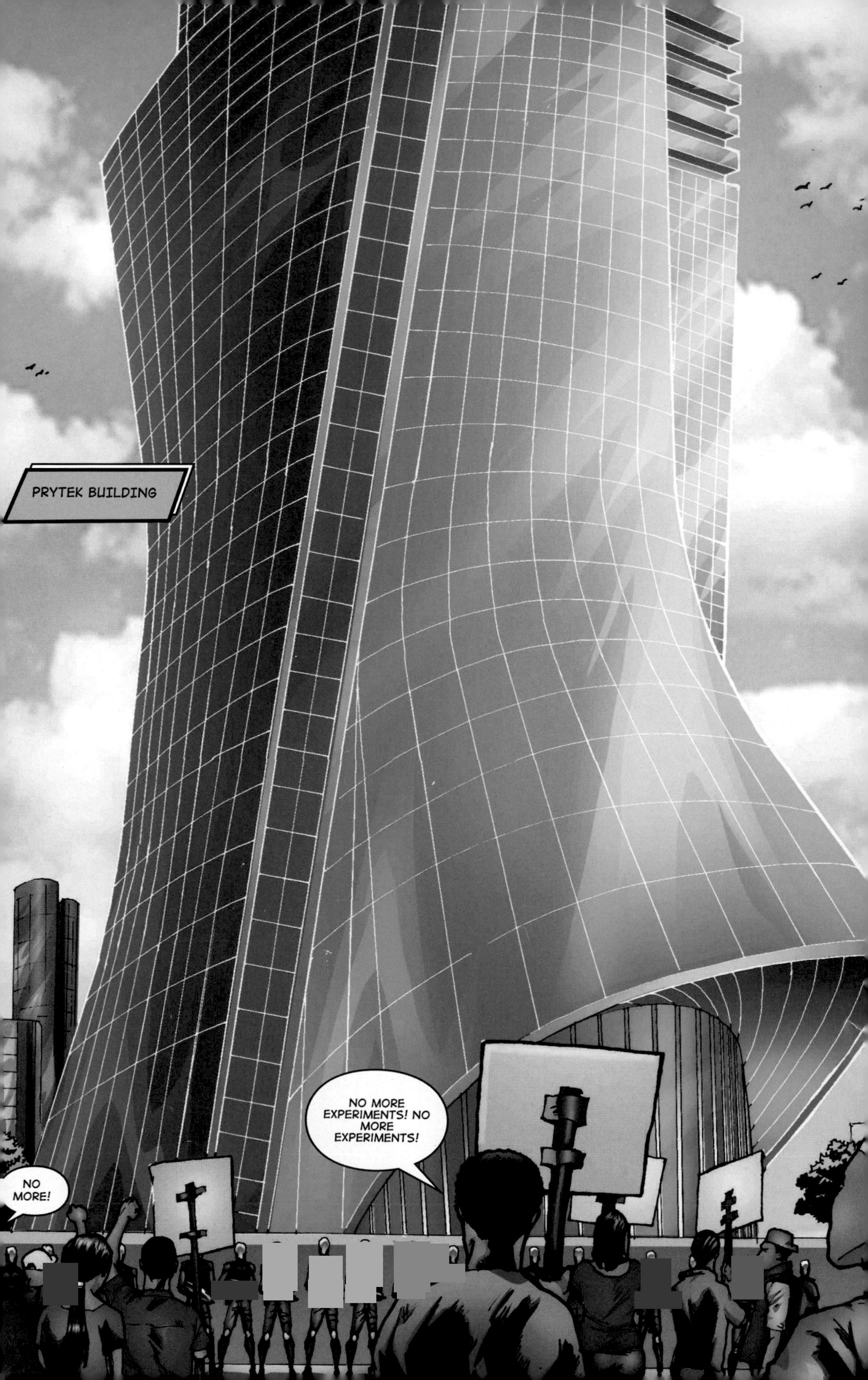
PRYTEK BUILDING
NO MORE EXPERIMENTS! NO MORE EXPERIMENTS!
NO MORE!

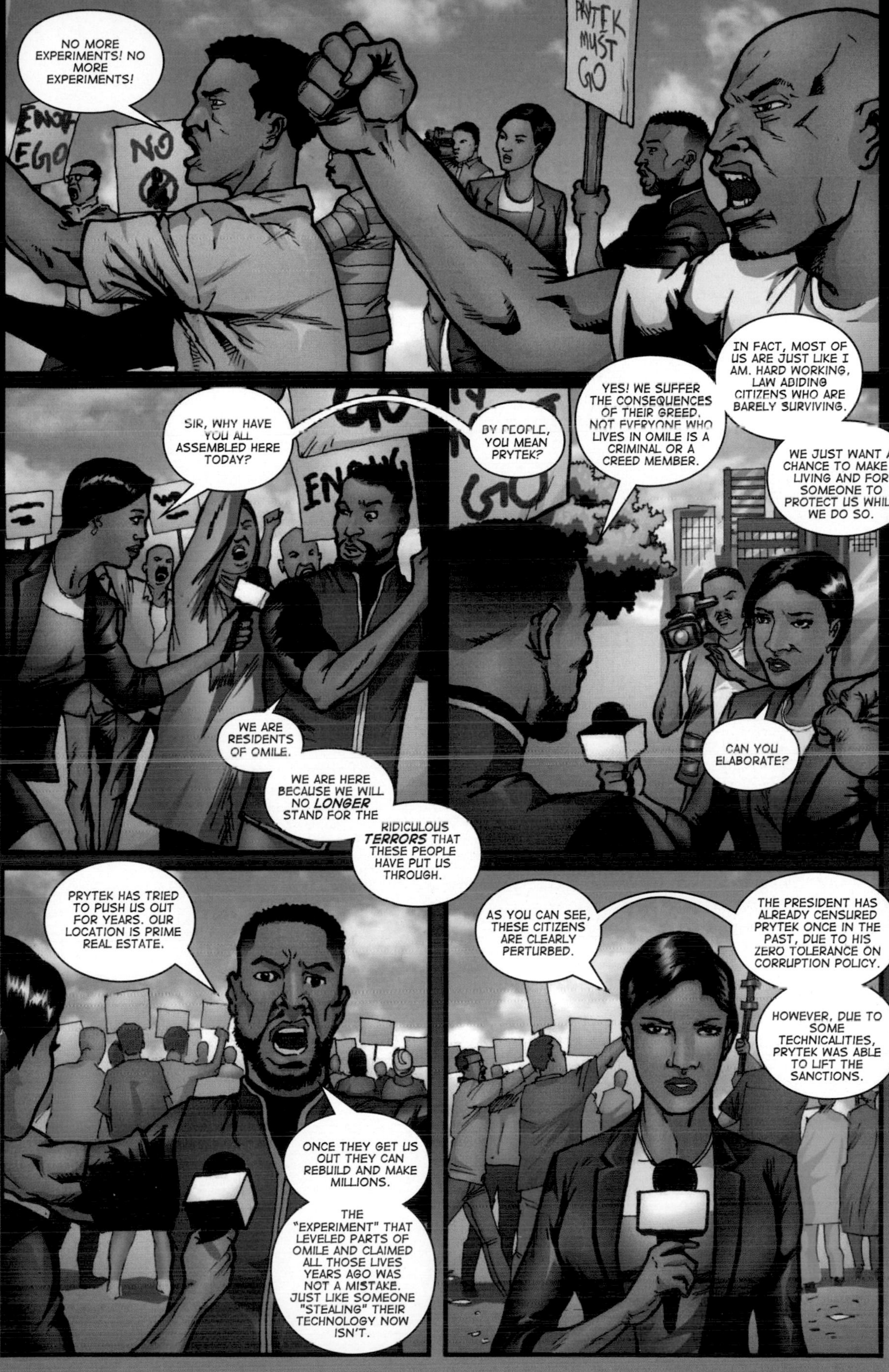
NO MORE EXPERIMENTS! NO MORE EXPERIMENTS!
PRYTEK MUST GO
NO
SIR, WHY HAVE YOU ALL ASSEMBLED HERE TODAY?
WE ARE RESIDENTS OF OMILE.
WE ARE HERE BECAUSE WE WILL NO LONGER STAND FOR THE RIDICULOUS TERRORS THAT THESE PEOPLE HAVE PUT US THROUGH.
BY PEOPLE, YOU MEAN PRYTEK?
YES! WE SUFFER THE CONSEQUENCES OF THEIR GREED. NOT EVERYONE WHO LIVES IN OMILE IS A CRIMINAL OR A CREED MEMBER.
IN FACT, MOST OF US ARE JUST LIKE I AM. HARD WORKING, LAW ABIDING CITIZENS WHO ARE BARELY SURVIVING.
WE JUST WANT A CHANCE TO MAKE A LIVING AND FOR SOMEONE TO PROTECT US WHILE WE DO SO.
CAN YOU ELABORATE?
PRYTEK HAS TRIED TO PUSH US OUT FOR YEARS. OUR LOCATION IS PRIME REAL ESTATE.
ONCE THEY GET US OUT THEY CAN REBUILD AND MAKE MILLIONS.
THE "EXPERIMENT" THAT LEVELED PARTS OF OMILE AND CLAIMED ALL THOSE LIVES YEARS AGO WAS NOT A MISTAKE. JUST LIKE SOMEONE "STEALING" THEIR TECHNOLOGY NOW ISN'T.
AS YOU CAN SEE, THESE CITIZENS ARE CLEARLY PERTURBED.
THE PRESIDENT HAS ALREADY CENSURED PRYTEK ONCE IN THE PAST, DUE TO HIS ZERO TOLERANCE ON CORRUPTION POLICY.
HOWEVER, DUE TO SOME TECHNICALITIES, PRYTEK WAS ABLE TO LIFT THE SANCTIONS.

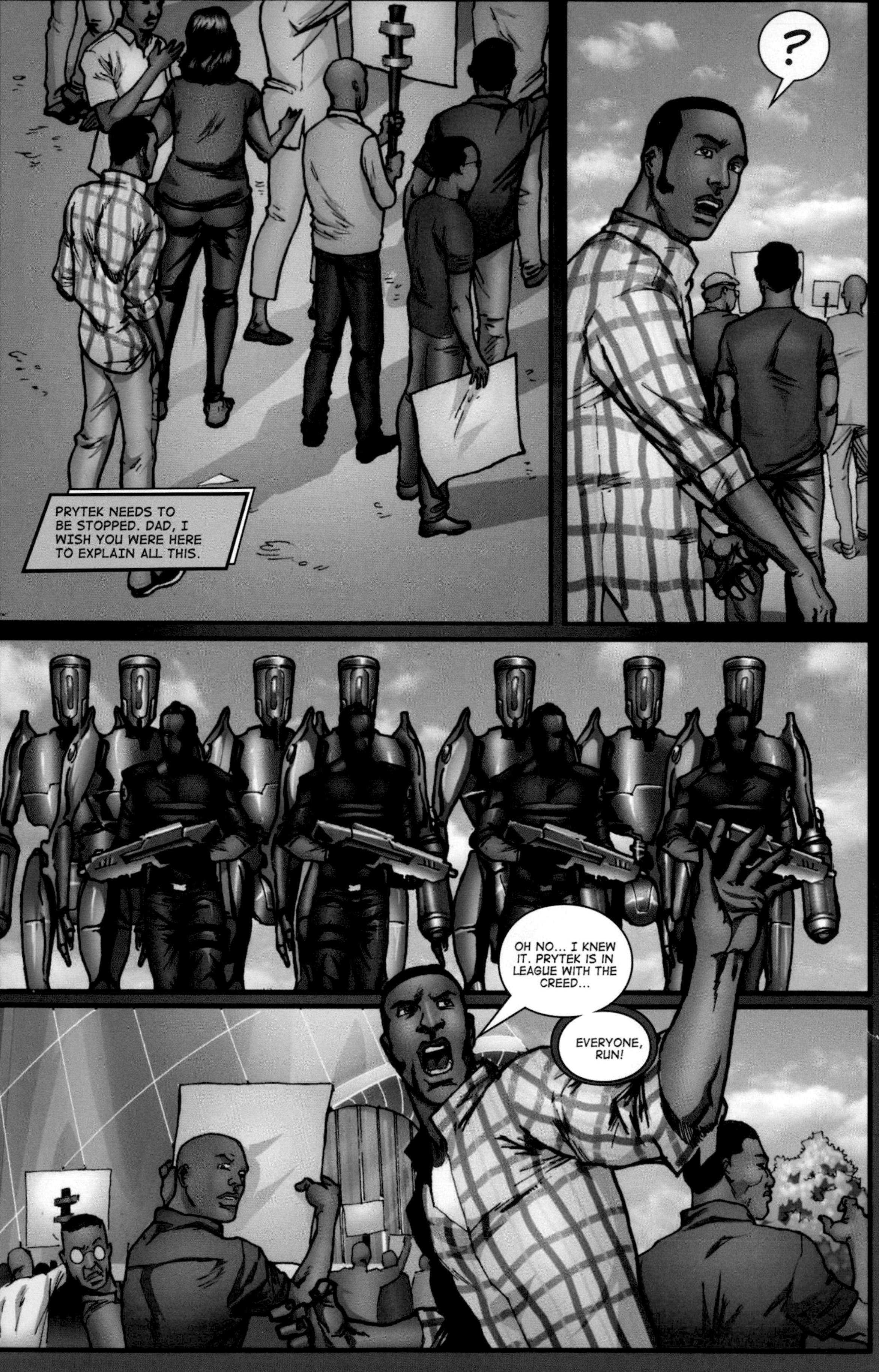
PRYTEK NEEDS TO BE STOPPED. DAD, I WISH YOU WERE HERE TO EXPLAIN ALL THIS.
?
OH NO... I KNEW IT. PRYTEK IS IN LEAGUE WITH THE CREED...
EVERYONE, RUN!

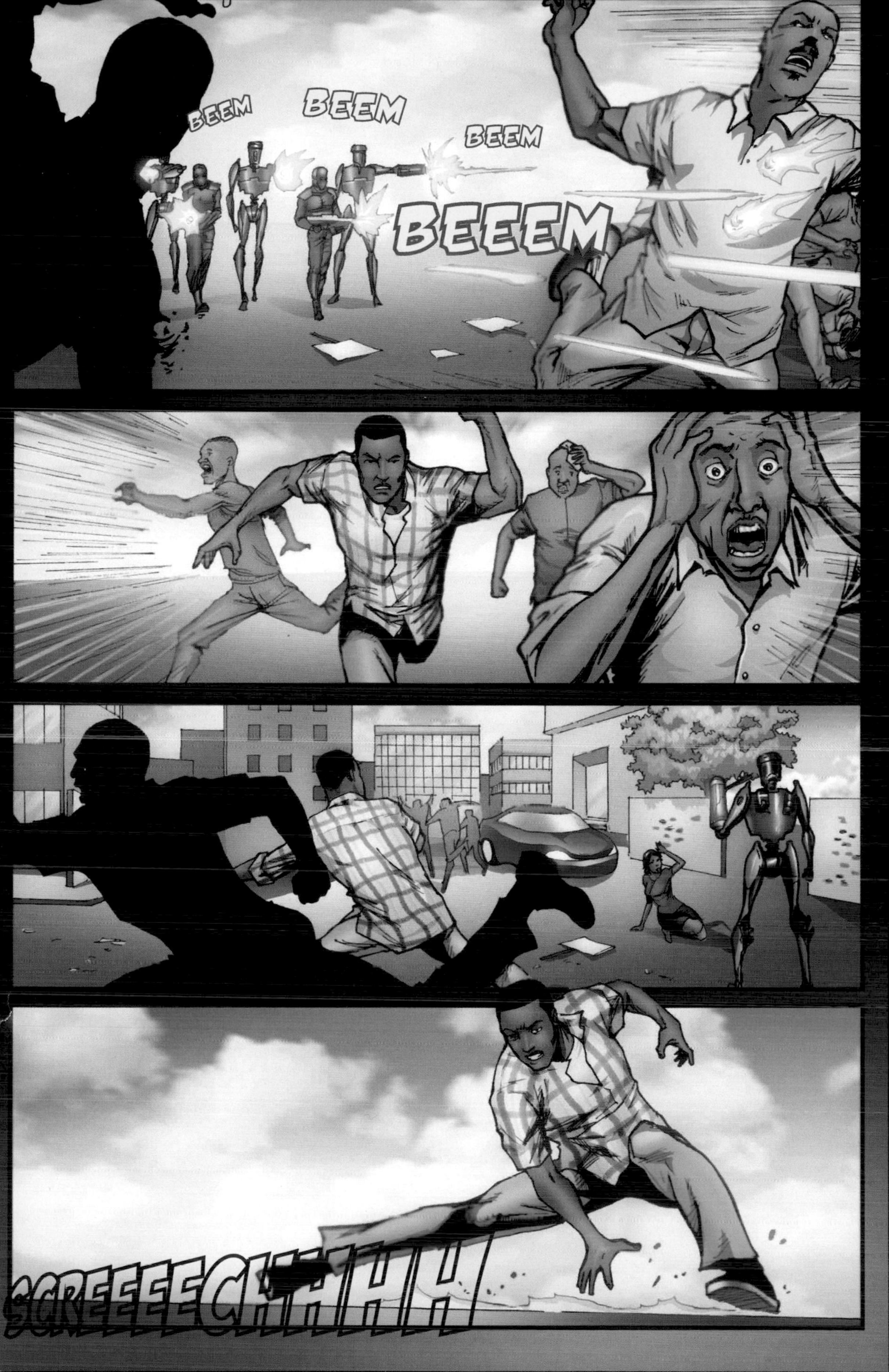
BEEM
BEEM
BEEM
BEEEM
SCREEEEECHHHHH

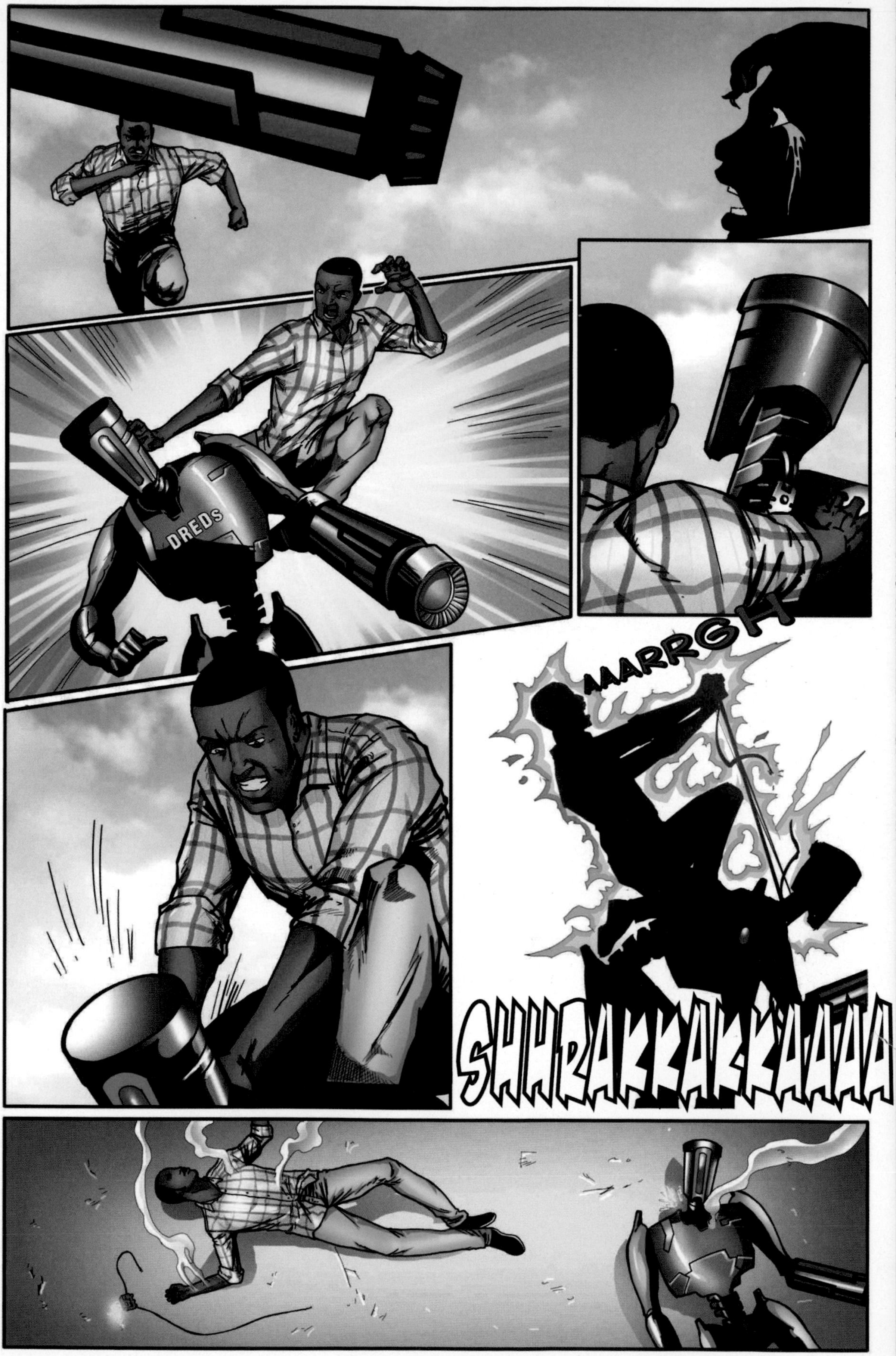
DREDS
AAARRGH
SHHRAKKAKKAAAA

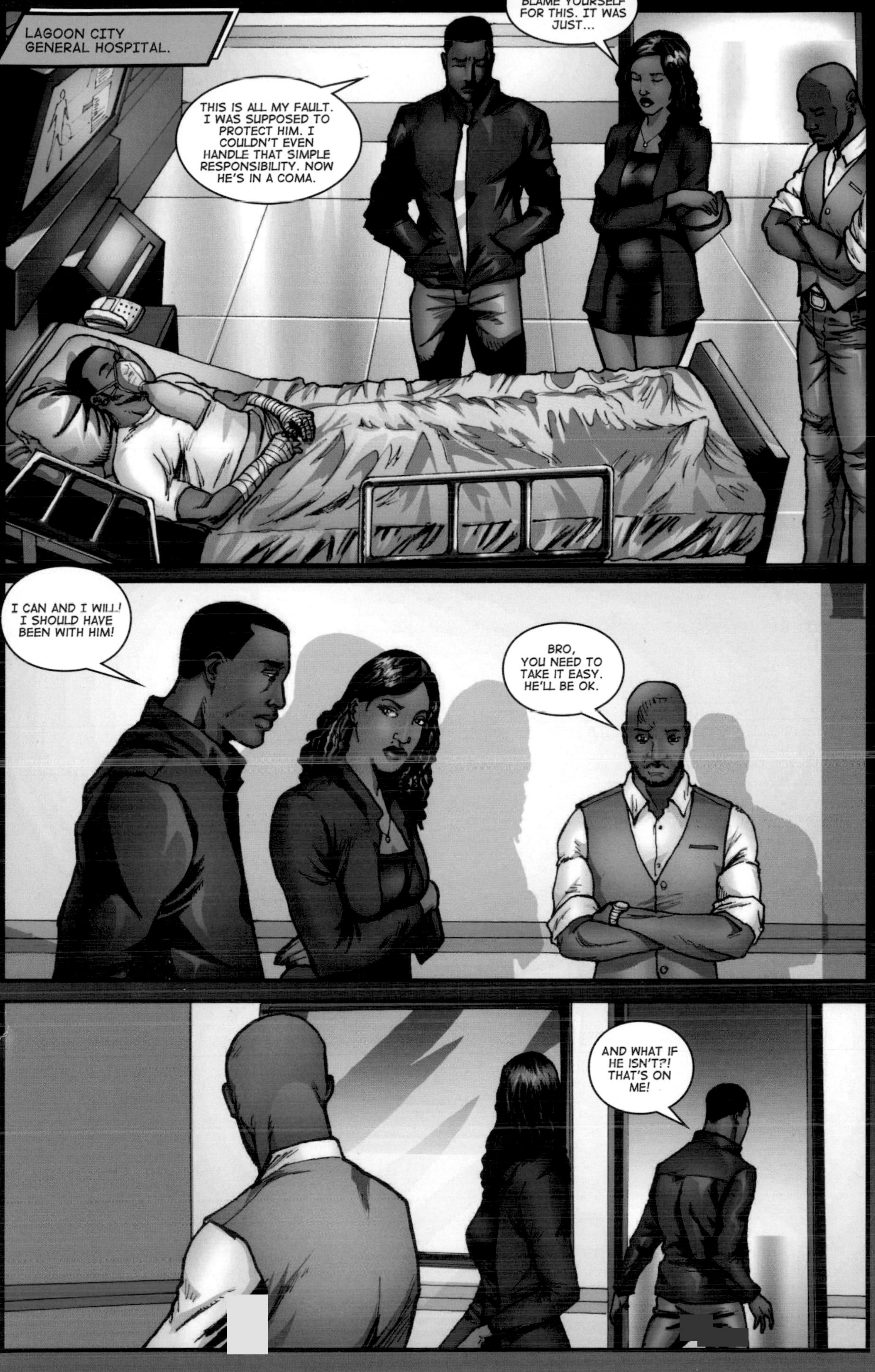
LAGOON CITY GENERAL HOSPITAL.
WALE, YOU CAN'T BLAME YOURSELF FOR THIS. IT WAS JUST...
THIS IS ALL MY FAULT. I WAS SUPPOSED TO PROTECT HIM. I COULDN'T EVEN HANDLE THAT SIMPLE RESPONSIBILITY. NOW HE'S IN A COMA.
I CAN AND I WILL! I SHOULD HAVE BEEN WITH HIM!
BRO, YOU NEED TO TAKE IT EASY. HE'LL BE OK.
AND WHAT IF HE ISN'T?! THAT'S ON ME!

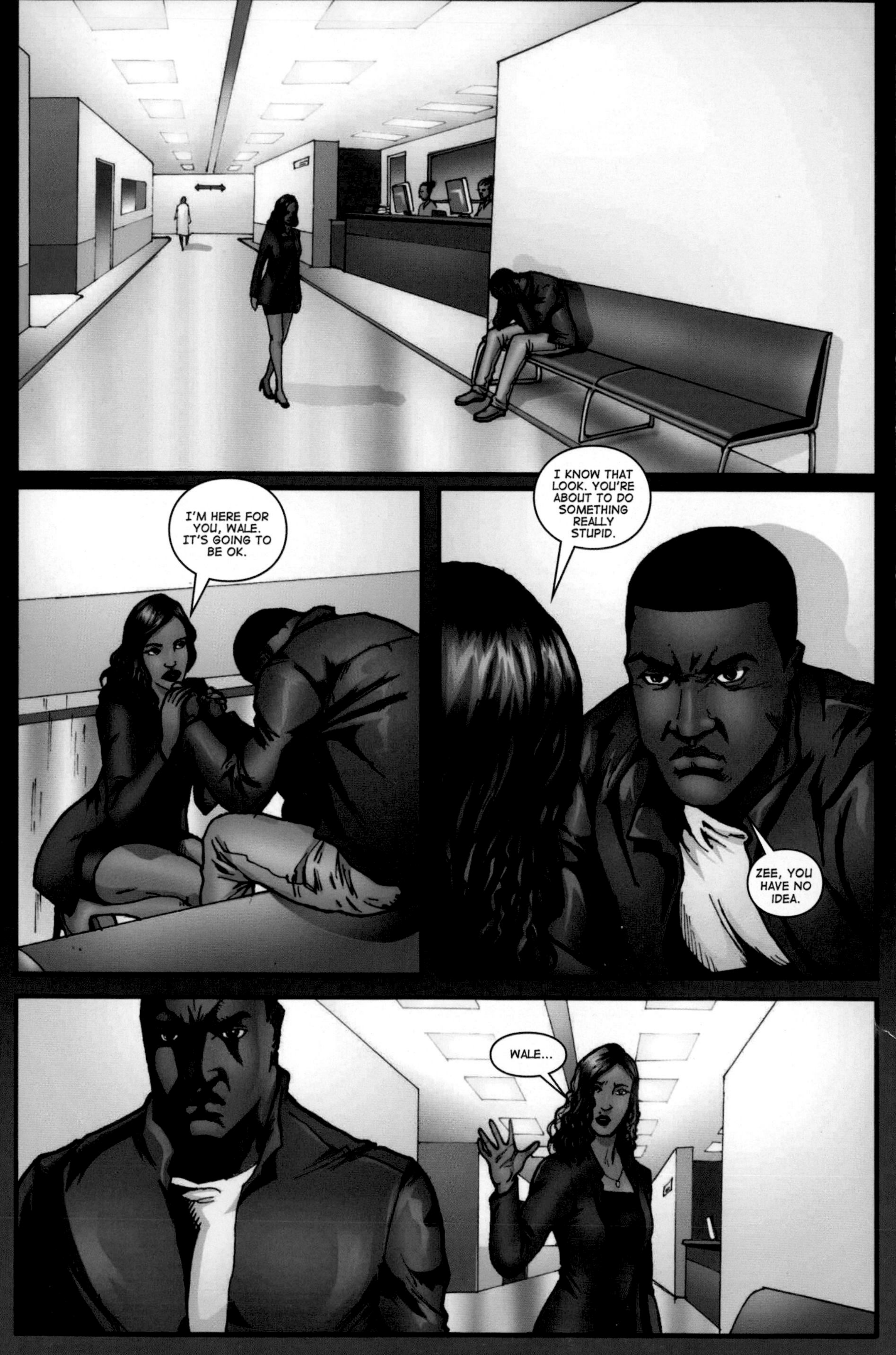
I'M HERE FOR YOU, WALE. IT'S GOING TO BE OK.
I KNOW THAT LOOK. YOU'RE ABOUT TO DO SOMETHING REALLY STUPID.
ZEE, YOU HAVE NO IDEA.
WALE...

CHAPTER FIVE

"This time, I won't go easy."

- *Fury*

# CHAPTER
# six

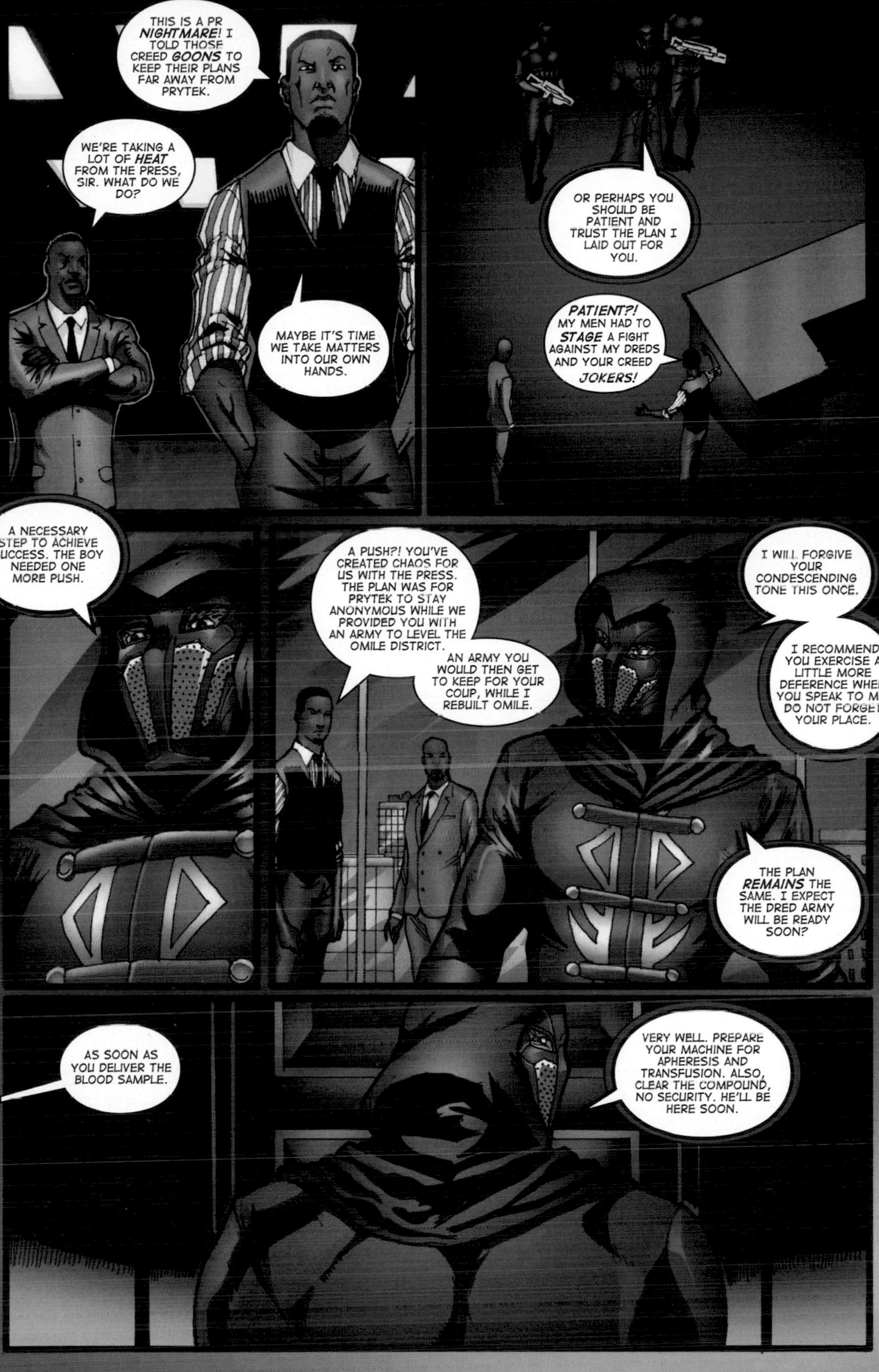
THIS IS A PR NIGHTMARE! I TOLD THOSE CREED GOONS TO KEEP THEIR PLANS FAR AWAY FROM PRYTEK.
WE'RE TAKING A LOT OF HEAT FROM THE PRESS, SIR. WHAT DO WE DO?
MAYBE IT'S TIME WE TAKE MATTERS INTO OUR OWN HANDS.
OR PERHAPS YOU SHOULD BE PATIENT AND TRUST THE PLAN I LAID OUT FOR YOU.
PATIENT?! MY MEN HAD TO STAGE A FIGHT AGAINST MY DREDS AND YOUR CREED JOKERS!
A NECESSARY STEP TO ACHIEVE SUCCESS. THE BOY NEEDED ONE MORE PUSH.
A PUSH?! YOU'VE CREATED CHAOS FOR US WITH THE PRESS. THE PLAN WAS FOR PRYTEK TO STAY ANONYMOUS WHILE WE PROVIDED YOU WITH AN ARMY TO LEVEL THE OMILE DISTRICT.
AN ARMY YOU WOULD THEN GET TO KEEP FOR YOUR COUP, WHILE I REBUILT OMILE.
I WILL FORGIVE YOUR CONDESCENDING TONE THIS ONCE.
I RECOMMEND YOU EXERCISE A LITTLE MORE DEFERENCE WHEN YOU SPEAK TO ME. DO NOT FORGET YOUR PLACE.
THE PLAN REMAINS THE SAME. I EXPECT THE DRED ARMY WILL BE READY SOON?
AS SOON AS YOU DELIVER THE BLOOD SAMPLE.
VERY WELL. PREPARE YOUR MACHINE FOR APHERESIS AND TRANSFUSION. ALSO, CLEAR THE COMPOUND, NO SECURITY. HE'LL BE HERE SOON.

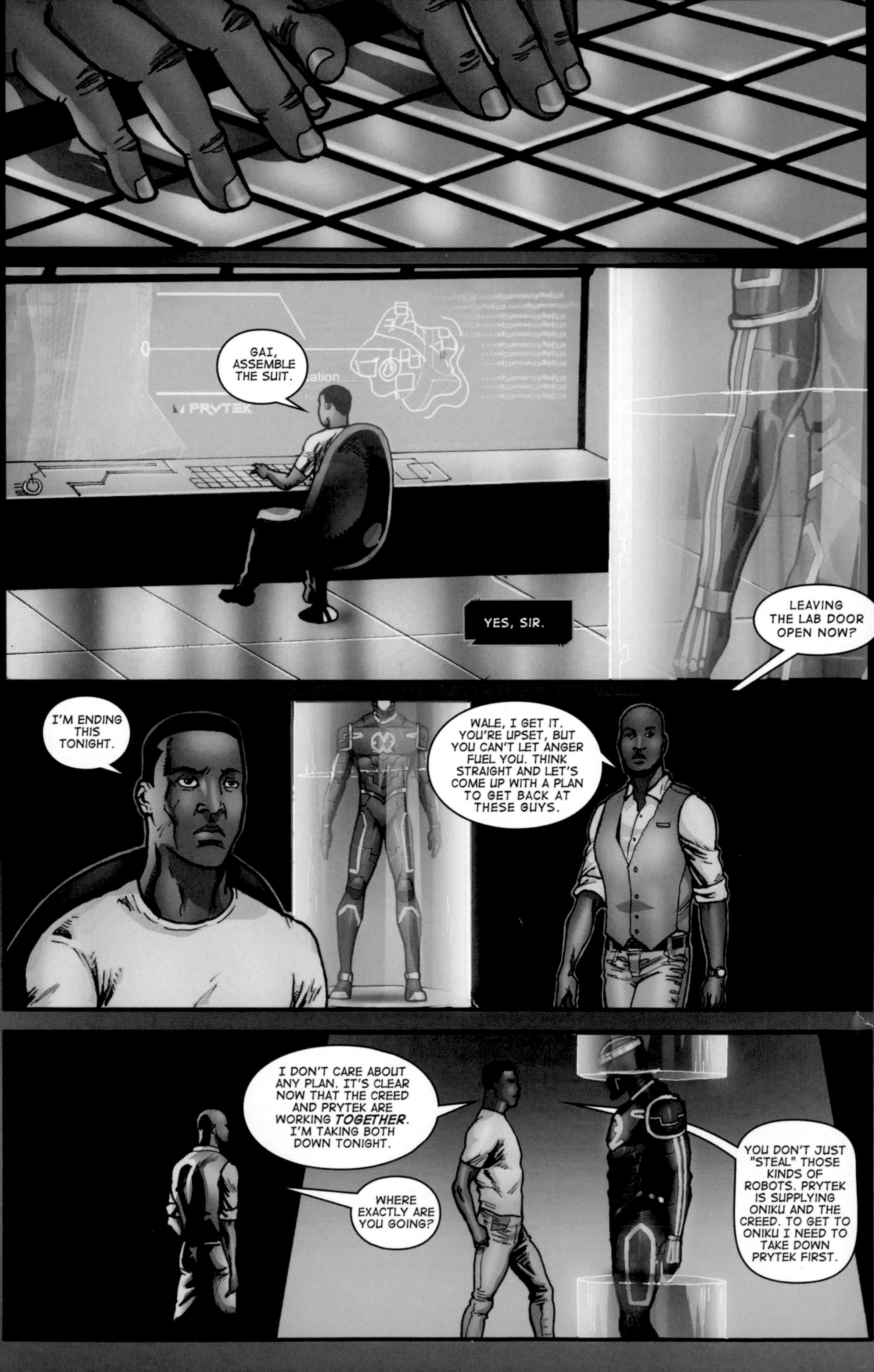

PRYTEK
GAI, ASSEMBLE THE SUIT.
YES, SIR.
LEAVING THE LAB DOOR OPEN NOW?
I'M ENDING THIS TONIGHT.
WALE, I GET IT. YOU'RE UPSET, BUT YOU CAN'T LET ANGER FUEL YOU. THINK STRAIGHT AND LET'S COME UP WITH A PLAN TO GET BACK AT THESE GUYS.
I DON'T CARE ABOUT ANY PLAN. IT'S CLEAR NOW THAT THE CREED AND PRYTEK ARE WORKING *TOGETHER*. I'M TAKING BOTH DOWN TONIGHT.
WHERE EXACTLY ARE YOU GOING?
YOU DON'T JUST "STEAL" THOSE KINDS OF ROBOTS. PRYTEK IS SUPPLYING ONIKU AND THE CREED. TO GET TO ONIKU I NEED TO TAKE DOWN PRYTEK FIRST.

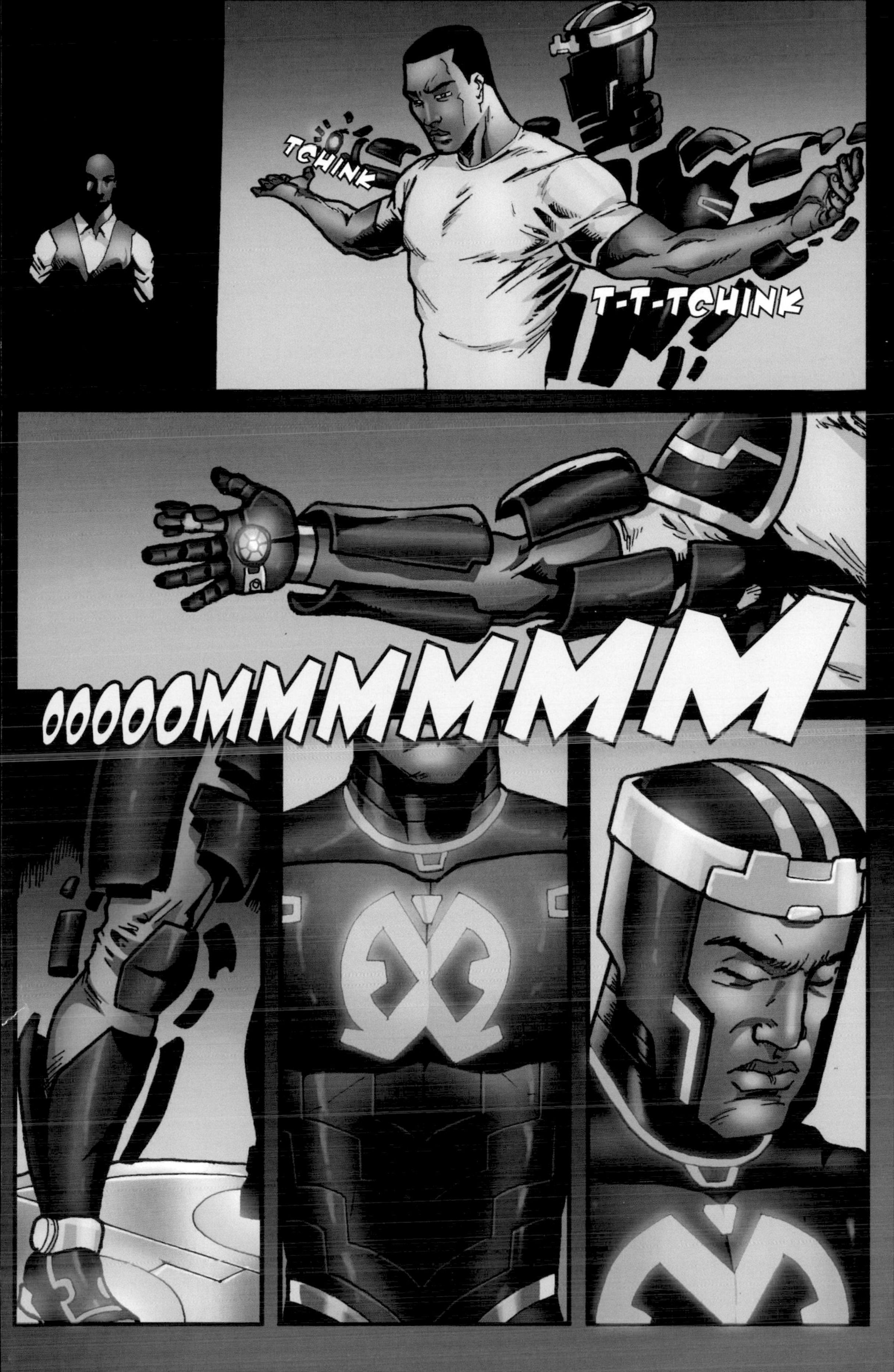
TCHINK
T-T-TCHINK
OOOOOMMMMMMM

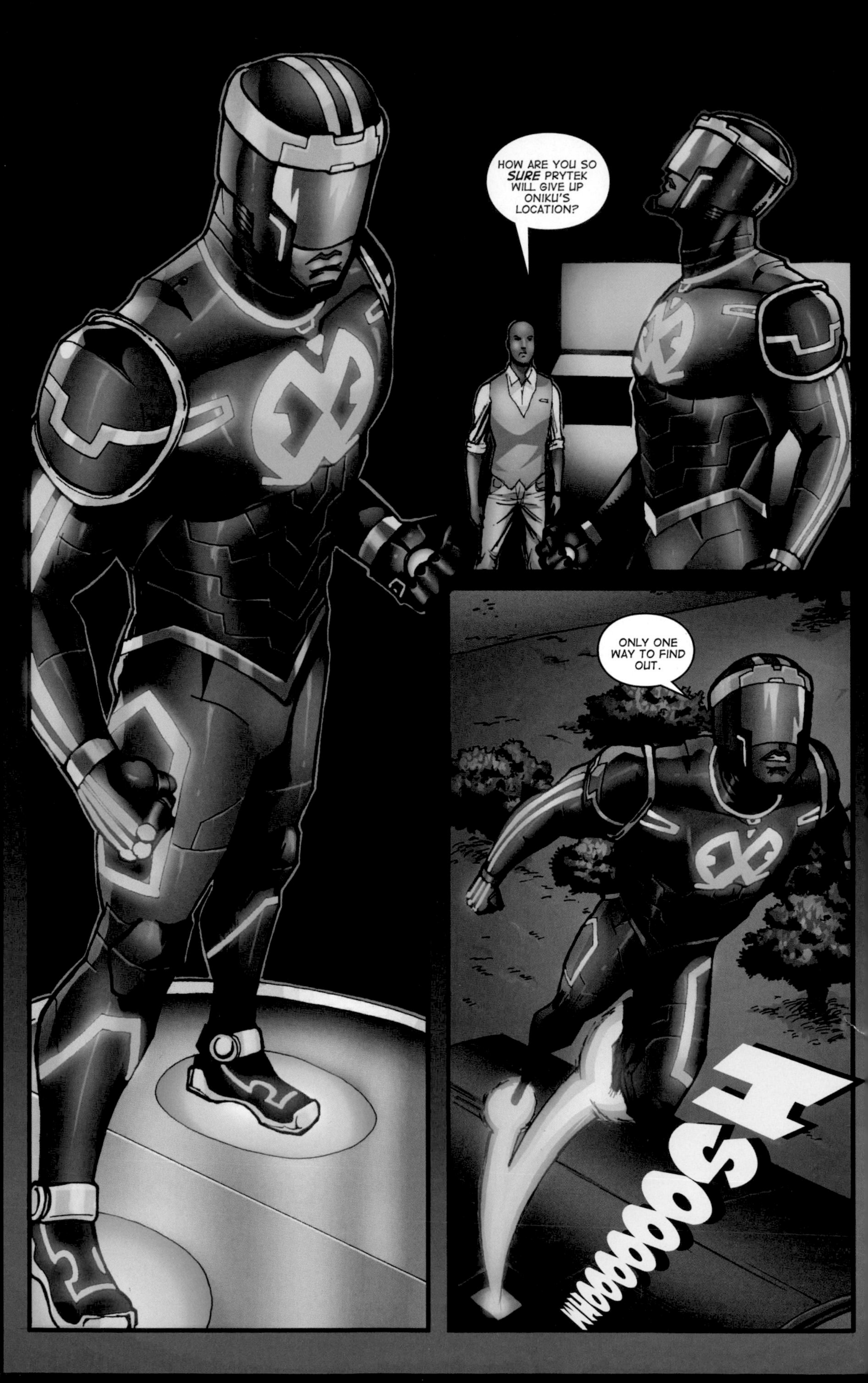
HOW ARE YOU SO SURE PRYTEK WILL GIVE UP ONIKU'S LOCATION?
ONLY ONE WAY TO FIND OUT.
WHOOOOOOOSH

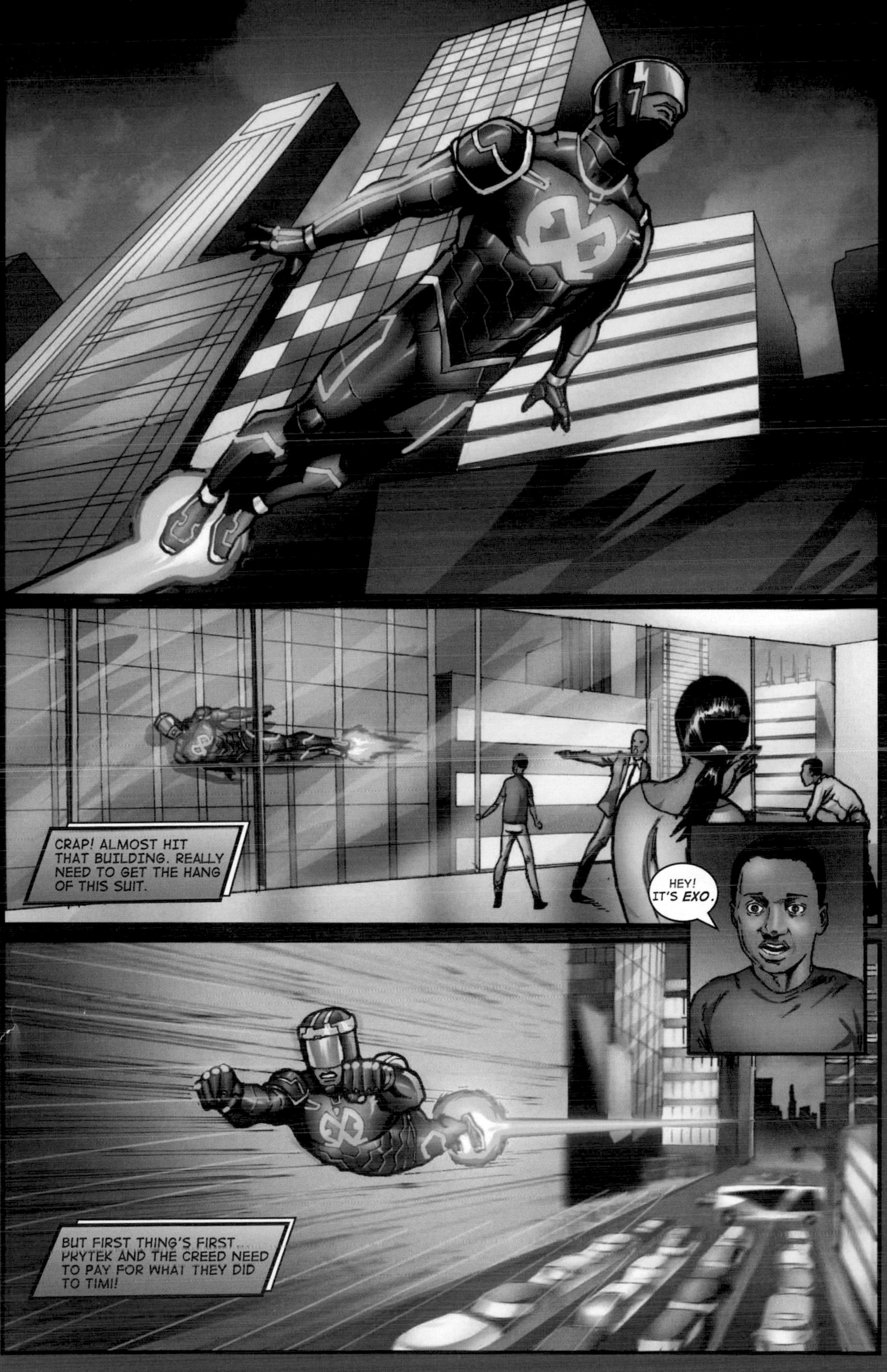
CRAP! ALMOST HIT THAT BUILDING. REALLY NEED TO GET THE HANG OF THIS SUIT.
HEY! IT'S EXO.
BUT FIRST THING'S FIRST... PRYTEK AND THE CREED NEED TO PAY FOR WHAT THEY DID TO TIMI!

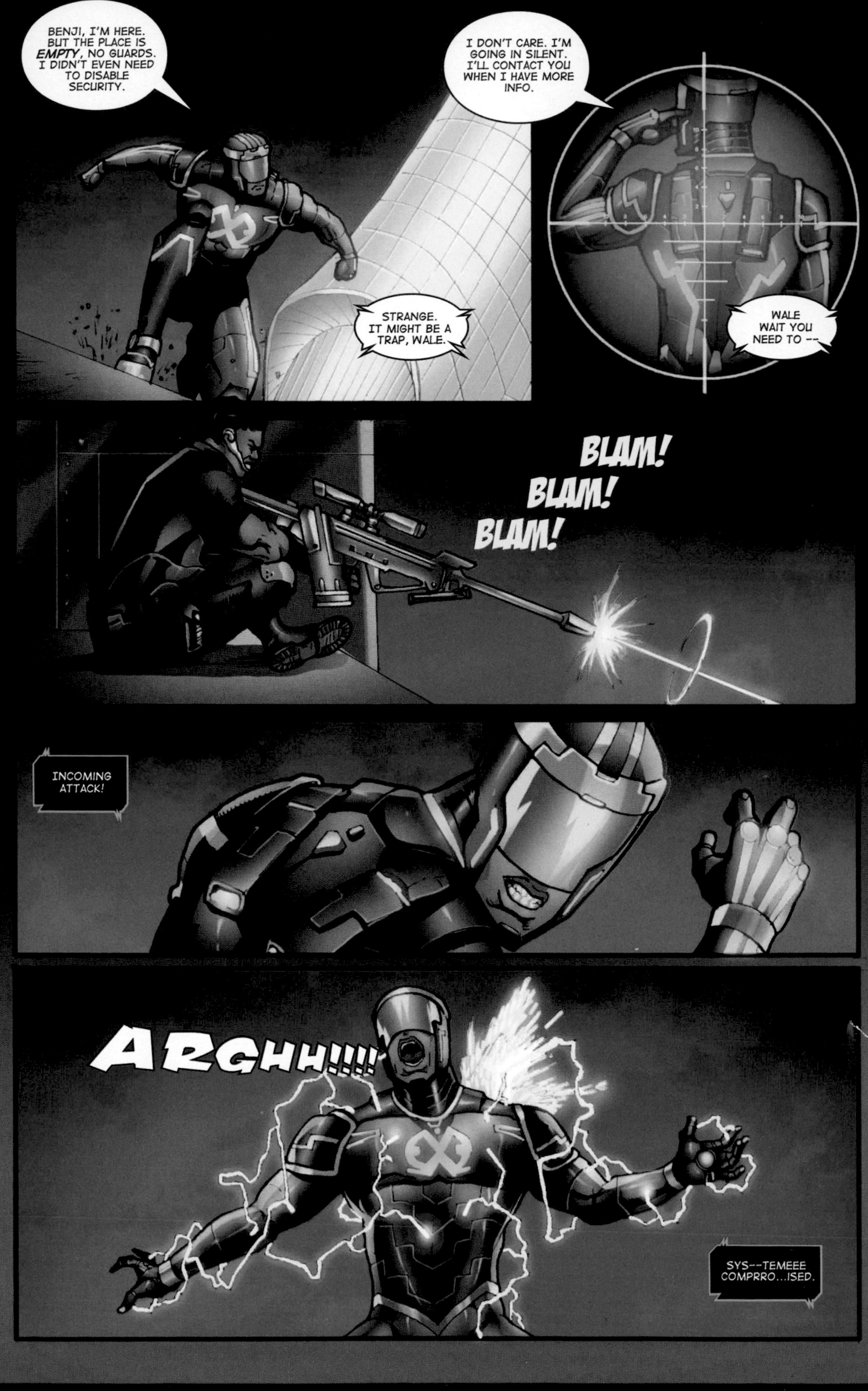
BENJI, I'M HERE. BUT THE PLACE IS *EMPTY*, NO GUARDS. I DIDN'T EVEN NEED TO DISABLE SECURITY.
STRANGE. IT MIGHT BE A TRAP, WALE.
I DON'T CARE. I'M GOING IN SILENT. I'LL CONTACT YOU WHEN I HAVE MORE INFO.
WALE WAIT YOU NEED TO --
BLAM!
BLAM!
BLAM!
INCOMING ATTACK!
ARGHH!!!!
SYS--TEMEEE COMPRRO...ISED.

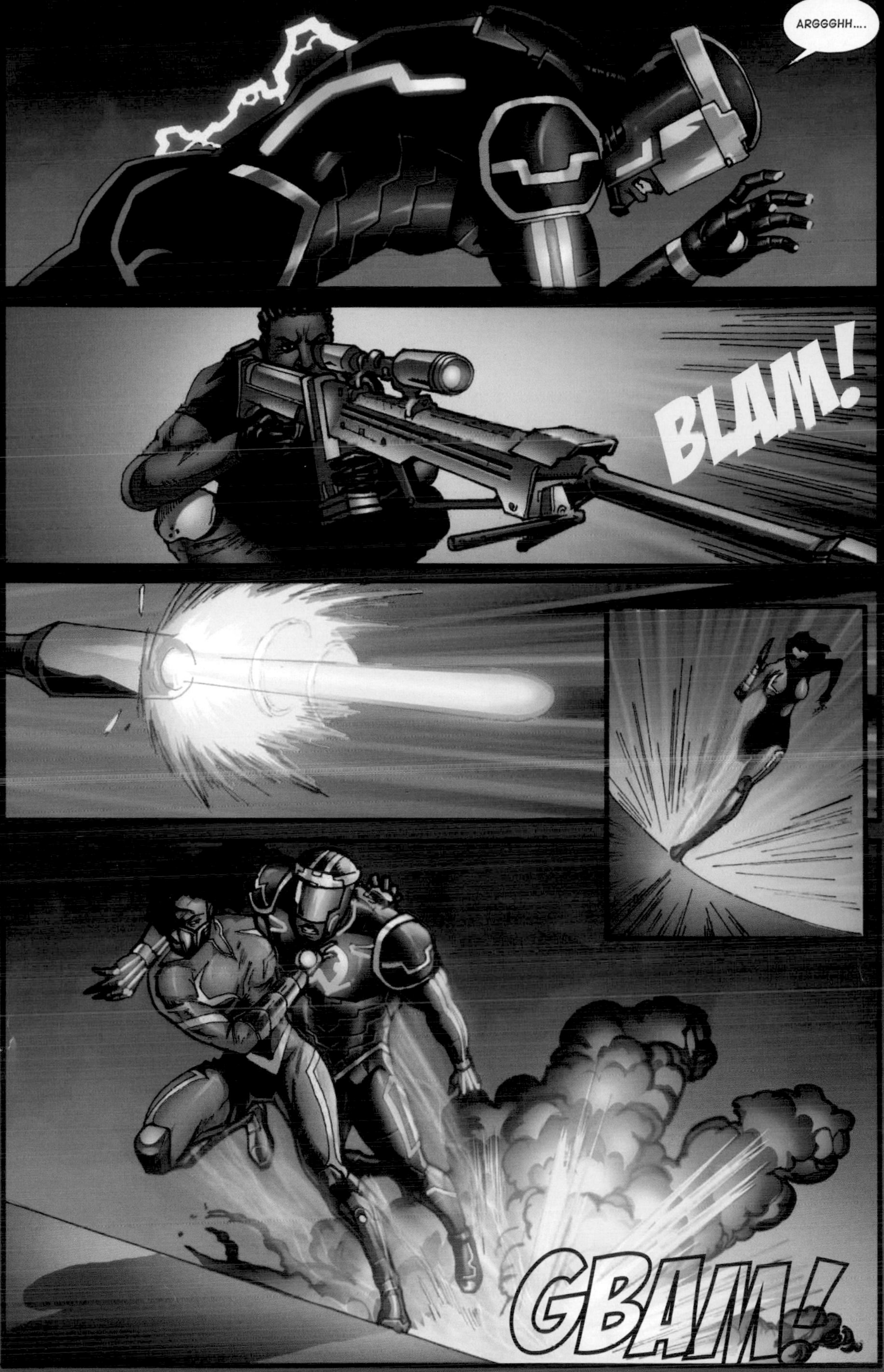
ARGGGHH....
BLAM!
GBAM!

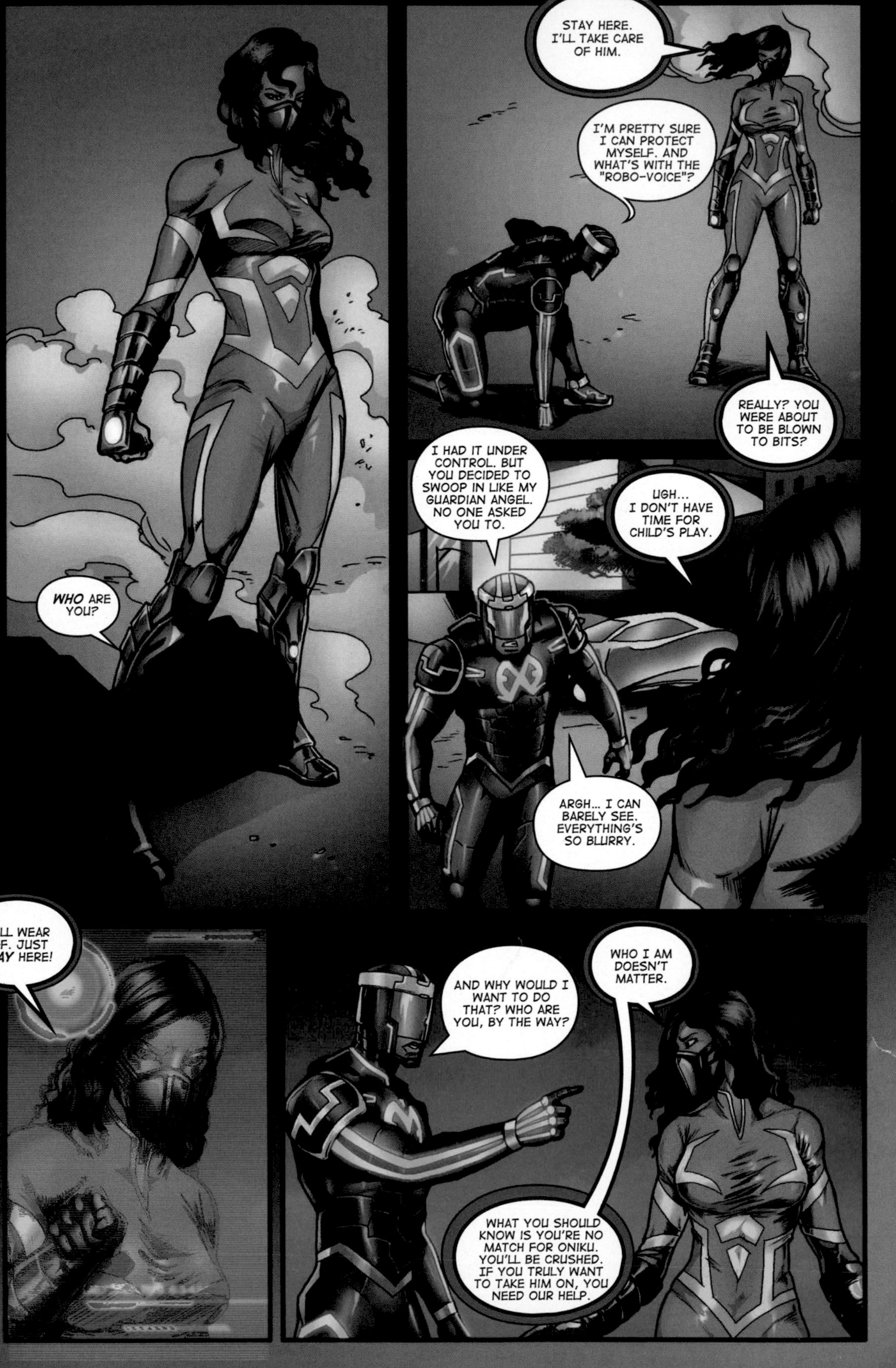

WHO ARE YOU?
STAY HERE. I'LL TAKE CARE OF HIM.
I'M PRETTY SURE I CAN PROTECT MYSELF. AND WHAT'S WITH THE "ROBO-VOICE"?
REALLY? YOU WERE ABOUT TO BE BLOWN TO BITS?
I HAD IT UNDER CONTROL. BUT YOU DECIDED TO SWOOP IN LIKE MY GUARDIAN ANGEL. NO ONE ASKED YOU TO.
UGH... I DON'T HAVE TIME FOR CHILD'S PLAY.
ARGH... I CAN BARELY SEE. EVERYTHING'S SO BLURRY.
IT'LL WEAR OFF. JUST STAY HERE!
AND WHY WOULD I WANT TO DO THAT? WHO ARE YOU, BY THE WAY?
WHO I AM DOESN'T MATTER.
WHAT YOU SHOULD KNOW IS YOU'RE NO MATCH FOR ONIKU. YOU'LL BE CRUSHED. IF YOU TRULY WANT TO TAKE HIM ON, YOU NEED OUR HELP.

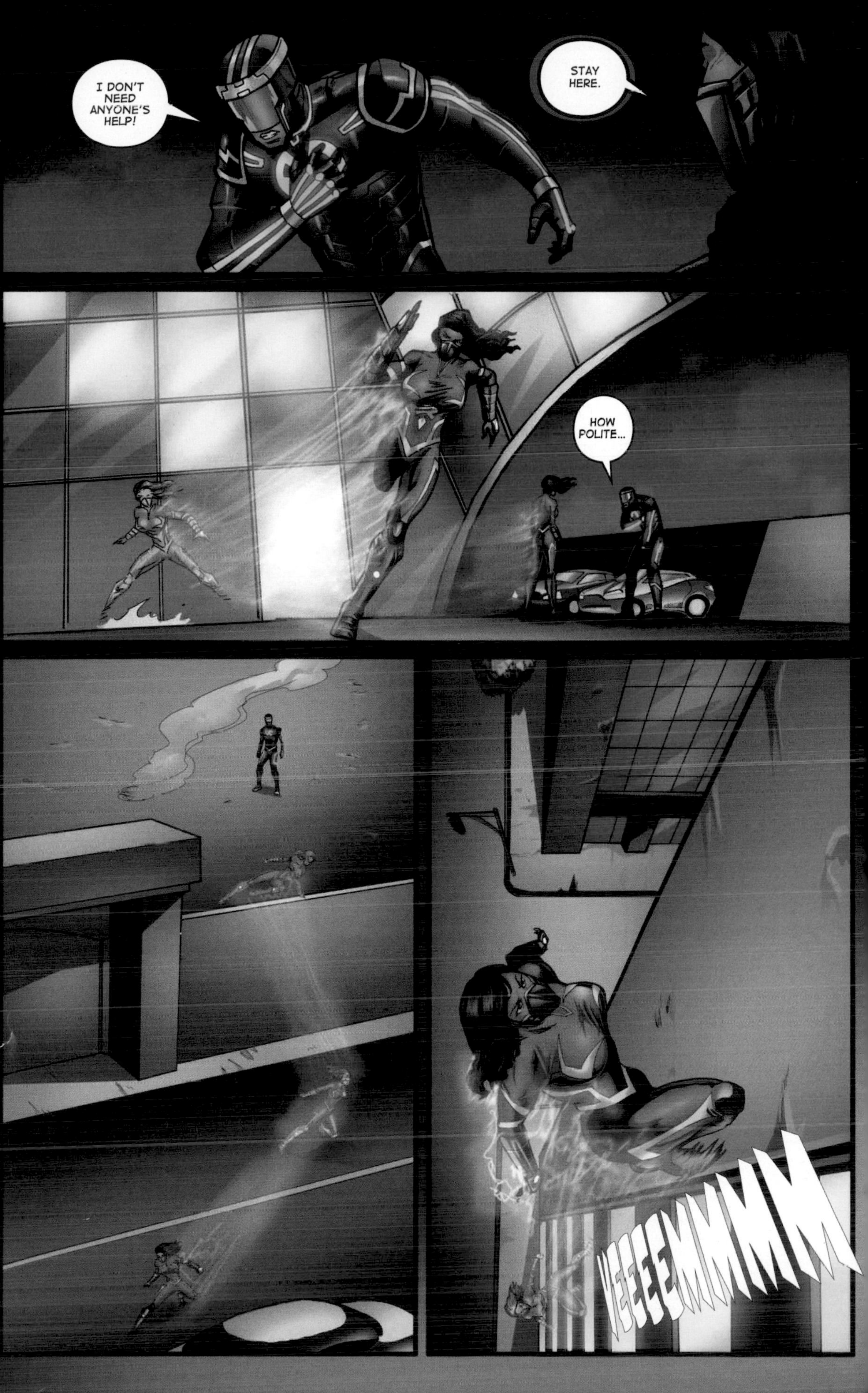
I DON'T NEED ANYONE'S HELP!
STAY HERE.
HOW POLITE...
VEEEEMMMMM

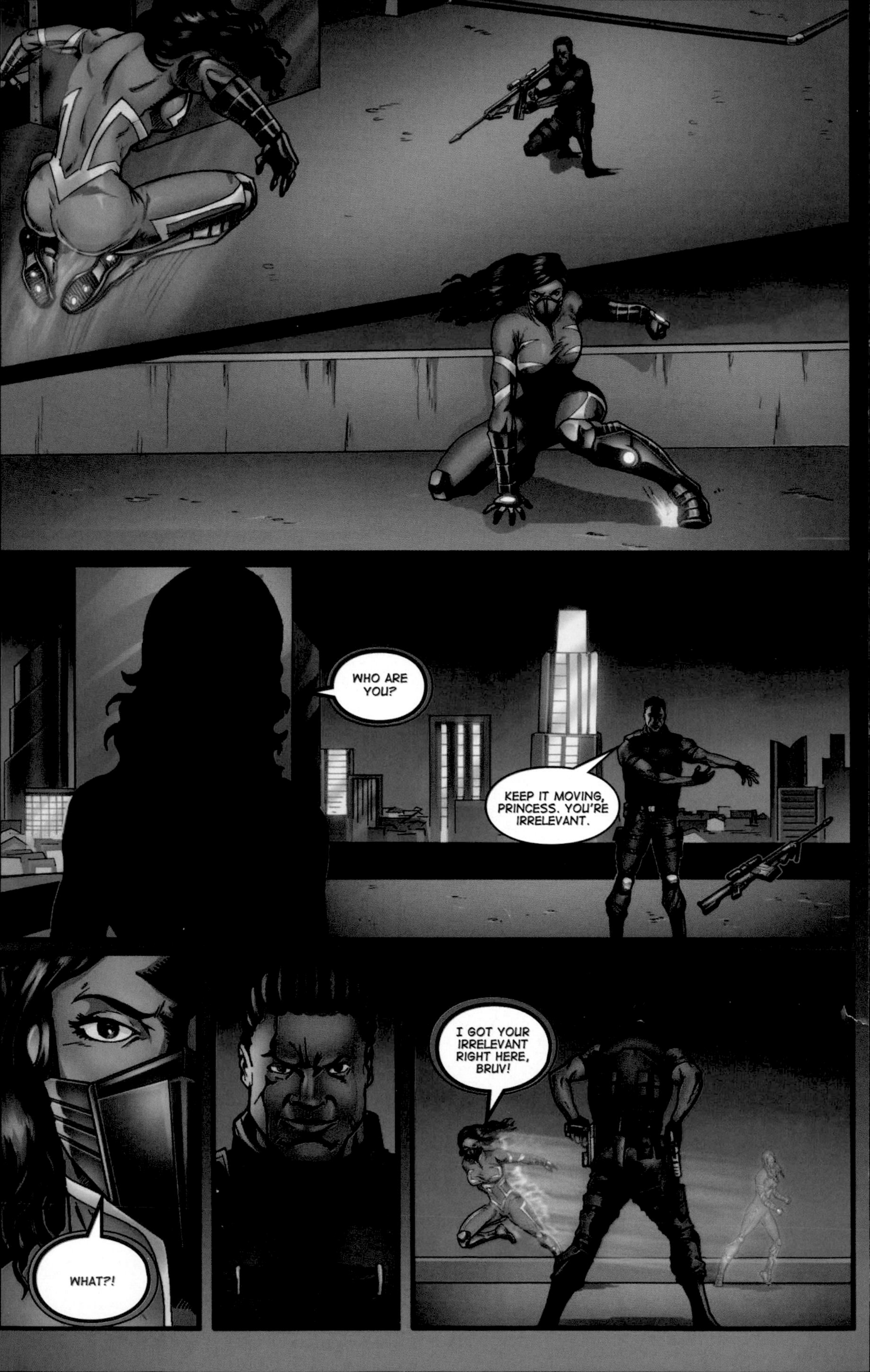
WHO ARE YOU?
KEEP IT MOVING, PRINCESS. YOU'RE IRRELEVANT.
WHAT?!
I GOT YOUR IRRELEVANT RIGHT HERE, BRUV!

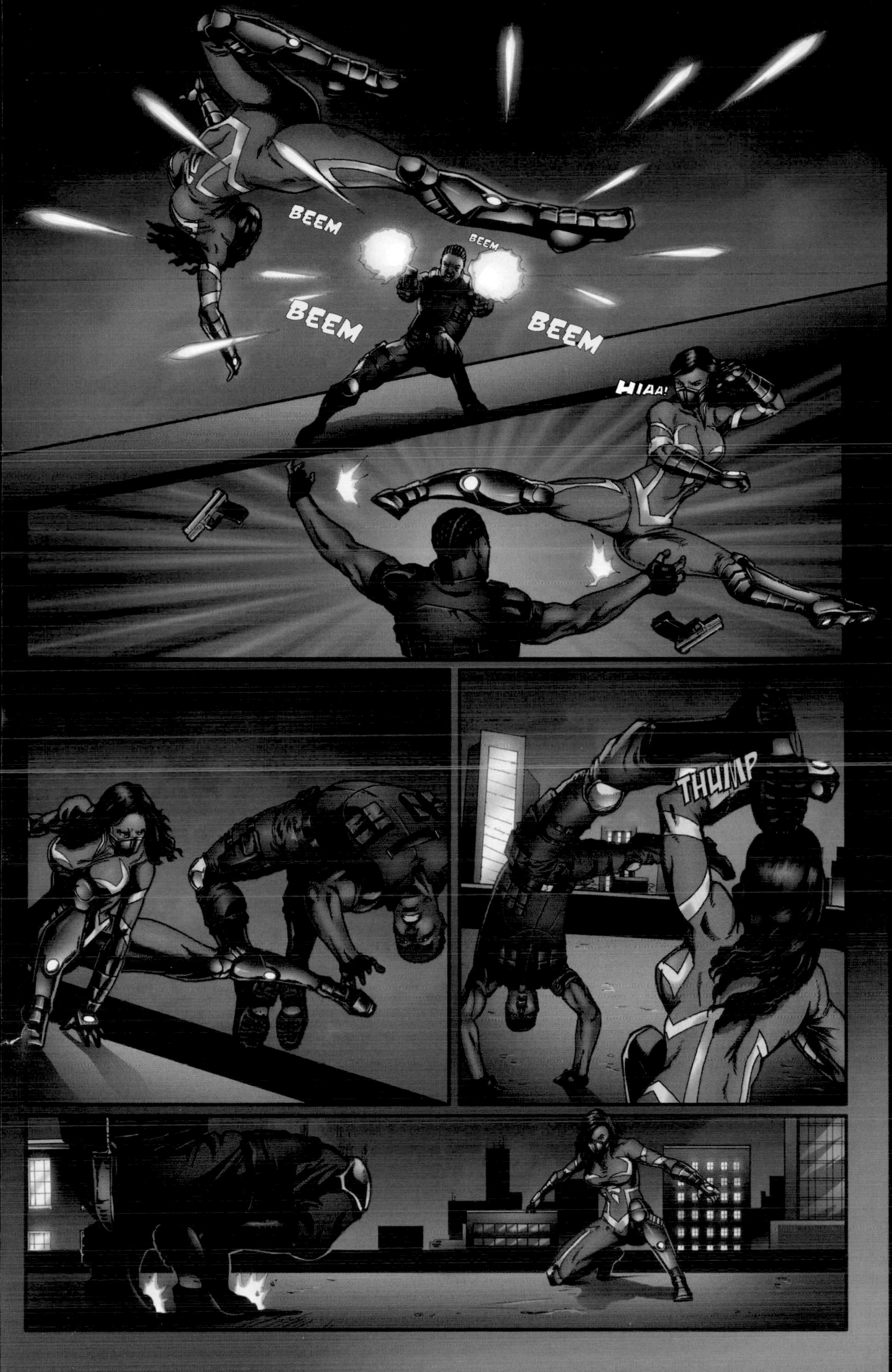
BEEM
BEEM
BEEM
BEEM
HIAA!
THUMP

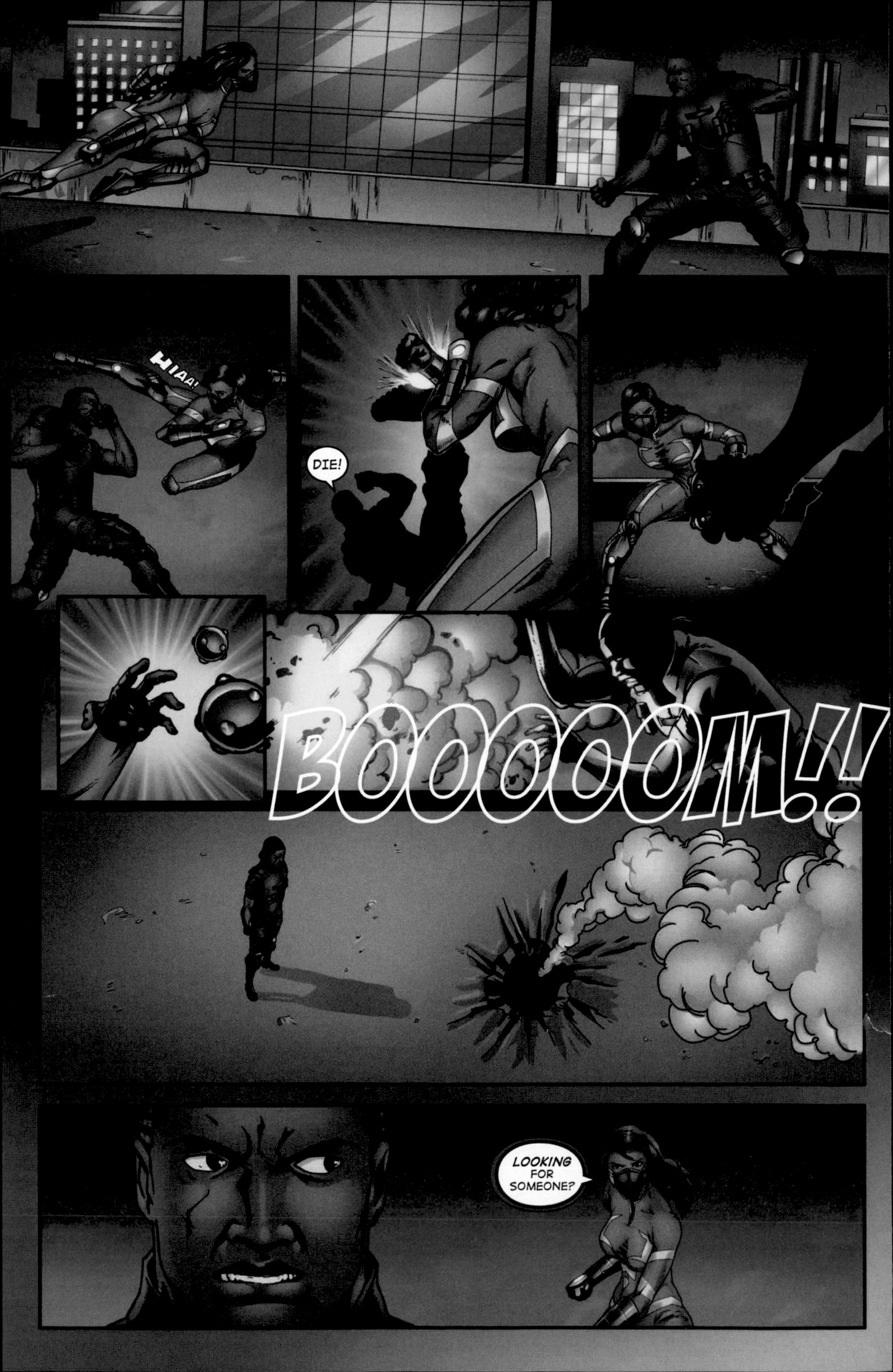
HIAA!
DIE!
BOOOOOM!!
LOOKING FOR SOMEONE?

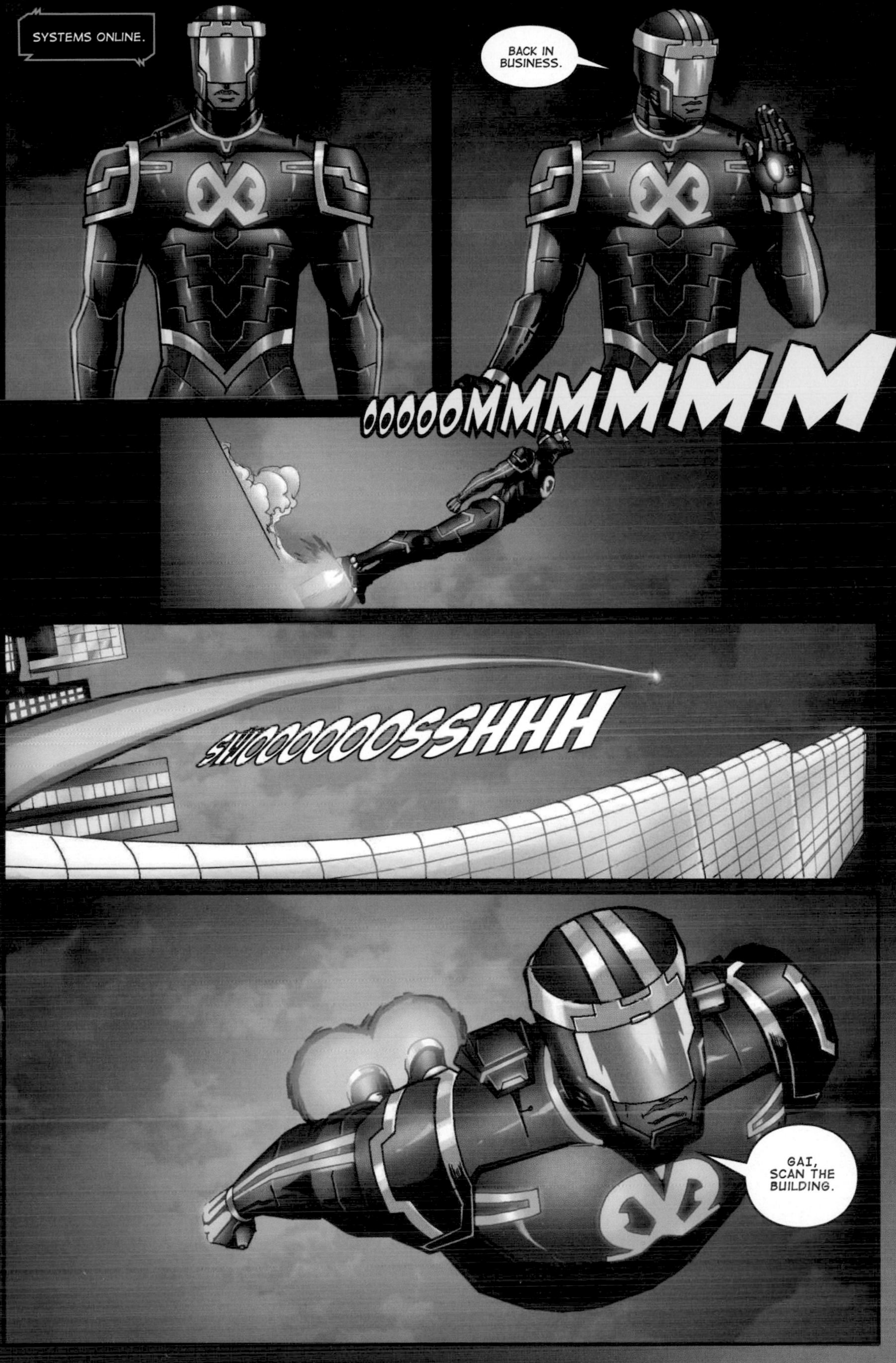
SYSTEMS ONLINE.
BACK IN BUSINESS.
OOOOOMMMMMMM
SHOOOOOOOOSSHHH
GAI, SCAN THE BUILDING.

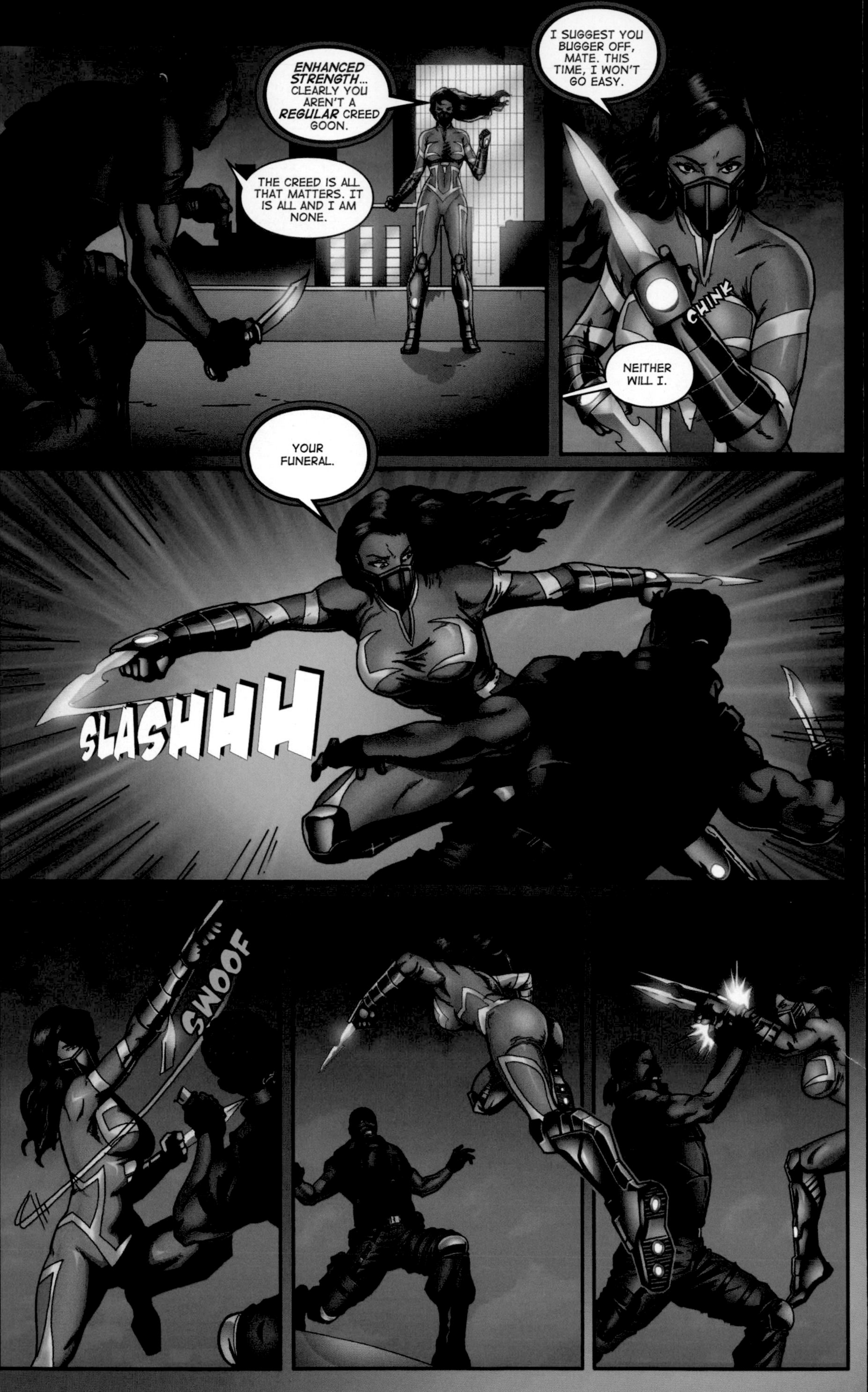
ENHANCED STRENGTH... CLEARLY YOU AREN'T A REGULAR CREED GOON.
THE CREED IS ALL THAT MATTERS. IT IS ALL AND I AM NONE.
I SUGGEST YOU BUGGER OFF, MATE. THIS TIME, I WON'T GO EASY.
CHINK
NEITHER WILL I.
YOUR FUNERAL.
SLASHHH
SWOOF

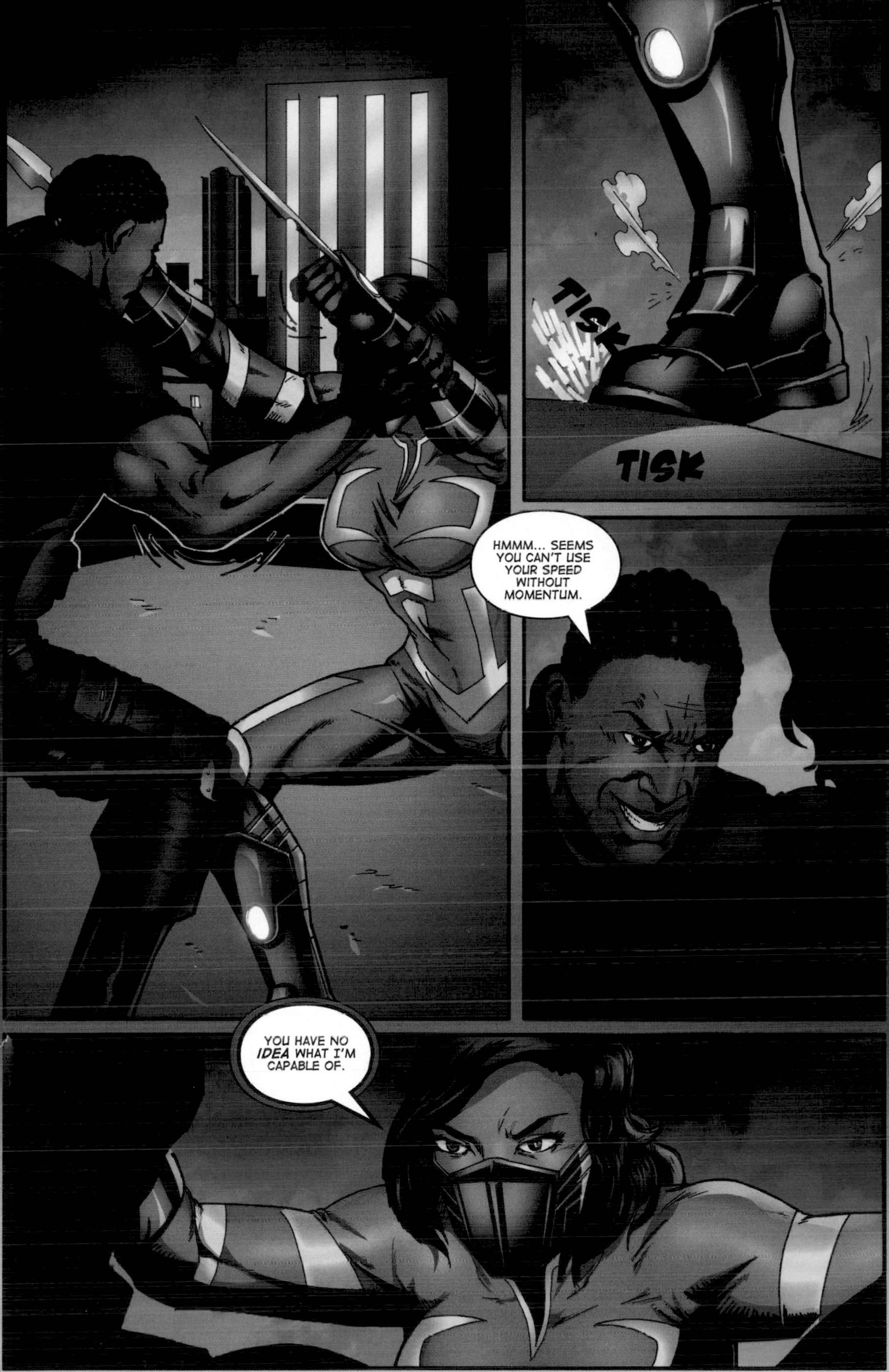
TISK
TISK
HMMM... SEEMS YOU CAN'T USE YOUR SPEED WITHOUT MOMENTUM.
YOU HAVE NO *IDEA* WHAT I'M CAPABLE OF.

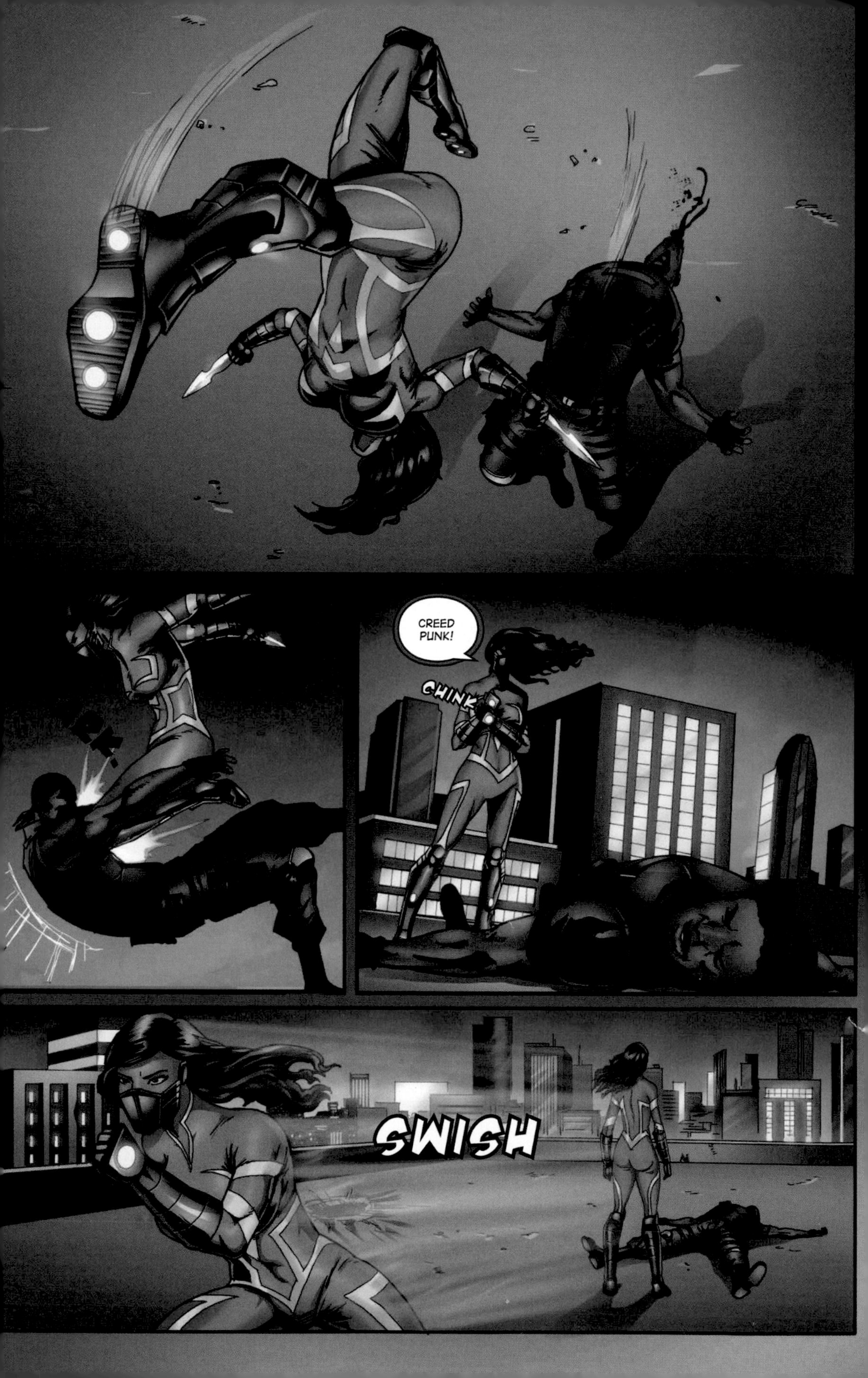
CREED PUNK!
CHINK
SWISH

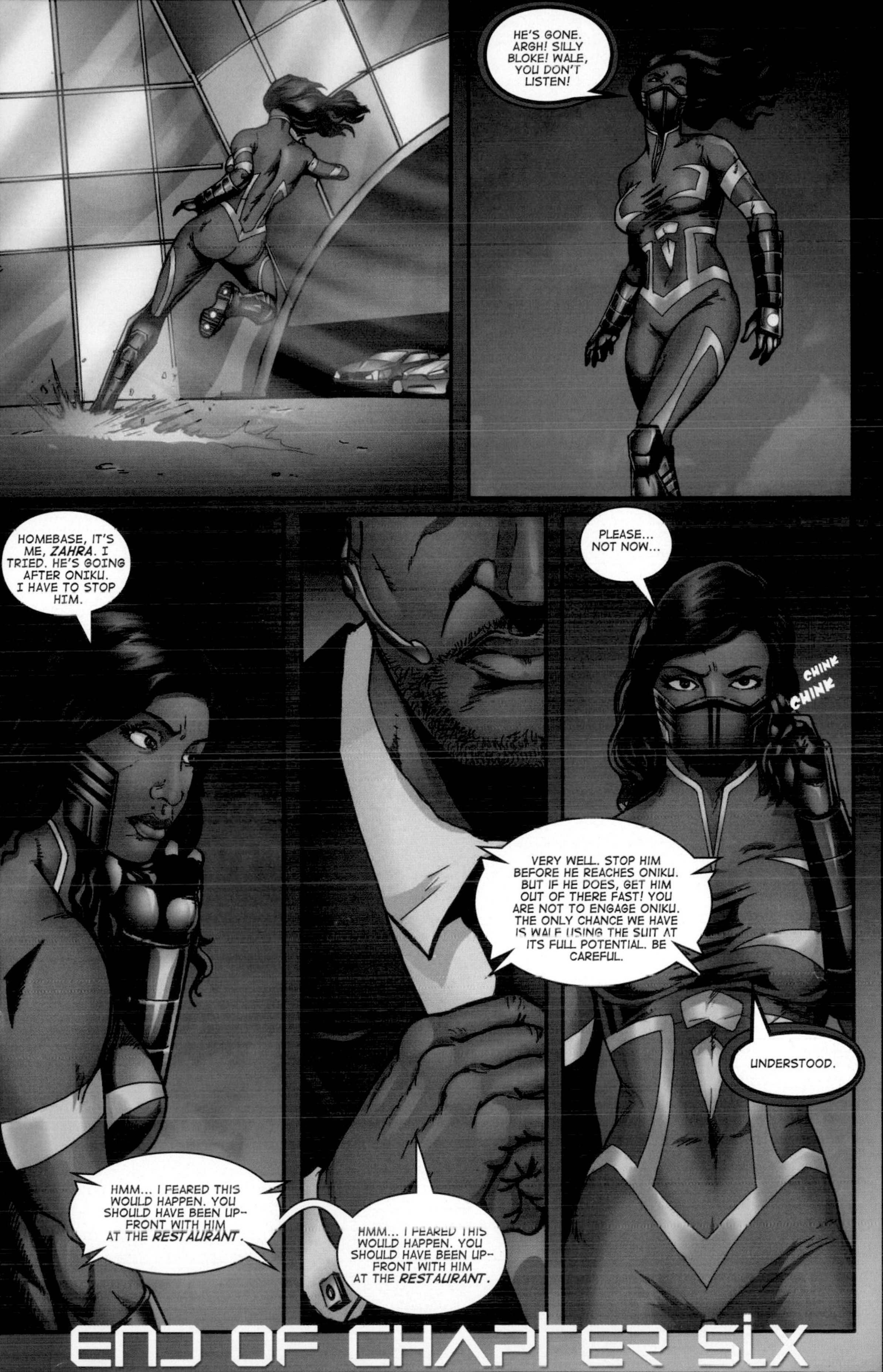
HE'S GONE. ARGH! SILLY BLOKE! WALE, YOU DON'T LISTEN!
HOMEBASE, IT'S ME, ZAHRA. I TRIED. HE'S GOING AFTER ONIKU. I HAVE TO STOP HIM.
HMM... I FEARED THIS WOULD HAPPEN. YOU SHOULD HAVE BEEN UP-FRONT WITH HIM AT THE RESTAURANT.
HMM... I FEARED THIS WOULD HAPPEN. YOU SHOULD HAVE BEEN UP-FRONT WITH HIM AT THE RESTAURANT.
PLEASE... NOT NOW...
CHINK
CHINK
VERY WELL. STOP HIM BEFORE HE REACHES ONIKU. BUT IF HE DOES, GET HIM OUT OF THERE FAST! YOU ARE NOT TO ENGAGE ONIKU. THE ONLY CHANCE WE HAVE IS WALE USING THE SUIT AT ITS FULL POTENTIAL. BE CAREFUL.
UNDERSTOOD.
END OF CHAPTER SIX

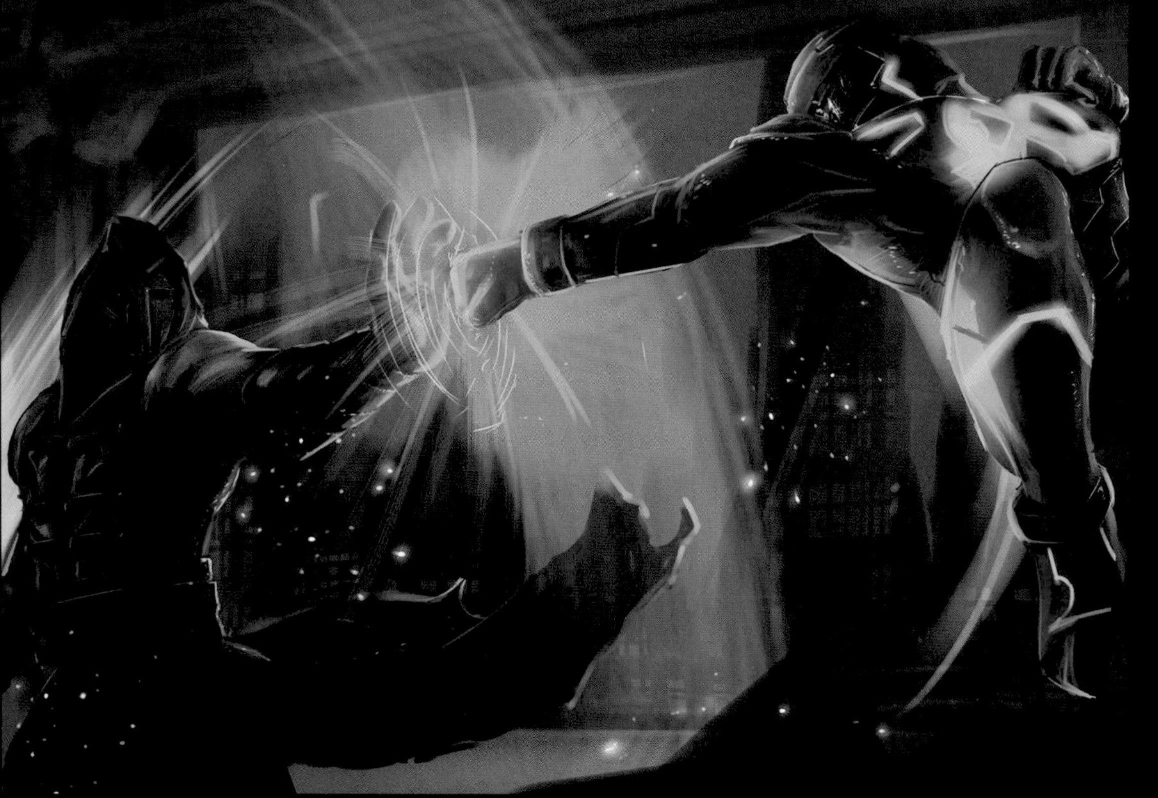

"If you think I'm just going to sit back while you kill innocent people, you're out of your mind!"

- *EXO*

# CHAPTER SEVEN

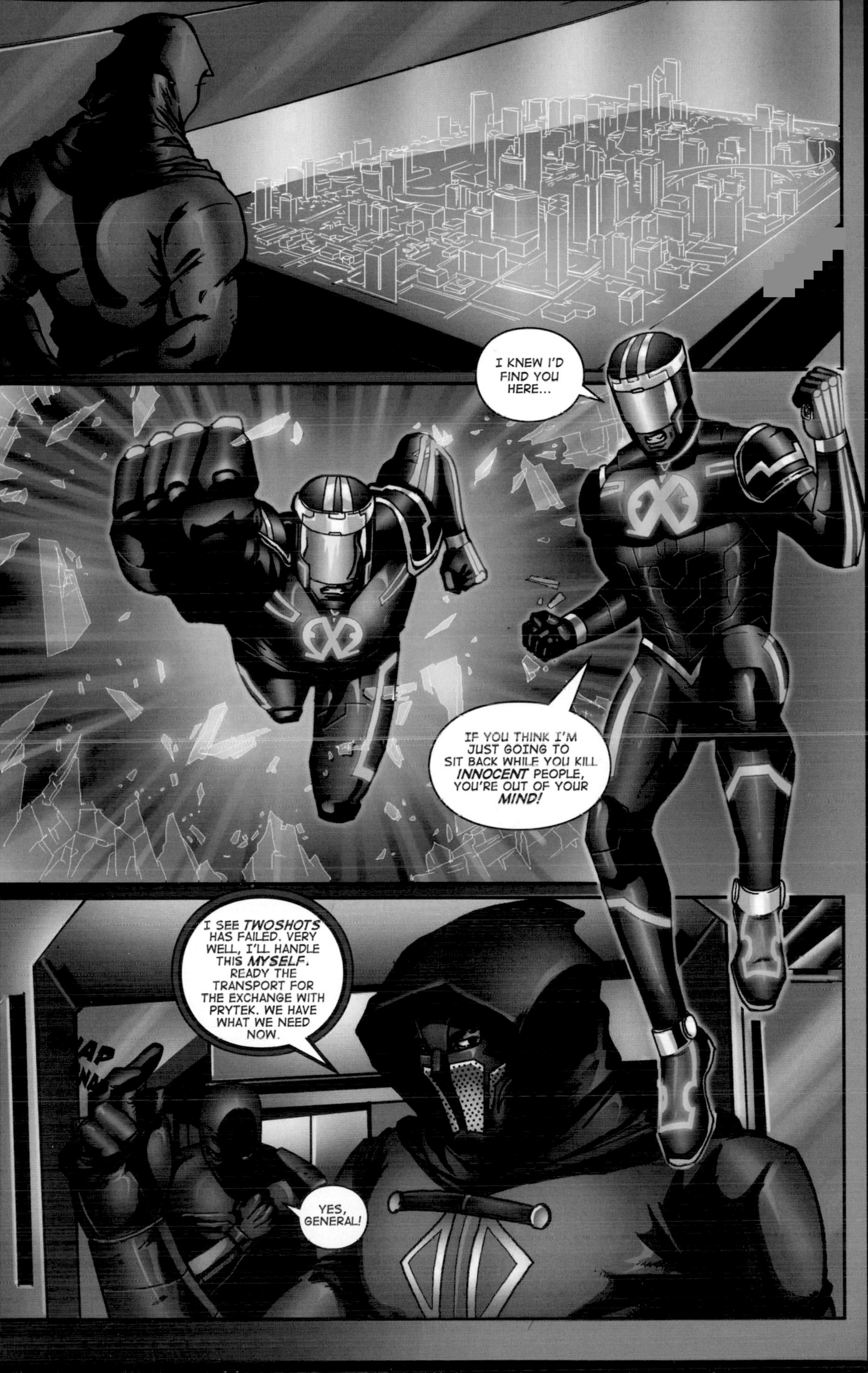
I KNEW I'D FIND YOU HERE...
IF YOU THINK I'M JUST GOING TO SIT BACK WHILE YOU KILL *INNOCENT* PEOPLE, YOU'RE OUT OF YOUR *MIND!*
I SEE *TWOSHOTS* HAS FAILED. VERY WELL, I'LL HANDLE THIS *MYSELF*. READY THE TRANSPORT FOR THE EXCHANGE WITH PRYTEK. WE HAVE WHAT WE NEED NOW.
YES, GENERAL!

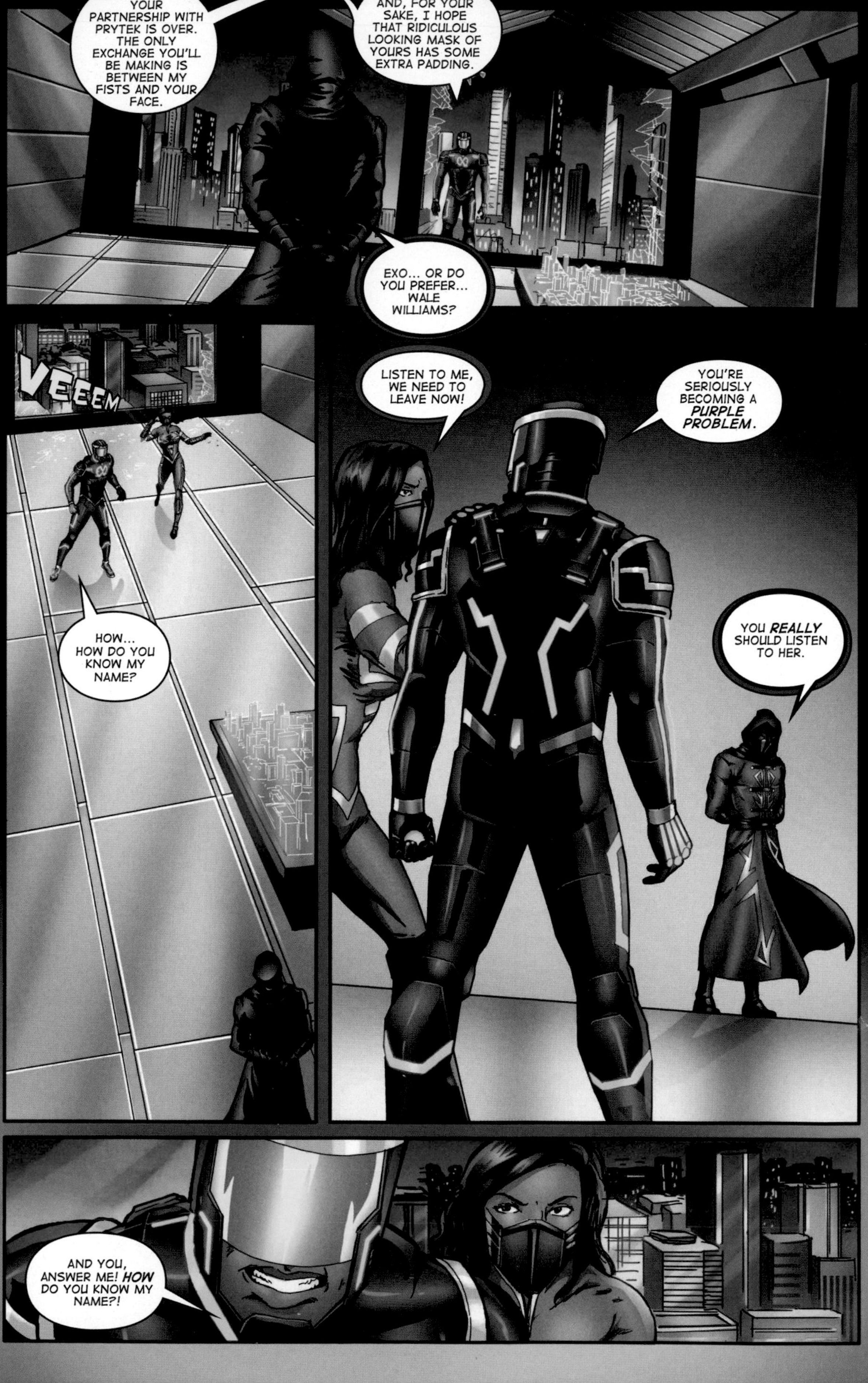
YOUR PARTNERSHIP WITH PRYTEK IS OVER. THE ONLY EXCHANGE YOU'LL BE MAKING IS BETWEEN MY FISTS AND YOUR FACE.
AND, FOR YOUR SAKE, I HOPE THAT RIDICULOUS LOOKING MASK OF YOURS HAS SOME EXTRA PADDING.
EXO... OR DO YOU PREFER... WALE WILLIAMS?
VEEEM
HOW... HOW DO YOU KNOW MY NAME?
LISTEN TO ME, WE NEED TO LEAVE NOW!
YOU'RE SERIOUSLY BECOMING A PURPLE PROBLEM.
YOU REALLY SHOULD LISTEN TO HER.
AND YOU, ANSWER ME! HOW DO YOU KNOW MY NAME?!

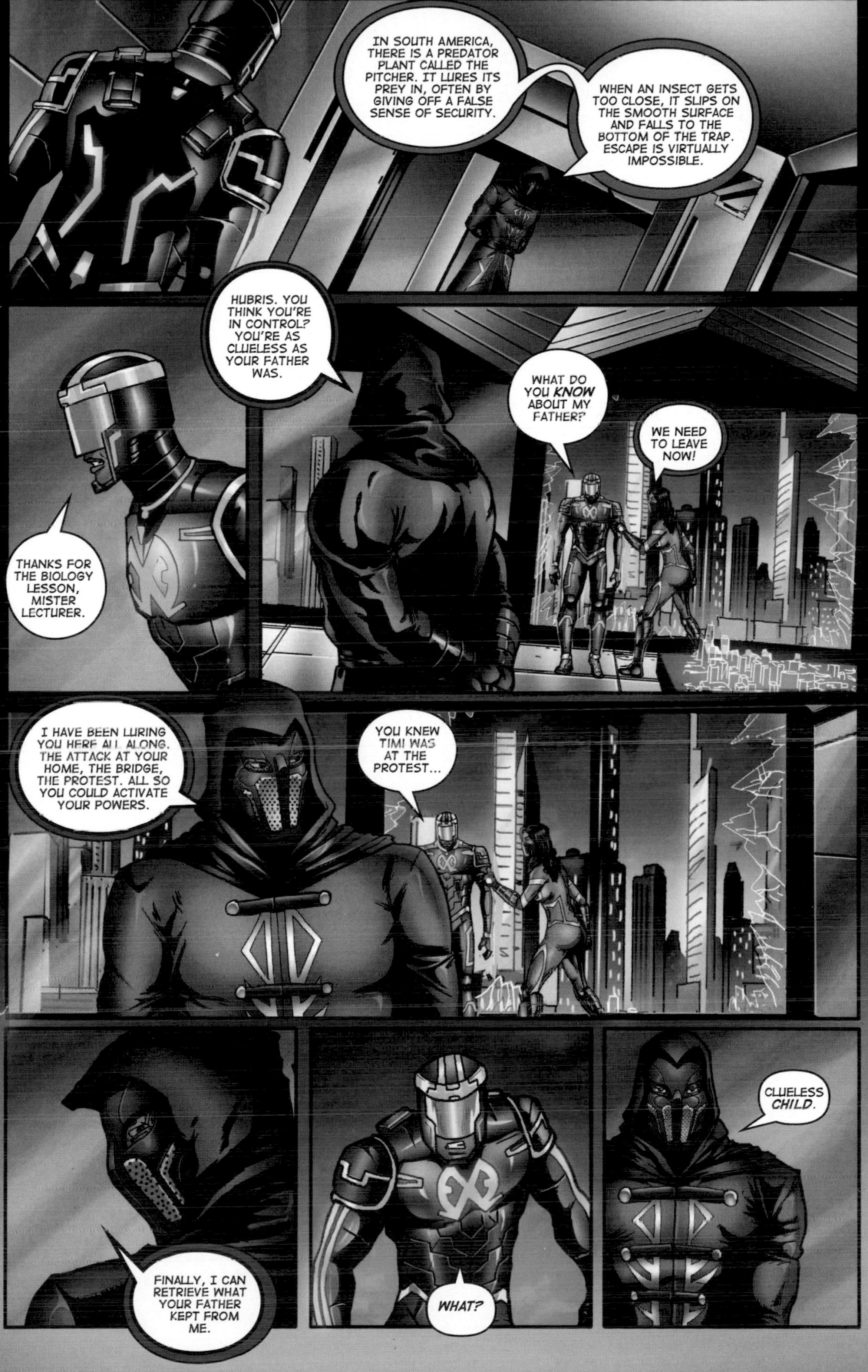
IN SOUTH AMERICA, THERE IS A PREDATOR PLANT CALLED THE PITCHER. IT LURES ITS PREY IN, OFTEN BY GIVING OFF A FALSE SENSE OF SECURITY.
WHEN AN INSECT GETS TOO CLOSE, IT SLIPS ON THE SMOOTH SURFACE AND FALLS TO THE BOTTOM OF THE TRAP. ESCAPE IS VIRTUALLY IMPOSSIBLE.
THANKS FOR THE BIOLOGY LESSON, MISTER LECTURER.
HUBRIS. YOU THINK YOU'RE IN CONTROL? YOU'RE AS CLUELESS AS YOUR FATHER WAS.
WHAT DO YOU *KNOW* ABOUT MY FATHER?
WE NEED TO LEAVE NOW!
I HAVE BEEN LURING YOU HERE ALL ALONG. THE ATTACK AT YOUR HOME, THE BRIDGE, THE PROTEST. ALL SO YOU COULD ACTIVATE YOUR POWERS.
YOU KNEW TIMI WAS AT THE PROTEST...
FINALLY, I CAN RETRIEVE WHAT YOUR FATHER KEPT FROM ME.
*WHAT?*
CLUELESS *CHILD*.

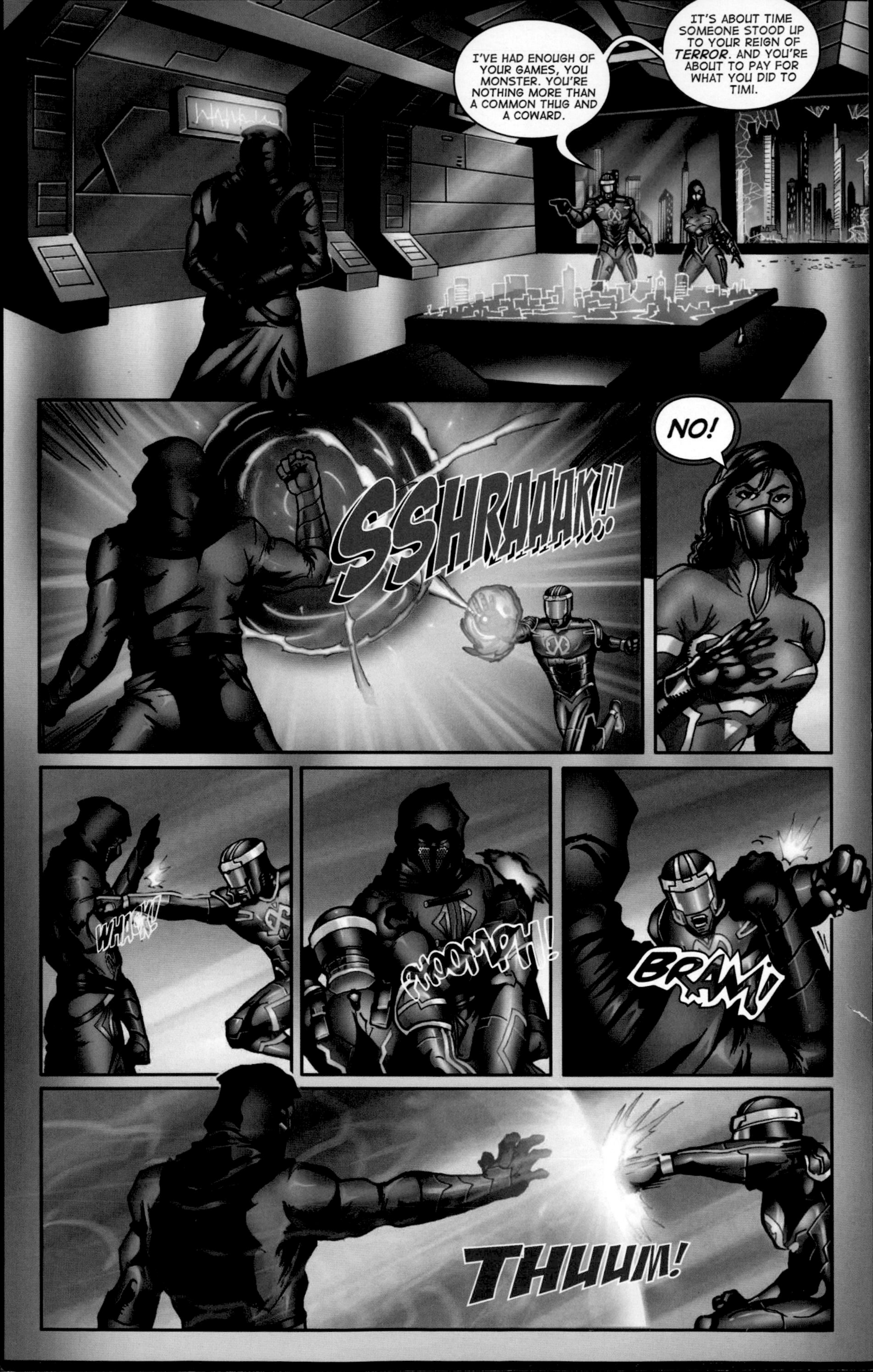
I'VE HAD ENOUGH OF YOUR GAMES, YOU MONSTER. YOU'RE NOTHING MORE THAN A COMMON THUG AND A COWARD.
IT'S ABOUT TIME SOMEONE STOOD UP TO YOUR REIGN OF *TERROR*. AND YOU'RE ABOUT TO PAY FOR WHAT YOU DID TO TIMI.
SSHRAAAK!!
NO!
WHACK!
FHOOMPH!
BRAM!
THUUM!

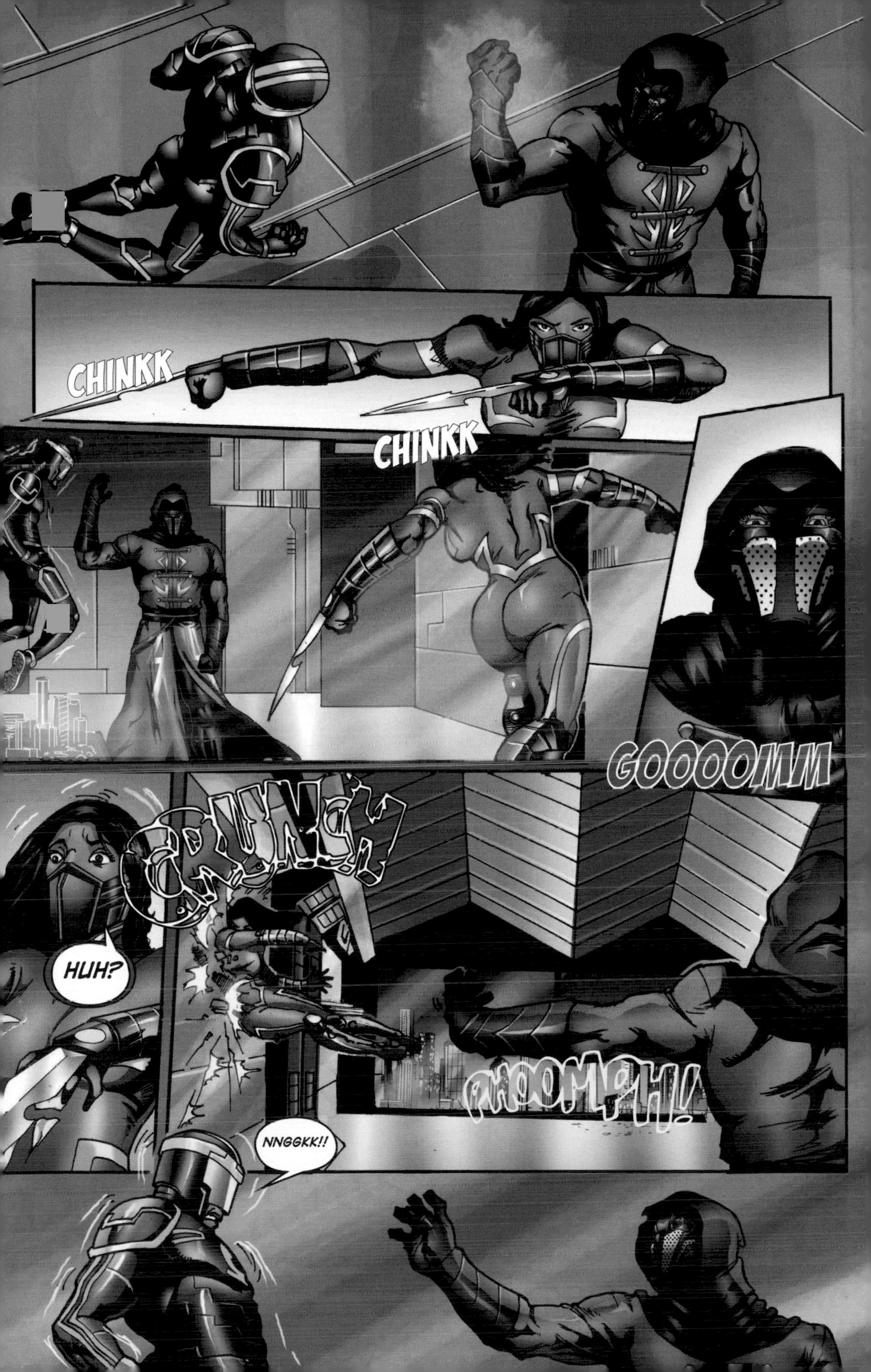
CHINKK
CHINKK
GOOOOMM
CRUNCH
HUH?
PHOOMPH!
NNGGKK!!

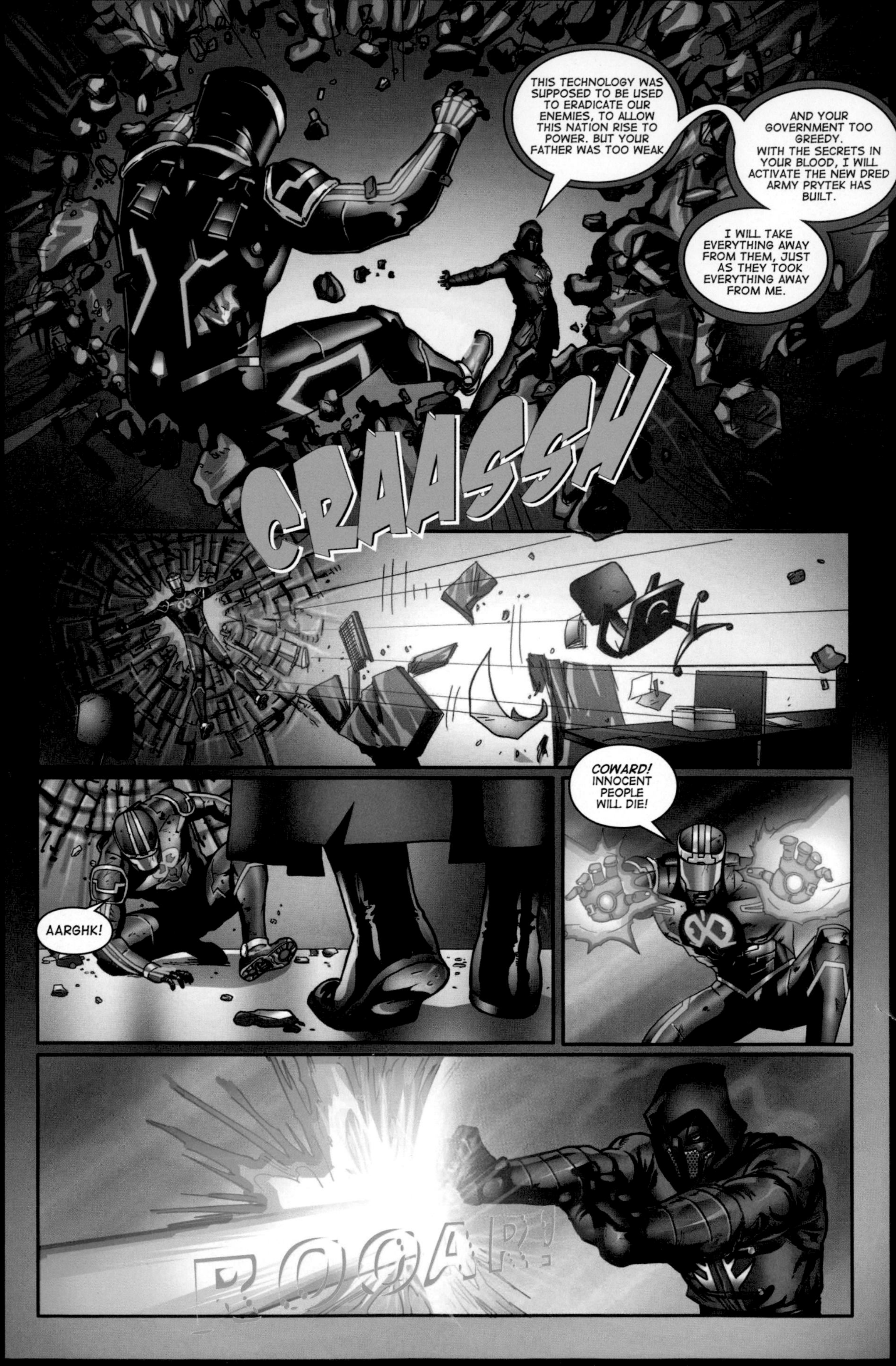
THIS TECHNOLOGY WAS SUPPOSED TO BE USED TO ERADICATE OUR ENEMIES, TO ALLOW THIS NATION RISE TO POWER. BUT YOUR FATHER WAS TOO WEAK
AND YOUR GOVERNMENT TOO GREEDY. WITH THE SECRETS IN YOUR BLOOD, I WILL ACTIVATE THE NEW DRED ARMY PRYTEK HAS BUILT.
I WILL TAKE EVERYTHING AWAY FROM THEM, JUST AS THEY TOOK EVERYTHING AWAY FROM ME.
CRAASSH
AARGHK!
COWARD! INNOCENT PEOPLE WILL DIE!
BOOOM!

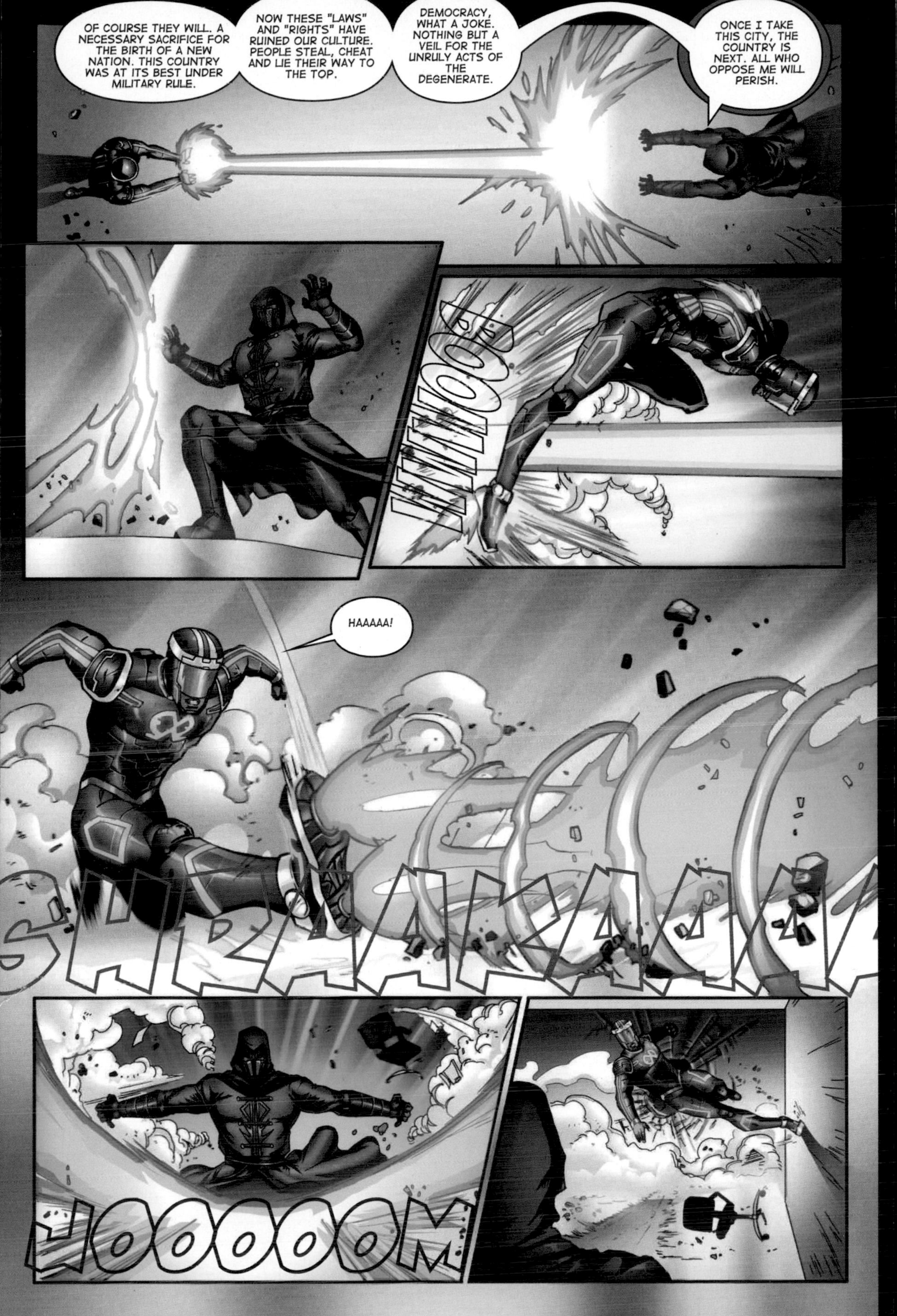

OF COURSE THEY WILL. A NECESSARY SACRIFICE FOR THE BIRTH OF A NEW NATION. THIS COUNTRY WAS AT ITS BEST UNDER MILITARY RULE.
NOW THESE "LAWS" AND "RIGHTS" HAVE RUINED OUR CULTURE. PEOPLE STEAL, CHEAT AND LIE THEIR WAY TO THE TOP.
DEMOCRACY, WHAT A JOKE. NOTHING BUT A VEIL FOR THE UNRULY ACTS OF THE DEGENERATE.
ONCE I TAKE THIS CITY, THE COUNTRY IS NEXT. ALL WHO OPPOSE ME WILL PERISH.
HAAAAA!
JOOOOOM

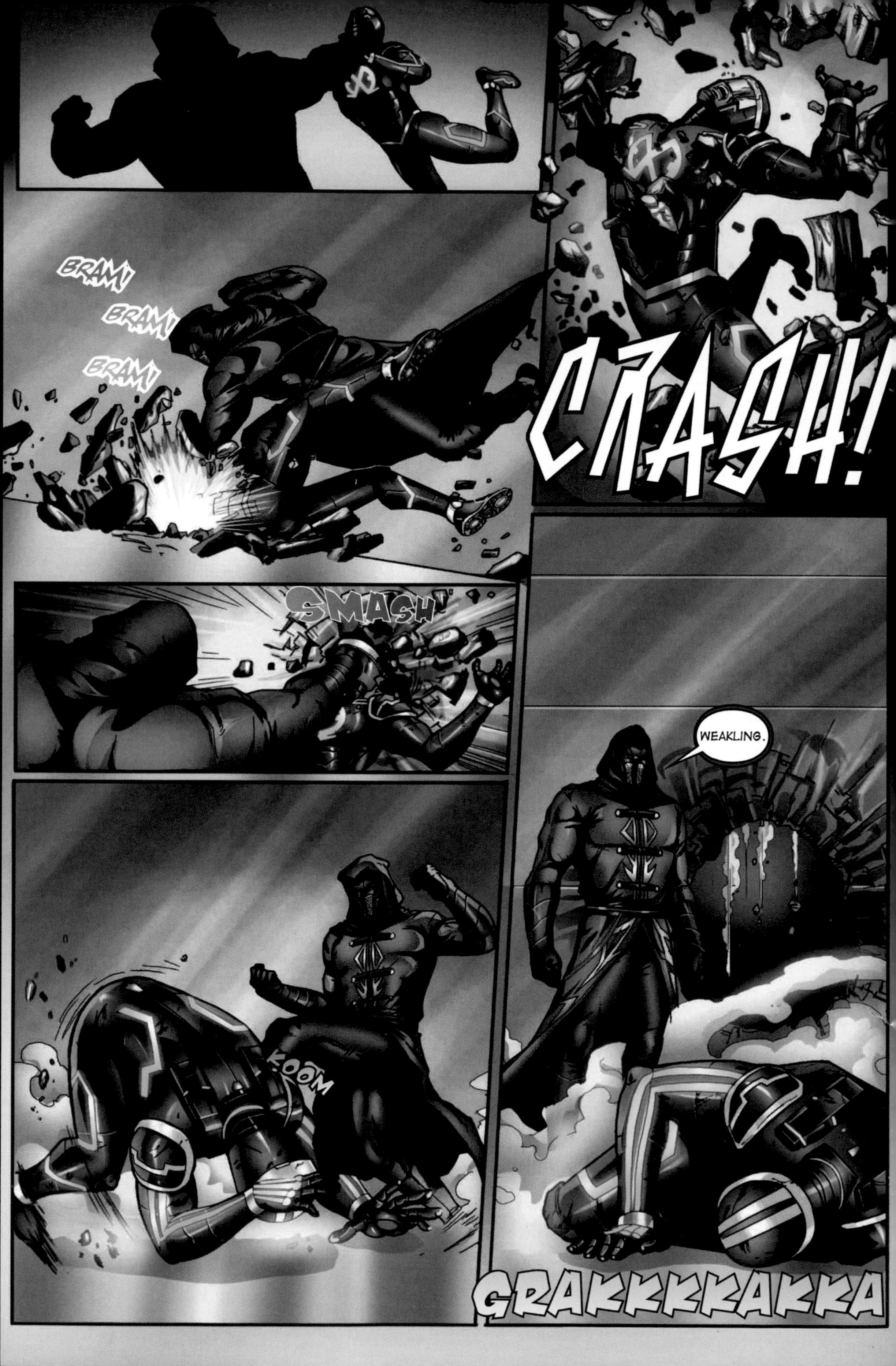

BRAM!
BRAM!
BRAM!
CRASH!
SMASH
KOOM
WEAKLING.
GRAKKKAKKA

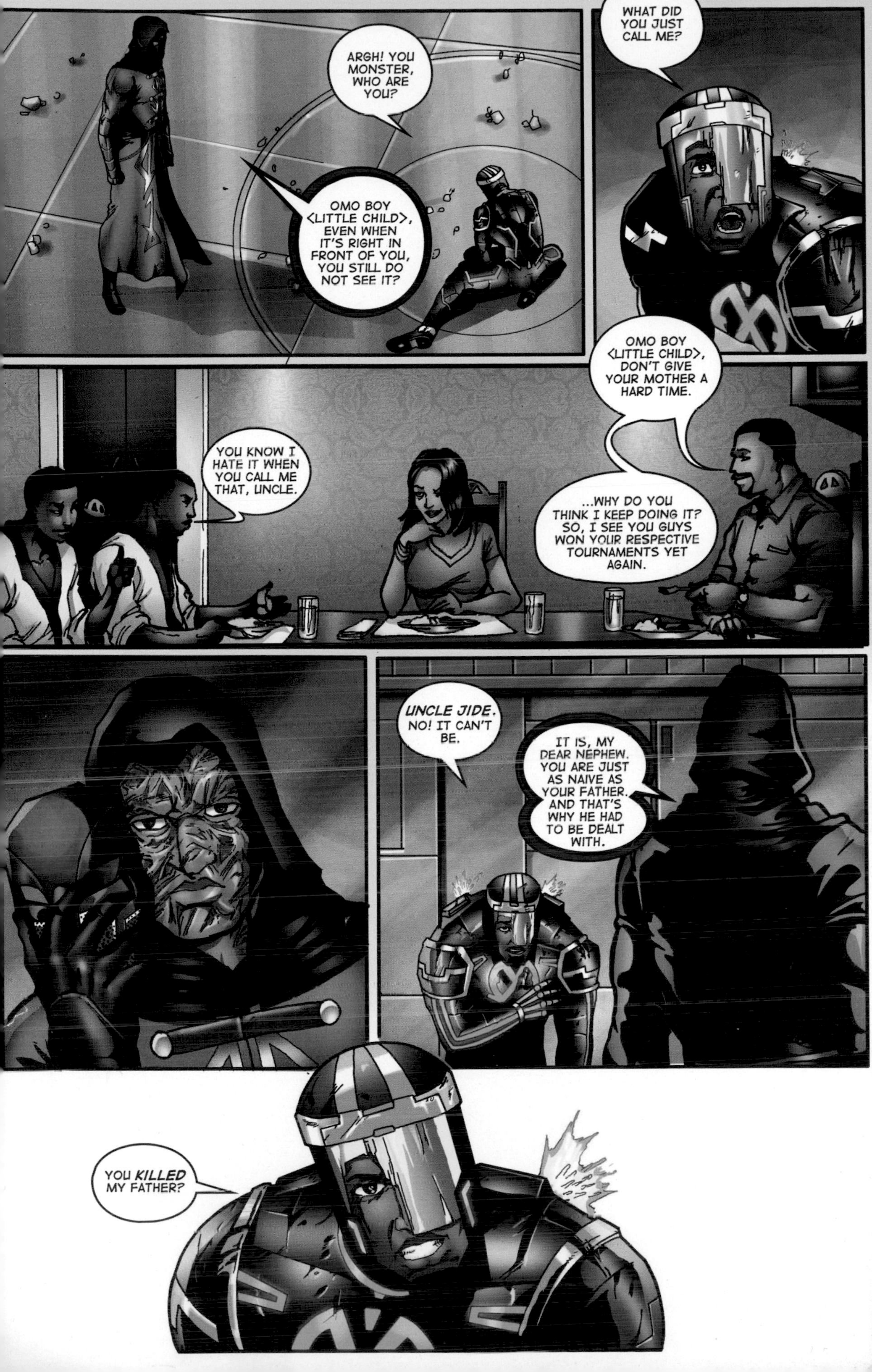
ARGH! YOU MONSTER, WHO ARE YOU?
OMO BOY <LITTLE CHILD>, EVEN WHEN IT'S RIGHT IN FRONT OF YOU, YOU STILL DO NOT SEE IT?
WHAT DID YOU JUST CALL ME?
OMO BOY <LITTLE CHILD>, DON'T GIVE YOUR MOTHER A HARD TIME.
YOU KNOW I HATE IT WHEN YOU CALL ME THAT, UNCLE.
...WHY DO YOU THINK I KEEP DOING IT? SO, I SEE YOU GUYS WON YOUR RESPECTIVE TOURNAMENTS YET AGAIN.
UNCLE JIDE. NO! IT CAN'T BE.
IT IS, MY DEAR NEPHEW. YOU ARE JUST AS NAIVE AS YOUR FATHER. AND THAT'S WHY HE HAD TO BE DEALT WITH.
YOU KILLED MY FATHER?

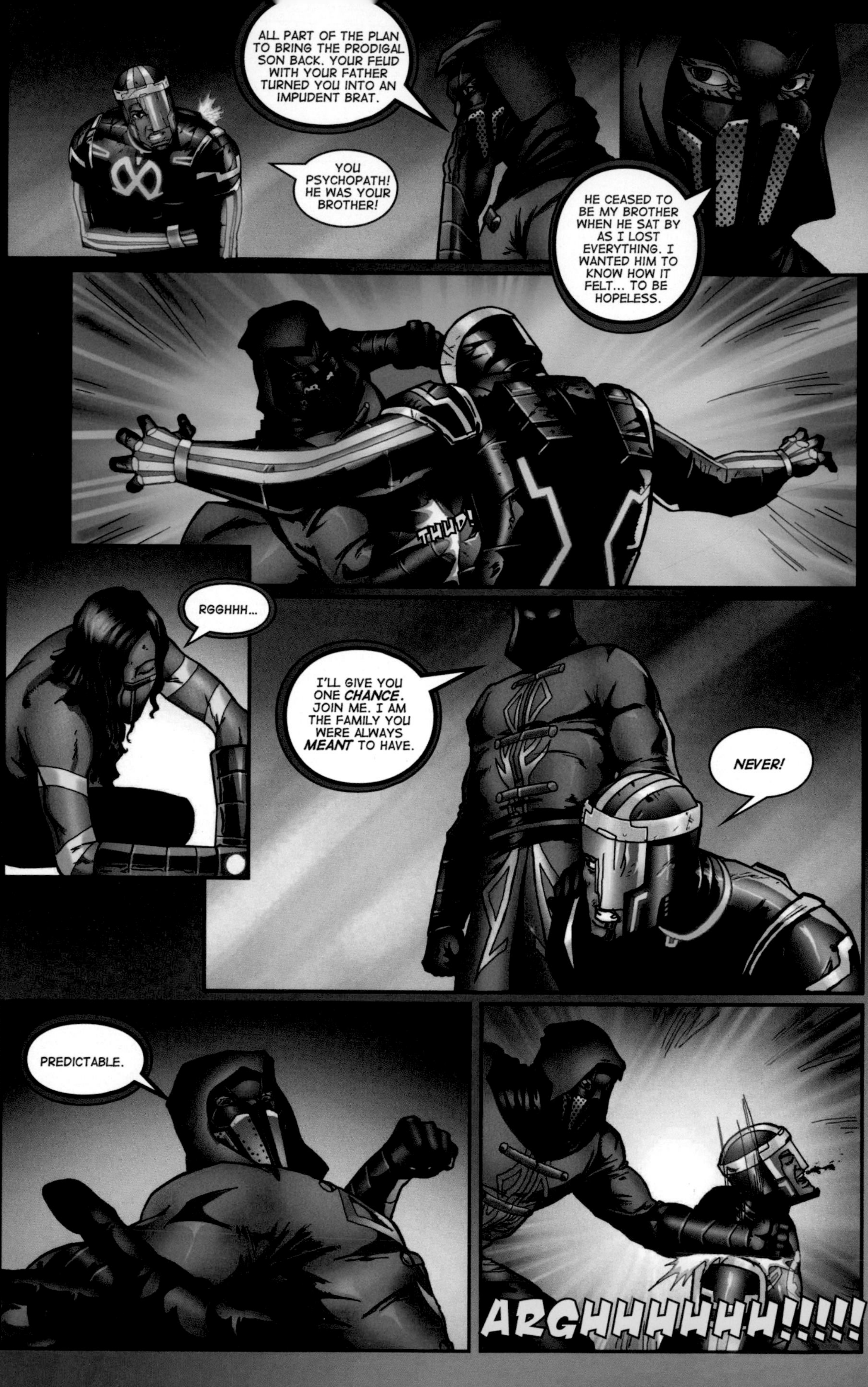
ALL PART OF THE PLAN TO BRING THE PRODIGAL SON BACK. YOUR FEUD WITH YOUR FATHER TURNED YOU INTO AN IMPUDENT BRAT.
YOU PSYCHOPATH! HE WAS YOUR BROTHER!
HE CEASED TO BE MY BROTHER WHEN HE SAT BY AS I LOST EVERYTHING. I WANTED HIM TO KNOW HOW IT FELT... TO BE HOPELESS.
THUD!
RGGHHH...
I'LL GIVE YOU ONE CHANCE. JOIN ME. I AM THE FAMILY YOU WERE ALWAYS MEANT TO HAVE.
NEVER!
PREDICTABLE.
ARGHHHHHH!!!!!

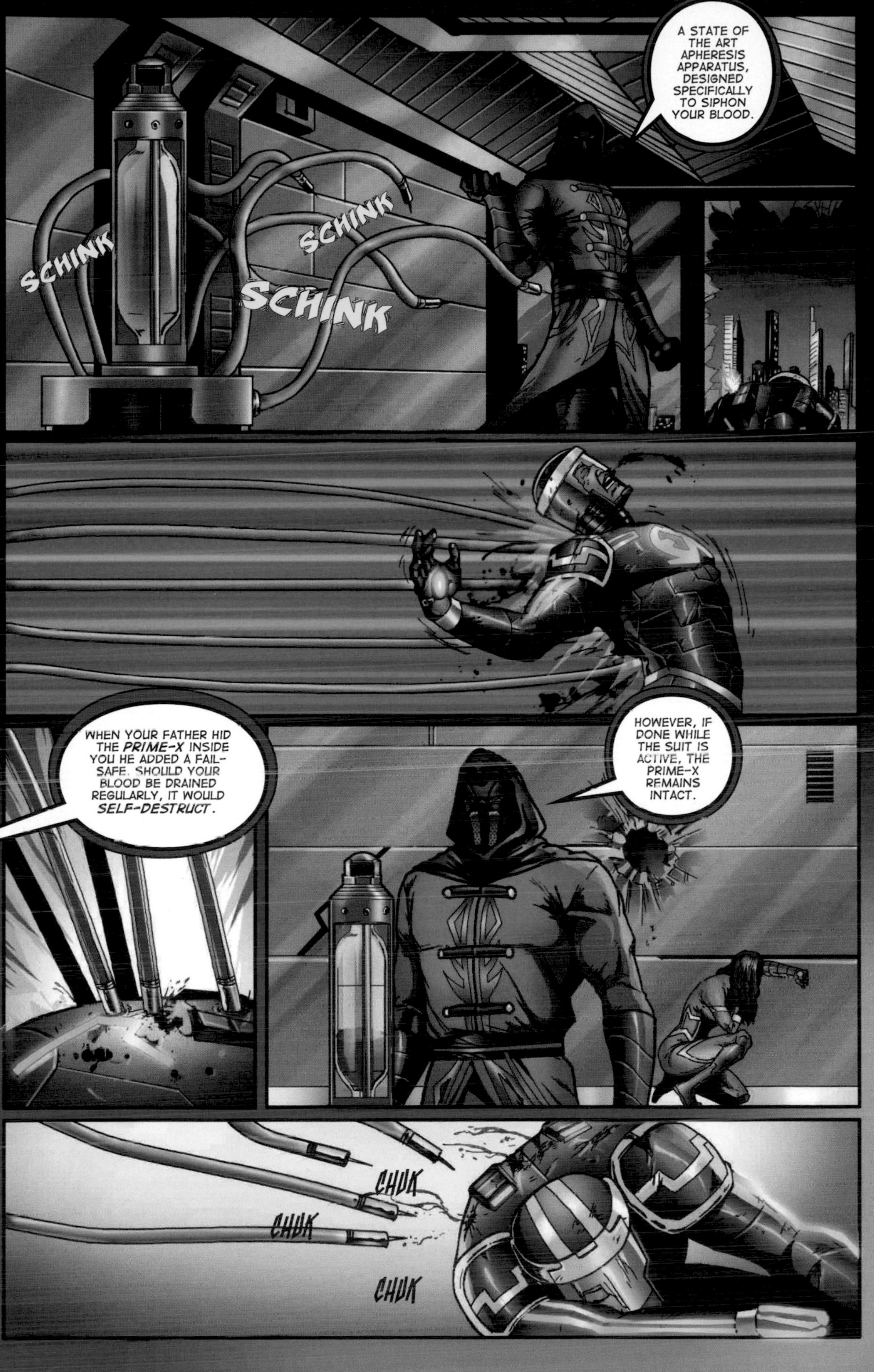
A STATE OF THE ART APHERESIS APPARATUS, DESIGNED SPECIFICALLY TO SIPHON YOUR BLOOD.
SCHINK
SCHINK
SCHINK
SCHINK
WHEN YOUR FATHER HID THE PRIME-X INSIDE YOU HE ADDED A FAIL-SAFE. SHOULD YOUR BLOOD BE DRAINED REGULARLY, IT WOULD SELF-DESTRUCT.
HOWEVER, IF DONE WHILE THE SUIT IS ACTIVE, THE PRIME-X REMAINS INTACT.
CHUK
CHUK
CHUK

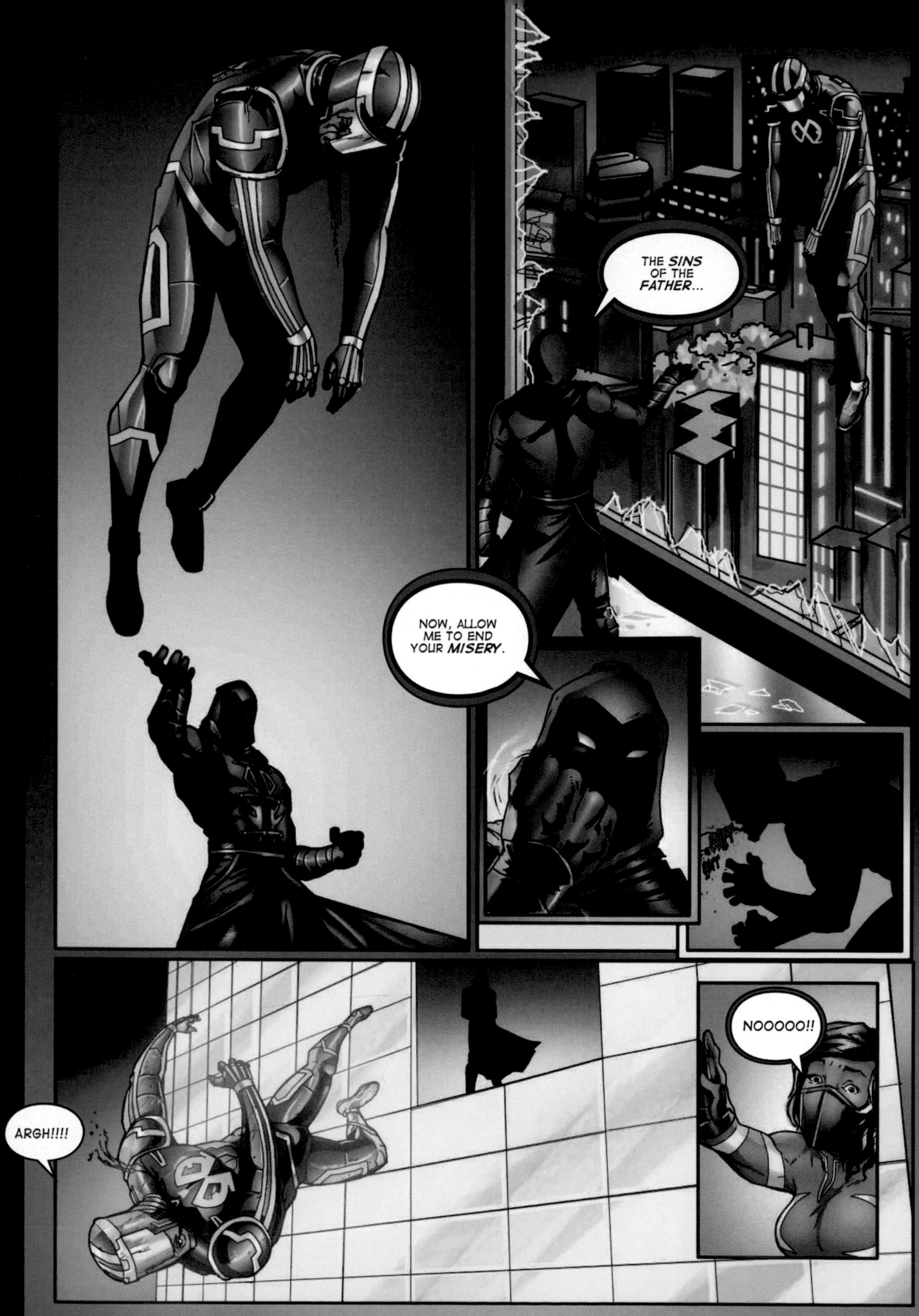
THE *SINS* OF THE *FATHER*...
NOW, ALLOW ME TO END YOUR *MISERY*.
ARGH!!!!
NOOOOO!!

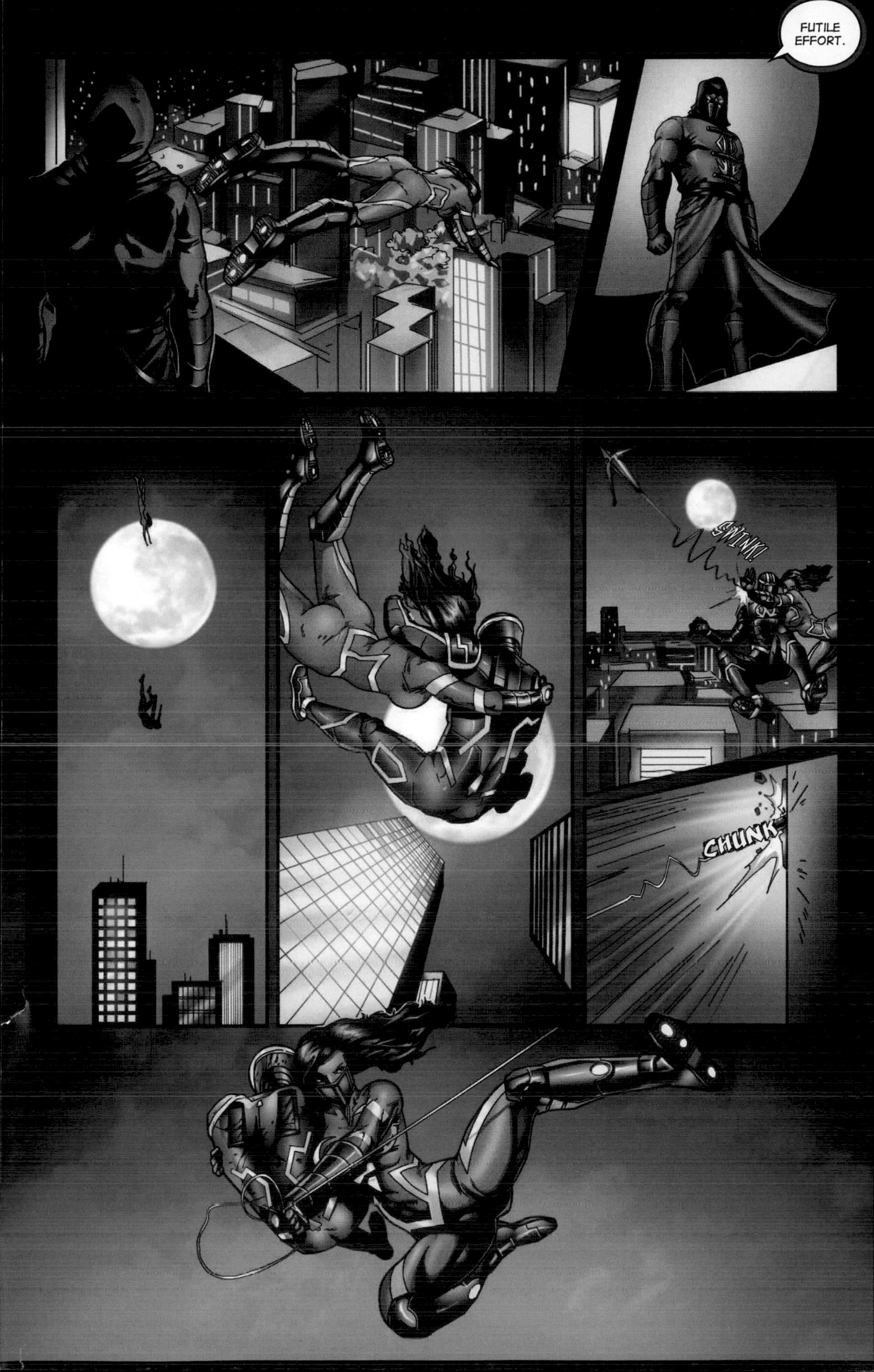
FUTILE EFFORT.
SWINK!
CHUNK

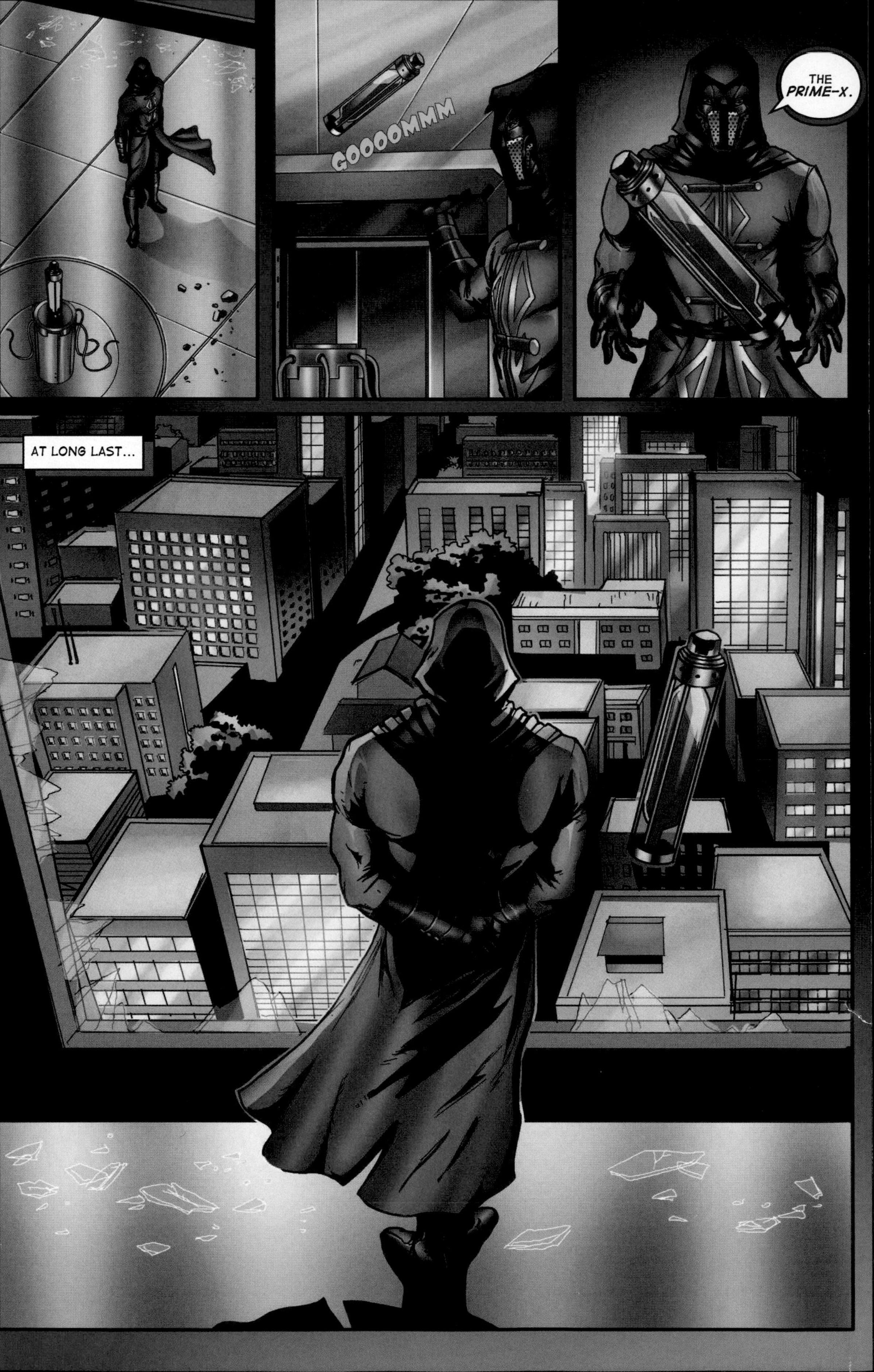
GOOOOMMM
THE PRIME-X.
AT LONG LAST...

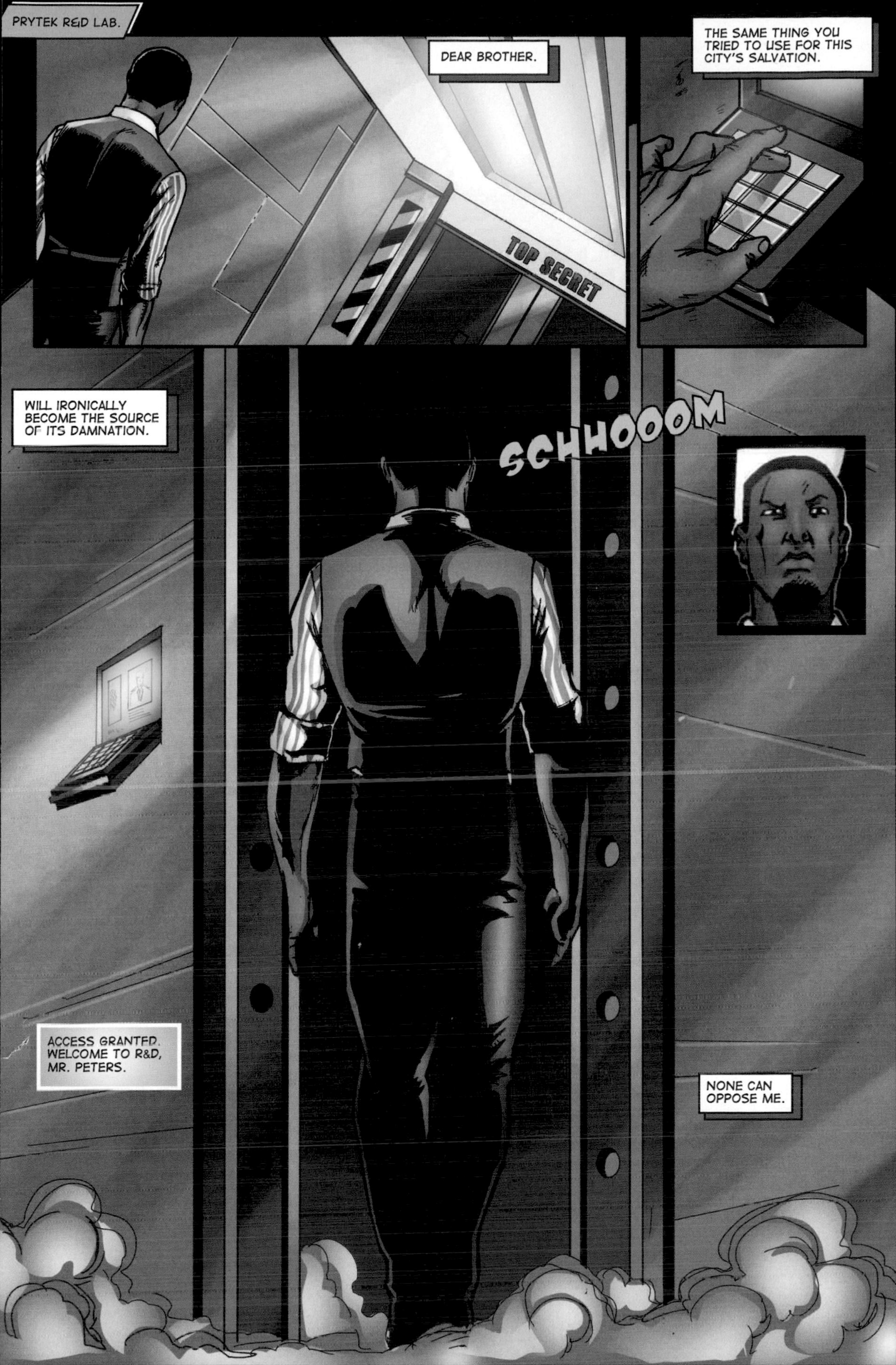
PRYTEK R&D LAB.
DEAR BROTHER.
TOP SECRET
THE SAME THING YOU TRIED TO USE FOR THIS CITY'S SALVATION.
WILL IRONICALLY BECOME THE SOURCE OF ITS DAMNATION.
SCHHOOOM
ACCESS GRANTED. WELCOME TO R&D, MR. PETERS.
NONE CAN OPPOSE ME.

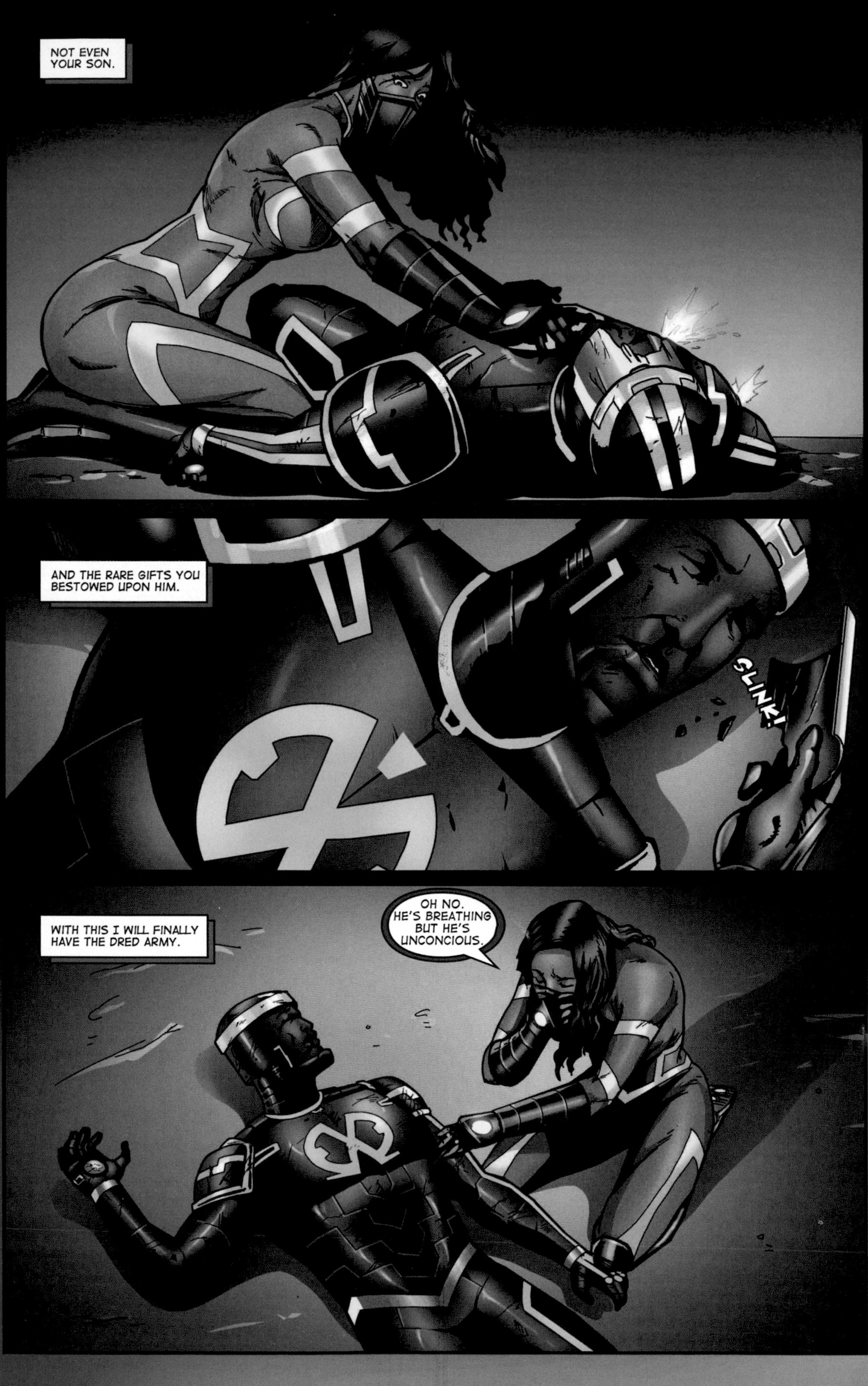
NOT EVEN YOUR SON.
AND THE RARE GIFTS YOU BESTOWED UPON HIM.
CLINK!
WITH THIS I WILL FINALLY HAVE THE DRED ARMY.
OH NO. HE'S BREATHING BUT HE'S UNCONCIOUS.

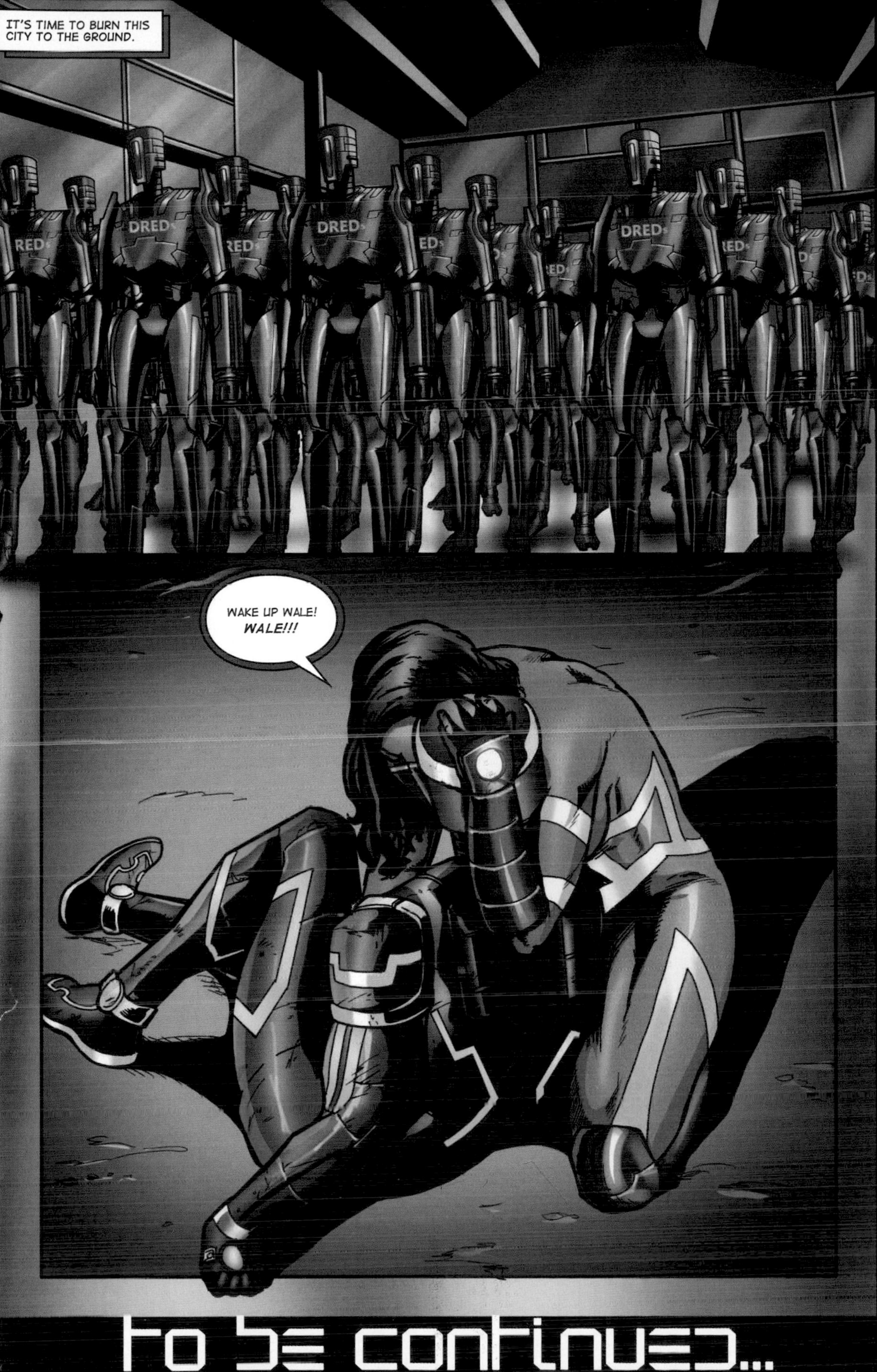
IT'S TIME TO BURN THIS CITY TO THE GROUND.
DREDs
WAKE UP WALE! WALE!!!
to be continued...

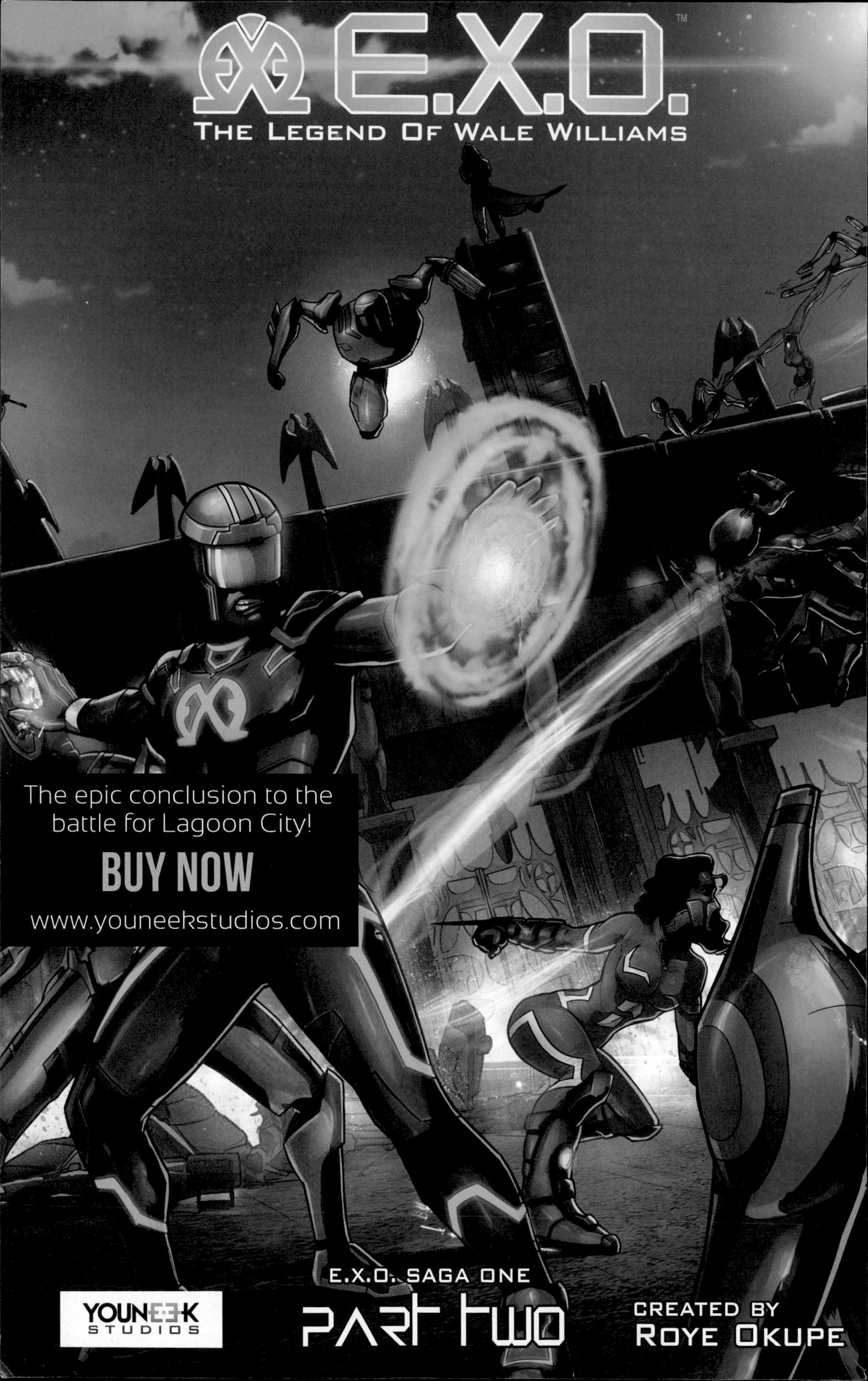
E.X.O.™
THE LEGEND OF WALE WILLIAMS
The epic conclusion to the battle for Lagoon City!
BUY NOW
www.youneekstudios.com
E.X.O. SAGA ONE
PART TWO
YOUNEEK STUDIOS
CREATED BY
ROYE OKUPE

# A SPECIAL THANK YOU TO OUR SPONSORS

AOTECHNOLOGY

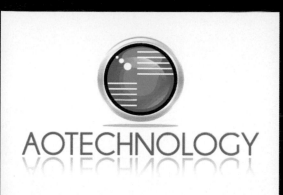

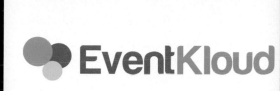

Mobile Application Development, Cloud based ERP software, Automation Software, Systems Integration, Website Creation.

www.aotechnology.co.uk
www.linkedin.com/company/aotechnology-ltd

EventKloud

EventKloud is an audience-driven marketing & advertising automation platform for events.

www.eventkloud.com

beat casa

SOUL BULLET ENTERTAINMENT©

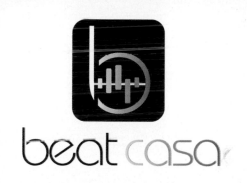

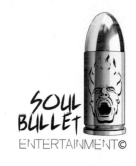

# A SPECIAL THANK YOU TO OUR KICKSTARTER BACKERS

| | | |
|---|---|---|
| Femi Agunbiade | Niyi Fajemidupe | @D3Artist |
| Chris "C I" Nwanze | Paul Pemberton | Jacob "Ryoku" Walker |
| Marcus Currie | Olukayode Malomo | Opeyemi Boroffice |
| Ayo Ojerinola, | Irvin Redezey Agbasi | Ema Bassey |
| Omotola Thomas | Edward Williams | Heath Fogelman |
| EventKloud | Gavin Kam-Young | Jiba Molei Anderson |
| Bello's | Matt Kansy | Torrence Davis |
| Michael J Ryan (tracker1) | Gary Simmons | Steven McGlone Jr |
| Jose Pahissa | Adam DeKraker | Jack Norris |
| A. Rahman Ford | Len "Zeppelin" Ahgeak | Jose Angel "Dr. Death" Lara |
| Teju Sanusi | Jimi Ogunduyile | Bambi Odumosu |
| Niyi Adisa | Jason Murdock | Remi Fayomi a.k.a. Negromaestro |
| Andrew akindlee | Chykie | Bruno Sauce |
| Emery Ortiz | Holly Hartman | Glenn Fayard |
| Kunle Malomo | Malaika Mose | Anonymous |
| Brian Loebig | William Anderson | chiamaka ezenwa |
| Tunde Adegboyo | Dallas Rico | Joel Maurinier |
| Yemisi Onibokun | Cas Thomas | Eghosa Osahon |
| Dayo O | Scott Blasingame | Patrick Reitz |
| Pelumi & Shade Olatinpo | Paolo Butera | Kenneth A. Brown |
| Vomoz Communications | Matt Carson | Hameed Catel (Kirucomics) |
| Wale and Lola Akingbade | Jason A Longden | Adefolami Odusanya |
| Abimbola Adeniranye | Emeka Ikwueze | Aaron Wakem |
| Tyrone Ross | Lewej Jahlil | Ejieme Eromosele |
| Wale Odusanya aka "Wollywood" | Meta Nabou Cisse (Brussels) | Brainchild Publications |
| Ayobami Oluokun | Dwain Pannell | Adetola Adewodu |
| Renee Ford | Jonathan Fung | James Hutchinson |
| Adedamola Adefemi | Logan McLeod | C. Neil Milton |
| Tayymee | Jennifer Bishop | Ted Butler |
| Lennhoff Family | Jacob Roberts-Mensah | Leigh Taylor |
| Kenyeda Adams | Chad Bowden | Pharoah Bolding |
| Ismaila Togola | Desayo O. Ajisegiri | Marcus R Carson |
| Tayo Agunbiade | Wats-On Productions | Kyle Nelson |
| Wale Ogunwale | Tosin Fakile | Anthony Blow ( @AnthonyGadgetX ) |
| Chichi Osuagwu | Brian Dysart | Michael King |
| Oluwatoyin Adewumi | Orielle Couttien | Marlon Banks |
| John T.Collins | Matt Benter | Eoin Smith |
| Dwayne Woodley | Shyvonne Adekoya | Adamu Waziri |
| Brendan Dahl | Ramel Rocket-Man Hill | Joseph Coat |
| Ashley Adewuyi | Cameron White | Miles Seppola |
| Landon Kortman | Nathan | E. Panzenboeck |
| Toks Akinsanmi | Dr. H.A. Nethery IV | Ben Halpern |
| CELT Business Solutions Ltd | Max Andrew Davis | Tim Adams |
| kalina vanderlei silva | Thomas B. Johnson II | KnightSeeker.com |
| Oseze Ekatah | Jaimel Hemphill | Karama "blerdgurl" Horne |
| Jason Matthew Eck | Carrie "Clips" McClain | Dare Ademola |
| Seyi Ogunyemi | Dorphise Jean | C.C. Azu |
| Ibijoke Oke | Josh Nowicki | J R Cannon |

# A SPECIAL THANK YOU TO OUR
## KICKSTARTER BACKERS

Kanayo Adibe

OKUPSY

Christopher M Demarest

Meg Fisher

Miracle Girl

Dwayne Simon

Steve Beaulieu

Caitlin Jane Hughes

Brandon Easton

Marielle Davis

Gary Lee Kuhre

Ryan Joseph

splendidgeek

Mayowa Ogundiyun

LeSean Thomas

Joe Walters

Erika Smith

T.Osinubi

Marizu Onwu

Oluwakemi Oso

Roosevelt Pitt, Jr.

David Neal Eriksen

Jorge Ortiz ValentÃn

Gideon Arthur Wiesen

RLL, MD

Paris Gamble

Everard J. McBain Jr.

Benedict Okojie

Castle K

Isaac Kimmel

Jerry Skold

DJ Don X

Kurt McMahon

Josh Medin

Richard Gaulding

Gábor Horváth

Fred Herman

Damien Wellman

magdrion

Sijuwade Salami

Benny Bottema

John Hildebrand

Eileen Kaur Alden

Giovanna & Mahala

Stephen Olibenu Igwue

Yann Kieffoloh

Parnell Jones

Per Sjoden

Ola Agunbiade

Murani Lewis

Nick Allen

Jim Vargas

Oodon.com

Scott Gill-Jacobson

Genie Ruzicka

CulturalGrassroots.com

Andrew Wilson

H. Alexander Perez

Kirk Lindo

Thomas Werner

Irrevenant

Jamie Heidenreich

Andrew E. C. Head

Allen Herbert

Erin Subramanian

Shawn Pryor

Mandy Wultsch

Peta Fenton

Uche Barry Ajokubi

Sandy Gould

Oladapo Adeniranye

Omolola

Joseph Thomas

Have Hope

Tony Valdivieso

Ronald T. Jones

Alec Hauser

Charles Mosteller

Paul

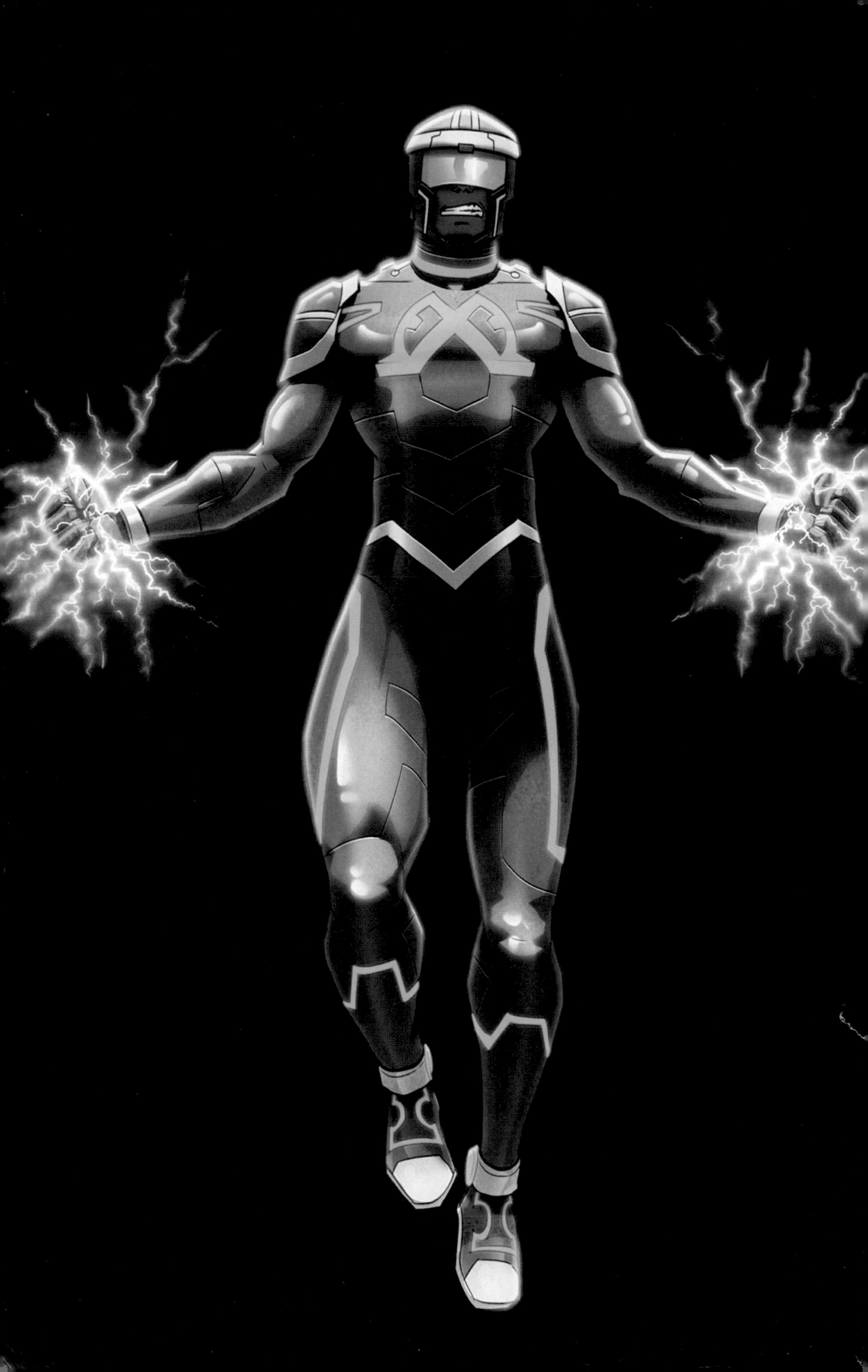

# E.X.O.® THE LEGEND OF WALE WILLIAMS PART TWO (AVAILABLE NOW)

ORDER OUR BOOKS TODAY - YOUNEEKSTUDIOS.COM

E.X.O.
THE LEGEND OF WALE WILLIAMS
YOUNEEK STUDIOS
E.X.O. SAGA ONE
PART TWO
CREATED BY
ROYE OKUPE

***FEATURED ON CBR, NBC, BLEEDING COOL, ABC7 & MORE!***

Part 2 continues to chronicle the journey of Wale Williams a.k.a EXO, who was last seen hanging on for dear life after his first encounter with the incredibly powerful and sinister Oniku, leader of the extremist group, The CREED. After his shocking revelation, Oniku now has all he needs to launch a crippling attack at the heart of Lagoon City, an attack that would be felt across the entire nation of Nigeria.

152 pages - $14.99
Second book in the YouNeek YouNiverse Continuity

"THIS IS A GOOD READ." - COMIXOLOGY

WOOOMMMM
ARGH. THANKS FOR THE UPDATE.
ARGGHHHHHH!
I WILL BREAK EVERY LAST BONE IN YOUR BODY AND EXTRACT THE REST OF WHAT IS MINE FROM YOUR CARCASS.
MUSTER ALL YOUR WISDOM AND ALL YOUR STRENGTH.
IT STILL PALES IN COMPARISON TO THE POWER I WIELD.

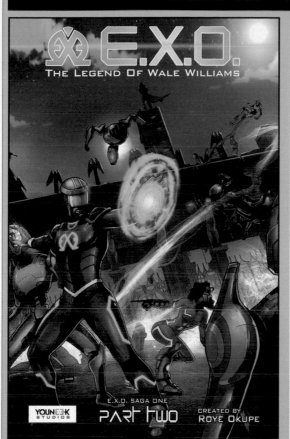

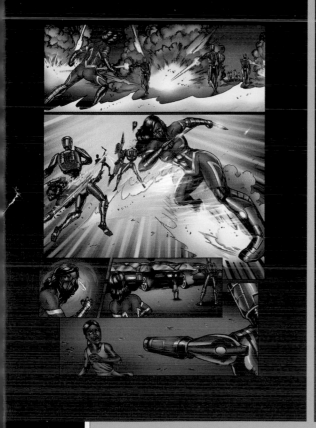

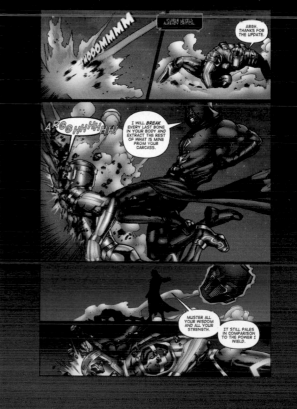

WINDMAKER™ – THE HISTORY OF ATALA (AVAILABLE NOW)

ORDER OUR BOOKS TODAY - YOUNEEKSTUDIOS.COM

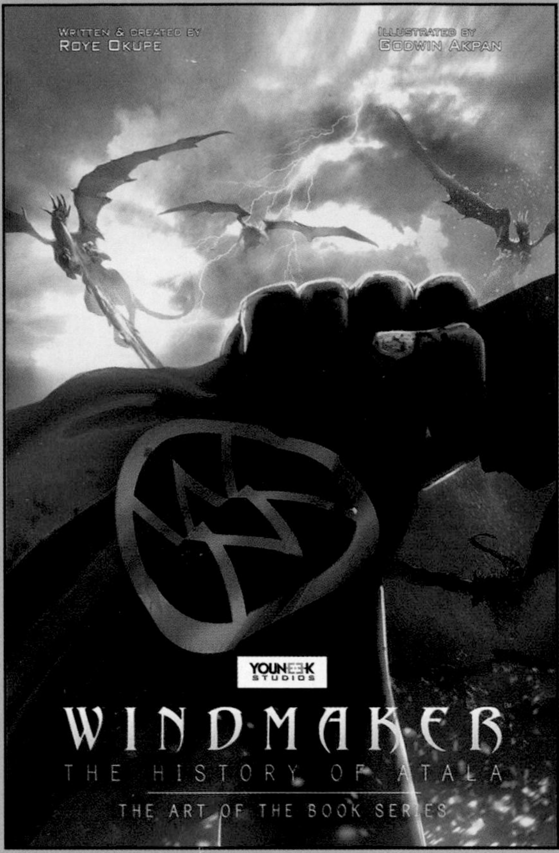

WRITTEN & CREATED BY
ROYE OKUPE
ILLUSTRATED BY
GODWIN AKPAN
YOUNEEK STUDIOS
WINDMAKER
THE HISTORY OF ATALA
THE ART OF THE BOOK SERIES


***FEATURED ON KONBINI & THE WASHINGTON POST!***

Inspired by African mythology, Windmaker: The History of Atala (Hardcover) pulls from the amazing depths of African history. With this art book, writer Roye Okupe sets the foundations for what is definitely a deep and meaningful universe of heroes. Illustrator Godwin Akpan's painting breathes life into the story in an amazing way. It's dragons, mythical relics, a feuding royal family & magical swords all mixed into in an awe inspiring African setting.

Hardcover Art Book - $24.99
Third book in the
YouNeek YouNiverse Continuity

## INSPIRED BY AFRICAN MYTHOLOGY

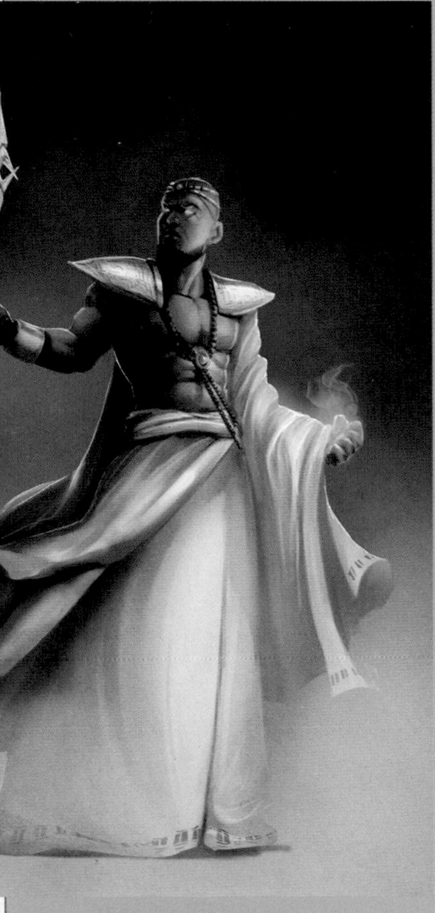

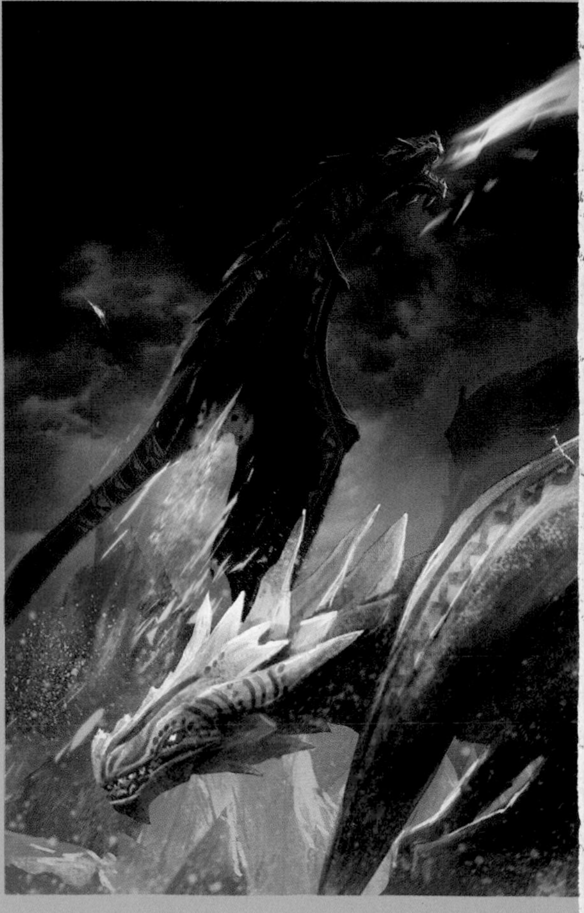